the knitter's handy **book of sweater patterns**

the knitter's handy book of sweater patterns

Basic Designs in Multiple Sizes & Gauges

Ann Budd

INTERWEAVE PRESS
www.interweave.com

technical editor Lori Gayle
editor Pam Allen
design Leigh Radford
illustration Ann Swanson
technical illustration Gayle Ford
production Dean Howes
photography Joe Coca
photo styling Ann Swanson
proofreader Nancy Arndt

 Interweave Press
201 East Fourth Street
Loveland, Colorado 80537-5655 USA
www.interweave.com

Printed and bound in China through Asia Pacific Offset

Library of Congress Cataloging-in-Publication Data

Budd, Ann.
   The knitter's handy book of sweater patterns : basic designs in multiple sizes & gauges / Ann
Budd.
      p. cm.
   ISBN 1-931499-43-8
   1. Knitting. I. Title.
   TT820.B878 2004
   746.43'20432—dc22

                                              2004003763

10 9 8 7 6 5 4 3 2 1

contents

Acknowledgments   vi
Introduction   1

Drop-Shoulder Sweaters   10
Child Sizes   13
Adult Sizes   19
Copy Cats   31

Modified Drop-Shoulder Sweaters   38
Child Sizes   41
Adult Sizes   47
Copy Cats   59

Set-In Sleeve Sweaters   70
Child Sizes   73
Adult Sizes   81
Copy Cats   97

Saddle-Shoulder Sweaters   106
Child Sizes   109
Adult Sizes   117
Copy Cats   132

Raglan Sweaters   140
Child Sizes   143
Adult Sizes   151
Copy Cats   166

Seamless Yoke Sweaters   172
Child Sizes   175
Adult Sizes   181
Copy Cats   192

Expanding Your Options   198

Glossary   204
Abbreviations   214
Yarn Sources   215
Index   216

acknowledgments

I've been lucky. In my job as managing editor of *Interweave Knits*, I've made friends with hundreds of knitters, from beginners to well-known designers. Whether or not they realize it, they have all contributed to this book.

A few people merit special attention. Melanie Falick, former editor of *Interweave Knits*, was generous in her suggestions for choosing color, styles, and finishing details in the early stages of this book, and in sage advice toward the end. Pam Allen, current editor of *Interweave Knits*, helped smooth the rough edges and lead to a cohesive and thorough book that I hope knitters will enjoy as a reference for years to come. As technical editor, Lori Gayle poured through endless columns of numbers, checked the math, and suggested modifications to improve the sweaters' fit, all with unwavering good sense punctuated with humor. My coworkers at Interweave Press, particularly the *Interweave Knits* editorial team—including Ivy Bigelow and Susan Sternlieb—patiently listened to my infinite musings about sweater shaping, yarn choices, stitch patterns, and finishing techniques, and provided valuable opinions and insight. Leigh Radford designed the pages to be clear and beautiful, despite the fact that she had little but numbers to work with. Finally, Lynn Gates helped by knitting several of the sweaters photographed.

The sweaters in this book couldn't have been knitted without the contributions of yarns from Baabajoes Wool Company, Classic Elite Yarns, GGH/Muench Yarns, Louet Sales, Plymouth Yarn Company, and Westminster Fibers.

Most of all, I am indebted to my husband, David, and our three sons, Alex, Eric, and Nicholas, who accept the big part of my life that is knitting, and bring joy to the other parts.

introduction

I learned to knit in 1968. Since then, I've evolved from a closet knitter, to a weekend knitter, to a devoted knitter. At one time I worked in a yarn store, and now I am managing editor of *Interweave Knits* magazine. Through it all, I've always favored basic patterns that allow me to add my own design ideas. This concept led to my first book, *The Knitter's Handy Book of Patterns*, a collection of easy-to-follow charted instructions for eight projects—mittens, gloves, hats, tams, scarves, socks, vests, and set-in-sleeve sweaters. Soon after that book was published in 2002, I sat knitting in my favorite chair and was hit with the idea that I should write another book—a book that begins where *The Knitter's Handy Book of Patterns* leaves off. I thought that knitters would be equally interested in easy-to-follow charted instructions for all the most common sweater constructions in multiple sizes and gauges. And that's how *The Knitter's Handy Book of Sweater Patterns* came about.

This is not your standard sweater pattern book, though you'll find detailed instructions for eighteen designs. Nor is this a design book, though it will guide you through creating the sweater of your choice in the yarn of your choice. This book offers instructions for the six most common sweater constructions—drop shoulder, modified drop shoulder, set-in sleeve, saddle shoulder, raglan, and seamless yoke. Each style is provided in fifteen sizes, in 2" (5-cm) increments from a 26" (66 cm) chest circumference appropriate for a child to a 54" (137 cm) chest circumference appropriate for a large adult. And each size is given in five possible gauges—3, 4, 5, 6, and 7 stitches per inch. That's a whopping 75 options for each of the six styles, or 450 patterns in all! Add the cardigan versions and you've got 900 possibilities, without counting neckline, edging, color, and stitch pattern variations.

The six sweater styles in this book differ in the way that the sleeves join the body. The first four styles are made by knitting the sweater pieces separately—one back, one or two front(s), and two sleeves. In general, the pieces are knitted back and forth in rows (though some designers have methods for working them in the round). The other two styles are worked in the round from the bottom up. The body is worked as a tube from the lower edge to the armholes, the sleeves are also worked as tubes to the armhole, the sleeves and body are joined, and the yoke is worked in a single piece to the neck.

The simplest style, the **drop shoulder**, consists of a rectangle for the front, another rectangle for the back, and two trapezoids for the sleeves. There is no armhole shaping and the tops of the sleeves are sewn directly onto the side edges above the marked armhole positions.

The **modified drop-shoulder** style uses rudimentary shaping to eliminate some excess width at the upper body above the armholes. Stitches are bound off at the base of each armhole on the front and back to form notches that accommodate the upper sleeves.

Set-in sleeve sweaters have the most tailored fit. Both the upper body and the tops of the sleeves are shaped to eliminate excess fabric at the armholes. On a well-fitting set-in-sleeve sweater, the armholes fall directly in line with the shoulder bone without pulling or puckering.

The **saddle shoulder** sweater in this book is closely related to the set-in-sleeve style (though other sweater styles can also have saddles). The difference between the two lies in the "saddle," an extension of the sleeve top, from the armhole to the neck.

The **raglan** style in this book is worked in the round. For the in-the-round method, the body and sleeves are each worked as tubes from the lower edge to the armholes, then joined for the yoke, which is also worked in the round to the neck. The yoke is shaped by decreases worked along four diagonal lines (two each on the front and back) that extend from armhole to neck.

Seamless yoke sweaters are worked in the round, as the raglan style, but the yoke is shaped by decreases that are placed evenly around the circumference of the yoke.

The instructions for each style are written for the most basic form of that style—a stockinette-stitch pullover or cardigan with a straight body, long sleeves, and crew- or V-neck. You can follow the instructions and schematics exactly as presented, or you can make adjustments to fit your needs. Add or subtract a few stitches to accommodate a color or texture pattern repeat, add edge stitches for easy seaming, tighten the fit, alter the sleeve or body length, or adjust the neck opening. These are the kinds of variations I have made in the eighteen sample sweaters, called Copy Cats, included in this book. In the detailed instructions for these sweaters, I've noted how and why I deviated from the charts. I hope these examples will give you the confidence to manipulate the basic patterns to accommodate your own design ideas.

Using the Charts
Instructions for each sweater style are divided into "child" sizes of 26"–34" (66–86.5 cm) chest circumference and "adult" sizes of 36"–54" (91.5–137 cm) chest circumference. Of course, depending on the amount of ease you want in the finished sweater, it's quite possible to follow a small size for an adult or a large size for a child. The instructions appear in chart, or grid, format with the possible sizes, from smallest to largest, in columns and the possible gauges, in stitches

per inch, in rows. Simply find your gauge along the left margin of the chart and follow across to your size.

For example, let's say you want to make a drop-shoulder sweater with a finished chest measurement of 42" (106.5 cm) at a gauge of 5 stitches to the inch. According to the adult drop-shoulder sweater chart on page 19, you'd follow the third row of numbers (for a gauge of 5 stitches to the inch) and the fourth column of numbers (for a finished size of 42" [106.5 cm]). For this example, you'd cast on 106 stitches and work the edging of your choice, then continue even until the piece measures about 14½" (37 cm) from the beginning. You may find it helpful to circle or highlight the numbers that apply to your size and gauge (on a photocopy of the pages if you don't want to write in the book) before you begin. When there is just one set of numbers in a row, it applies to all gauges.

Using the Schematics
All the instructions in this book were devised by calculating how many stitches would be needed to achieve a knitted piece of specific dimensions. Schematics are simply graphic representations of the finished

dimensions. They allow you to check your progress and assure that your piece is working out to the measurements specified. If you're confused by the instructions in a pattern, take a look at the schematic—often the picture is worth a thousand words.

Choosing a Size
The best way to choose which size to make is to measure a sweater that fits the future wearer well. Use those measurements as a guide for choosing a style and size from this book. To take accurate measurements, lay the sample sweater on a flat surface (a clean floor works well) and smooth out all the wrinkles. Use a yardstick (a tape measure can stretch and give inaccurate measurements) to measure the widest width below the armholes. This measurement is the finished circumference you'll want to duplicate. Other important measurements are the total body length measured from the back neck (excluding the neck edging) to the lower edge, and the length of the sleeve from the

general sweater measurements

child sizes 26"–34" (66–86.5 cm)

Finished Sweater Circumference

26	28	30	32	34"
66	71	76	81.5	86.5 cm

Actual Body Circumference

23	25	27	29	31"
58.5	63.5	68.5	73.5	78.5 cm

Body Length: Top Shoulder to Hem

14	16	18	20	22"
35.5	40.5	45.5	51	56 cm

Center Back Neck to Cuff

19	21	23	25	26½"
48.5	53.5	58.5	63.5	67.5 cm

Armhole Depth
Drop Shoulder, Modified Drop Shoulder

6½	7	7½	8	8½"
16.5	18	19	20.5	21.5 cm

Set-in, Saddle, Raglan, Yoke

5½	6½	7	7½	8"
14	16.5	18	19	20.5 cm

Front Neck Drop
Crewneck

2	2	2	2	2"
5	5	5	5	5 cm

V-Neck

5	5½	6	6	6"
12.5	14	15	15	15 cm

adult sizes 36"–44" (91.5–112 cm)

Finished Sweater Circumference

36	38	40	42	44"
91.5	96.5	101.5	106.5	112 cm

Actual Body Circumference

32	34	36	38	40"
81.5	86.5	91.5	96.5	101.5 cm

Body Length: Top Shoulder to Hem

22½	23	24	25	26"
57	58.5	61	63.5	66 cm

Center Back Neck to Cuff

28	29	30	31	32"
71	73.5	76	78.5	81.5 cm

Armhole Depth
Drop Shoulder, Modified Drop Shoulder

9	9½	10	10½	11"
23	24	25.5	26.5	28 cm

Set-in, Saddle, Raglan, Yoke

8½	9	9½	9¾	10"
21.5	23	24	25	25.5 cm

Front Neck Drop
Crewneck

2½	2½	2½	2½	2½"
6.5	6.5	6.5	6.5	6.5 cm

V-Neck

6	6½	6½	6¾	6¾"
15	16.5	16.5	17	17 cm

center back neck to the cuff. These key measurements are listed in the tables below for each of the fifteen sizes in this book. (Note: The measurements here differ slightly from those used in my first book, *The Knitter's Handy Book of Patterns*. For this book I needed to make some adjustments to keep the fit consistent between the six different sweater styles.) These measurements are loosely based on guidelines published by the Fashion Institute of Technology and examination of dozens of ready-made sweaters and sweater patterns. Of course, people come in all shapes and sizes, and although every attempt has been made to give the sweaters in this book a "standard" fit, you may find that some adjustments will be necessary to achieve the exact fit you want. In general, choose the circumference that matches your desired finished size. If necessary, you can adjust the total body length by adding or subtracting rows (and, therefore, inches) between the cast-on edge and the armhole. Likewise, you can adjust

adult sizes 46"–54" (117–137 cm)

Finished Sweater Circumference

46	48	50	52	54"
117	122	127	132	137 cm

Actual Body Circumference

42	44	46	48	50"
106.5	112	117	122	127 cm

Body Length: Top Shoulder to Hem

26½	27	27½	28	28½"
67.5	68.5	70	71	72.5 cm

Center Back Neck to Cuff

33	34	34½	35	35½"
84	86.5	87.5	89	90 cm

Armhole Depth
Drop Shoulder, Modified Drop Shoulder

11½	12	12½	13	13½"
29	30.5	31.5	33	34.5 cm

Set-in, Saddle, Raglan, Yoke

10¼	10½	10¾	11	11¼"
26	26.5	27.5	28	28.5cm

Front Neck Drop
Crewneck

3	3	3	3	3"
7.5	7.5	7.5	7.5	7.5 cm

V-Neck

7	7	7¼	7½	7½"
18	18	18.5	19	19 cm

the sleeve length by adding or subtracting rows between the cast-on edge and the armhole. I do not recommend adjusting the armholes or sleeve caps.

Knitting a Swatch and Measuring Gauge
Once you've chosen your yarn and sweater style, the first step in any knitting project is to knit a gauge swatch using the yarn, needles, and stitch pattern you've selected. The beauty of the instructions in this book is that they do not specify a particular yarn or yarn weight. You decide on the yarn and needles—and therefore, gauge—you want to use. Once you have chosen a yarn and needle size, you'll need to take an accurate gauge measurement of a knitted test swatch. The swatch will show you what the finished fabric will look and feel like and will indicate which row of the sweater chart you should follow.

To help you get started, try knitting a swatch with the needle size recommended on the ball band. The table below gives the gauges and needle sizes recommended for the six standard yarn categories provided by the Craft Yarn Council of America. Of course, all knitters have their own slightly unique way of holding the yarn and manipulating the stitches, and your way may affect the results. It is therefore important to keep in mind that the information in this table is a guide, or starting point, not a concrete set of rules. It is also important to note that although knitting needles come in standard sizes, the same size can vary from manufacturer to manufacturer. A size 5 needle from one company may closely resemble a size 6 or 4 from another. Moreover, your gauge may vary depending on whether you work on wooden or metal needles. If you plan to knit a raglan or yoke sweater in the round, you should knit your gauge swatch in the round. Many knitters experience a noticeable difference in gauge between knit and purl stitches so that a stockinette-stitch swatch worked back and forth in rows (in which it's necessary to alternate between rows of knit stitches and rows of purl stitches) will measure significantly different from a swatch worked in the round (in which the same side of the knitting always faces you and the stitches are always knitted). Knit a generous swatch—at least 4" (10 cm) square—using the stitch pattern you plan to use for your sweater. Some stitch patterns, particularly those involving twisted or crossed stitches, require more stitches per inch of knitting than stockinette stitch. Likewise, openwork stitch patterns (made with yarnovers) tend to stretch in width and can require fewer stitches per inch of knitting.

Most knitting patterns specify a gauge. It's up to you to adjust the

Standard Yarn Weights, Needle Sizes, and Gauges

Yarn Weight	Needle Size	Stitches/Inch
Sock, Baby, Fingering	1–3 (2.25–3.25 mm)	6.75–8
Sport, Baby	3–5 (3.25–3.75 mm)	5.75–6.5
DK, Light Worsted	5–7 (3.75–4.5 mm)	5.25–6
Worsted, Afghan, Aran	7–9 (4.5–5.5 mm)	4–5
Chunky, Craft, Rug	9–11 (5.5–8 mm)	3–3.75
Bulky, Roving	11+ (8+ mm)	1.5–2.75

measuring your swatch

Using a ruler as a guide, count the number of stitches, including partial stitches, in a 4" (10-cm) width of knitting. In this example, the gauge (measured on stockinette stitch) is 6 stitches per inch.

needle size until you achieve that gauge. The patterns in this book are different: You can knit a swatch that has the look and feel you like, then follow the instructions that match the gauge for that swatch. This method allows you to substitute stitch patterns or unusual yarns. Of course, you can always choose to achieve the gauge recommended on the ball band of your yarn and follow the instructions here that match that gauge.

Once you've knitted a suitable swatch, loosely bind off the stitches and wash and block the swatch just as you plan to wash and block the finished sweater. When the swatch is completely dry, take time to examine it critically. Does it have the look and feel you want in the finished sweater? Sometimes, especially if you've chosen to work a stitch pattern, you will not like the fabric created by the recommended needle size. For example, if the stitches look open or sloppy, you may want to try smaller needles for a tighter fabric. If you want a looser

fabric, try larger needles. It is not uncommon for a designer to work three or four swatches before settling on the optimum needle size.

When you have a swatch you like, measure the gauge—that is, measure the number of stitches in a set width. Most knitting books recommend measuring the number of stitches in a 4-inch (10-cm) width, then dividing by four to get the number of stitches in 1 inch (2.5 cm) of knitted width. To measure, lay the swatch on a flat surface. Place a ruler (not a tape measure, which can stretch and give inaccurate measurements) on top of the swatch and measure the number of stitches in a 4-inch (10-cm) width, including any partial stitches. Divide this number by four to get the number of stitches (including partial stitches) per inch. Repeat this process in a number of places on the swatch and take the average to account for uneven yarn or stitches. The resulting number is the number of stitches required to knit each inch

(2.5 cm) of width with the yarn, needles, and stitch pattern you've chosen.

The instructions in this book are based on gauges of full-number increments from 3 to 7 stitches per inch. Therefore, if your calculations give you a stitch gauge that includes a fraction of a stitch, you should adjust the needle size to get one of the gauges listed. Let's say you want to knit a sweater at a gauge of 4 stitches to the inch. If your swatch measures 4.25 stitches per inch, your stitches are too small and you should try again with larger needles. Conversely, if your swatch measures 3.75 stitches per inch, your stitches are too big and you should try again with smaller needles. If you decide that the yarn looks and feels best knitted at 4.25 stitches per inch, don't despair—turn to Adjusting for a Different Gauge on page 201.

Estimating Yarn Amounts

One of the most difficult tasks in writing sweater instructions is predicting how

much yarn is needed for each size given. In most cases, only one size has actually been knitted—the one in the photograph. For that sweater, and that sweater alone, the exact amount of yarn required is known—the sweater has been weighed or the knitter has kept track of the number of balls of yarn used. But it would be impractical to knit a sample sweater for each of the sizes provided. Therefore, the amount of yarn listed for the other sizes is an estimate based on how much the size differs, bigger or smaller, from the photographed sample.

The yardages listed in this book are no different. Of the 450 possible sweater options, only eighteen were actually knitted. The yarn yardage requirements for the others are estimates based on the number of square inches of knitted fabric in the finished sweater and the amount of yarn required to knit a square inch of fabric at each gauge. I'll save you the details of how I came up with these estimates, but it's worth noting that the estimates match the amount of yarn actually used in the eighteen sweaters that were knitted and photographed.

Of course, it's always a good idea to buy an extra ball of yarn, particularly if you plan to make adjustments to the instructions. And keep in mind that extra yarn is needed for color work, in which the unused yarn is carried across the back of the work, and for texture work, in which stitches clump together or cross over each other.

drop-shoulder sweaters

Of all the sweater shapes, the drop shoulder is the easiest to knit. The body is a simple rectangle without armhole shaping—the upper body is as wide as the lower body and the armhole seams fall, or drop, beyond the shoulders, and give the sweater its name. The wide upper body results in excess fabric at the armholes, which gives this type of sweater a loose fit and a casual, boxy look.

From a knitter's perspective, drop-shoulder sweaters are appealing because they are so easy to knit—just cast on and knit to the shoulders. Finishing is also a breeze—the seams are straight and can be worked stitch for stitch or row for row, reducing the chances of stretching or puckering. The clean rectangular shapes, uninterrupted by armholes, are good for texture and color patterns (see the Mistake Rib Cardigan on page 32). Although drop-shoulder sweaters are seductive in their simplicity, the lack of armhole shaping can give the sweater a somewhat sloppy look. This look can be exaggerated if the two sleeves are not sewn in to the same depth at the two sides—a potentially tricky proposition given that there is no structural guide for sleeve placement into the armholes.

Three sweater variations following the drop-shoulder chart. Top to bottom: Tweed V-Neck Pullover at 44" (112 cm) circumference and 5 stitches/inch, Mistake Rib Cardigan at 40" (101.5 cm) circumference and 5 stitches/inch, and Chunky Drop-Shoulder Turtleneck at 32" (81.5 cm) circumference and 3 stitches/inch. Step-by-step instructions for these sweaters begin on page 31.

basic anatomy

The following drop-shoulder sweater instructions closely parallel Elizabeth Zimmermann's Percentage System, which Elizabeth began playing with in the late 1950s and which was formally named EPS in issue #26 of *Wool Gathering* in 1982. (This ingenious do-it-yourself method of sweater sizing bases key dimensions on the body circumference at the widest point—i.e., the upper sleeve width is one-half the body circumference and the back neck and shoulder widths are each one-third of the body width.) Although all of Elizabeth's designs were knitted in the round, the drop-shoulder sweater here is worked in pieces—back, front(s), and sleeves—from the lower edges upward.

The back is a rectangle—the number of stitches bound off for the neck and shoulders is the same as the number cast on for the lower edge. For the pullover version, the front is worked the same as the back up to the point where stitches are bound off and/or decreased to the shape of a crew- or V-neck. For the cardigan version, the front consists of two pieces— each with half the number of stitches used for the back. The sleeves are widened for the upper arm by paired increases worked at specific intervals until the desired width is achieved. The stitches for the upper sleeve are bound off in a single step. After the pieces are blocked, the shoulder seams are joined, the neck finished off with the desired edging, and the sleeve tops are sewn into the upper portions of the side seams.

To use the following chart to make a drop-shoulder sweater, you need to choose yarn, determine your gauge (see page 6), and pick a size based on the desired finished bust/chest circumference. You'll also need straight needles in the size necessary to obtain the desired gauge (and needles one or two sizes smaller for edgings, if desired), a tapestry needle, and buttons for cardigan versions: 5 to 7 for child sizes, 7 to 9 for adult sizes. Gauge runs vertically along the left side of the chart; finished bust/chest circumference is listed horizontally across the top. The chart for children's sizes begins on page 13; schematics are on page 18. The chart for adult sizes begins on page 19; schematics are on page 30.

sizing child

Finished Chest Circumference

26	28	30	32	34"		26	28	30	32	34"
66	71	76	81.5	86.5 cm		66	71	76	81.5	86.5 cm

Yarn Requirement

GAUGE					
3	270	340	410	490	550 yd
	247	311	375	448	503 m
4	390	480	580	690	780
	357	439	530	631	713
5	490	610	730	870	990
	448	558	667	796	905
6	690	860	1030	1230	1400
	631	786	942	1125	1280
7	760	950	1140	1350	1540
	695	869	1042	1234	1408

Pullover Back

CO:

3	40	42	46	48	52 sts.
4	52	56	60	64	68
5	64	70	74	80	86
6	78	84	90	96	102
7	90	98	106	112	120

Work edging of choice (see pages 35–37), then cont even until piece measures desired length to armholes, or about:

7½	9	10½	12	13½"
19	23	26.5	30.5	34.5 cm

Mark Armholes

Mark each edge of last row for base of armhole. Cont even until armholes measure:

6½	7	7½	8	8½"
16.5	18	19	20.5	21.5 cm

Shape Shoulders and Neck

BO all sts, marking first and last:

3	13	13	14	15	17 sts.
4	17	17	18	20	22
5	20	21	22	25	27
6	25	25	27	30	33
7	28	30	32	35	38

for each shoulder and rem sts for back neck:

3	14	16	18	18	18 sts.
4	18	22	24	24	24
5	24	28	30	30	30
6	28	34	36	36	36
7	34	38	42	42	44

Pullover Front with Crewneck

(For V-neck option, see page 14.) Work as for back, ending with a WS row, until armholes measure:

4½	5	5½	6	6½"
11.5	12.5	14	15	16.5 cm

Shape Crewneck

With RS facing, work across:

3	17	17	18	19	21 sts,
4	22	23	23	25	27
5	27	28	29	32	35
6	33	34	35	38	41
7	38	39	41	44	48

join new yarn and BO for front neck:

3	6	8	10	10	10 sts,
4	8	10	14	14	14
5	10	14	16	16	16
6	12	16	20	20	20
7	14	20	24	24	24

Finished Chest Circumference

26	28	30	32	34"		26	28	30	32	34"
66	71	76	81.5	86.5 cm		66	71	76	81.5	86.5 cm

work to end. There will be the foll number of sts at each side:

3	17	17	18	19	21 sts.
4	22	23	23	25	27
5	27	28	29	32	35
6	33	34	35	38	41
7	38	39	41	44	48

Working each side separately, at each neck edge BO 3 sts (if number is zero, omit these rows):

3	0	0	0	0	0 time(s).
4	0	0	0	0	0
5	1	1	1	1	1
6	1	1	1	1	1
7	1	1	1	1	1

Then BO 2 sts:

3	1	1	1	1	1 time(s).
4	2	2	1	1	1
5	1	1	1	1	1
6	2	2	1	1	1
7	2	2	2	2	2

Then dec 1 st every RS row:

3	2	2	2	2	2 time(s).
4	1	2	3	3	3
5	2	2	2	2	2
6	1	2	3	3	3
7	3	2	2	2	3

There will rem the foll number of sts at each side:

3	13	13	14	15	17 sts.
4	17	17	18	20	22
5	20	21	22	25	28
6	25	25	27	30	33
7	28	30	32	35	38

Work even until armholes measure same as back to shoulder.

Shape Shoulders
BO all sts.

Pullover Front with V-Neck
Work as for back until armholes measure:

1½	1½	1½	2	2½"
3.8	3.8	3.8	5	6.5 cm

With RS facing, work to center of row. Turn and work these sts only to shoulder (place rem sts on a holder to work later). Dec 1 st at neck edge every RS row:

3	3	4	4	4	4 times.
4	4	6	7	7	7
5	8	11	10	10	10
6	9	13	13	13	13
7	13	15	16	16	18

Then dec 1 st at neck edge every 4 rows:

3	4	4	5	5	5 times.
4	5	5	5	5	5
5	4	3	5	5	5
6	5	4	5	5	5
7	4	4	5	5	4

There will remain:

3	13	13	14	15	17 sts.
4	17	17	18	20	22
5	20	21	22	25	28
6	25	25	27	30	33
7	28	30	32	35	38

Work even until armhole measures same as back to shoulder. Shape shoulder as for back. Rejoin yarn at neck edge of held sts and work

Finished Chest Circumference

26	28	30	32	34"
66	71	76	81.5	86.5 cm

as for first half, reversing neck and shoulder shaping.

Sleeves

CO:

3	18	20	22	22	24 sts.
4	24	26	28	30	32
5	30	32	36	38	40
6	36	40	42	46	48
7	42	46	48	52	56

Work edging of choice until piece measures:

1½	1½	1½	2	2"
3.8	3.8	3.8	5	5 cm

Change to St st and inc 1 st each end of needle every 2 rows (if number is zero, omit these rows):

3	0	0	0	0	0 times.
4	0	0	0	0	0
5	2	0	0	0	0
6	3	0	0	0	0
7	6	2	0	0	0

Then inc 1 st each end of needle every 4 rows:

3	9	5	6	5	6 times.
4	14	11	11	11	11
5	16	19	17	16	18
6	18	21	22	21	23
7	19	24	29	29	29

Then inc 1 st each end of needle every 6 rows (if number is zero, omit these rows):

3	2	6	6	8	8 time(s).
4	0	4	5	6	7
5	0	0	3	5	5
6	0	1	2	4	4
7	0	0	0	1	3

Finished Chest Circumference

26	28	30	32	34"
66	71	76	81.5	86.5 cm

There will be:

3	40	42	46	48	52 sts.
4	52	56	60	64	68
5	66	70	76	80	86
6	78	84	90	96	102
7	92	98	106	112	120

Work even, if necessary, until piece measures:

12½	14	15½	17	18"
31.5	35.5	39.5	43	45.5 cm

BO all sts.

Finishing

Block pieces to measurements. With yarn threaded on a tapestry needle, sew one shoulder seam.

Neckband: Choose a crewneck finish on pages 66–67 or a V-neck finish on pages 68–69. With smaller needles, RS facing, and beg at other shoulder, pick up and knit 1 st for each BO st and about 3 sts for every 4 rows along sloped edges around neck opening. Adjust st count if necessary to achieve a full multiple of the edging patt you've chosen, plus 2 extra "seam" sts. Work in chosen pattern until neckband measures ¾" (2 cm), or desired length. BO all sts in patt.

Seams: Sew rem shoulder and neckband seam. Measure down (6½, 7, 7½, 8, 8½)" (16.5 [18, 19, 20.5, 21.5] cm) from shoulder seam and mark front and back for sleeve placement. Lay garment flat with RS facing upward. Fold sleeve in half lengthwise to locate shoulder point (center of BO edge), and pin RS of sleeve to body without stretching or easing the fabric, matching shoulder points, and making sure that front and back armholes are the same length. With yarn threaded on a tapestry needle and beginning at the shoulder point (leave sufficient yarn

Finished Chest Circumference

26	28	30	32	34"		26	28	30	32	34"
66	71	76	81.5	86.5 cm		66	71	76	81.5	86.5 cm

at the beginning of the seam to be used later to work the other half), sew sleeve to back armhole to the underarm. Repeat for front half of armhole. Sew sleeve and side seams in a continuous line.

Weave in loose ends. Block again, if desired.

Cardigan Back
Work as for pullover version.

Cardigan Left Front with Crewneck
CO:

3	20	21	23	24	26 sts.
4	26	28	30	32	34
5	33	35	38	40	43
6	39	42	45	48	51
7	46	49	53	56	60

Work edging of choice (as for back), then cont even until piece measures same length as back to armhole. Mark beg of RS row for armhole placement. Cont even until armhole measures:

4½	5	5½	6	6½"
11.5	12.5	14	15	16.5 cm

Shape Crewneck
At beg of next WS row BO:

3	3	4	5	5	5 sts,
4	4	5	7	7	7
5	5	7	8	8	8
6	6	8	10	10	10
7	7	10	12	12	12

work to end. At neck edge, BO 3 sts (if number is zero, omit these rows):

3	0	0	0	0	0 time(s).
4	0	0	0	0	0
5	I	I	I	I	I
6	I	I	I	I	I
7	2	I	I	I	I

Then BO 2 sts:

3	I	I	I	I	I time(s).
4	2	2	I	I	I
5	I	I	I	I	I
6	2	2	I	I	I
7	2	2	2	2	2

Then dec 1 st at neck edge (end of RS rows) every RS row:

3	2	2	2	2	2 time(s).
4	I	2	3	3	3
5	3	2	3	2	2
6	I	2	3	3	3
7	I	2	2	2	3

There will remain:

3	13	13	14	15	17 sts.
4	17	17	18	20	22
5	20	21	22	25	28
6	25	25	27	30	33
7	28	30	32	35	38

Cont even until piece measures same as back to shoulder.

Shape Shoulder
With RS facing, BO all sts.

Cardigan Right Front with Crewneck
Work as for left front but reverse shaping (i.e., shape neck at beg of RS rows and BO for shoulder at beg of WS row).

Cardigan Left Front with V-Neck
Work as for crewneck version until armholes measure:

1½	1½	1½	2	2½"
3.8	3.8	3.8	5	6.5 cm

Finished Chest Circumference

26	28	30	32	34"		26	28	30	32	34"
66	71	76	81.5	86.5 cm		66	71	76	81.5	86.5 cm

Dec 1 st at neck edge (end of RS rows) every RS row:

3	3	4	4	4	4 times.
4	5	5	7	7	7
5	9	9	12	10	10
6	10	13	13	13	13
7	15	15	18	16	18

Then dec 1 st at neck edge every 4 rows:

3	4	4	5	5	5 times.
4	4	6	5	5	5
5	4	5	4	5	5
6	4	4	5	5	5
7	3	4	4	5	4

There will remain:

3	13	13	14	15	17 sts.
4	17	17	18	20	22
5	20	21	22	25	28
6	25	25	27	30	33
7	28	30	32	35	38

Work even until piece measures same as back to shoulder. Shape shoulder as for back.

Cardigan Right Front with V-Neck

Work as for left front with V-neck but reverse shaping (i.e., shape neck at beg of RS rows and BO for shoulder at beg of WS row).

Finishing

Block pieces to measurements. With yarn threaded on a tapestry needle, sew shoulder seams.

Neckband: With smaller needles, RS facing, and beg at center front, pick up and knit 1 st for every BO st and about 3 sts for every 4 rows along sloped edges around neck opening for a crewneck. (Combine neckband with button and buttonhole bands for a V-neck version.) Adjust st count if necessary to achieve a full multiple of the edging patt you've chosen. Work in chosen pattern until neckband measures ¾" (2 cm), or desired length. BO all sts in patt.

Seams: Measure down (6½, 7, 7½, 8, 8½)" (16.5 [18, 19, 20.5, 21.5] cm) from shoulder seams and mark front and back for sleeve placement. Lay the garment flat with the RS facing upward. Fold the sleeve in half lengthwise to find the shoulder point (center of the BO edge), and pin the right side of the sleeve against the body without stretching or easing of the fabric, matching the shoulder points and making sure that the front and back armholes are the same length. With yarn threaded on a tapestry needle and beginning at the shoulder point (leave sufficient yarn at the beginning of the seam to be used later to work the other half), sew the sleeve to armhole to the underarm. Repeat for the other half of the armhole. Sew the sleeve and side seams in a continuous line.

Button band: (on left front for females; right front for males) With smaller needles and RS facing, pick up and knit about 3 sts for every 4 rows along center front edge. Adjust st count if necessary to achieve a full multiple of the edging pattern you've chosen. Work in chosen pattern until band measures ¾" (2 cm). BO all sts in patt. Mark placement of 5 to 7 buttons, one ½" (1.3 cm) up from CO edge, one at beg of neck shaping, and the others evenly spaced in between.

Buttonhole band: (on right front for females; left front for males) Work as for button band, working one-row buttonholes (see Glossary) opposite markers when band measures between ¼" and ½" (.6 and 1.3 cm). BO all sts in patt.

Weave in loose ends. Block again, if desired.

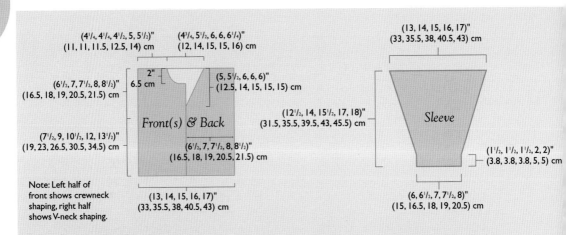

(4¼, 4¼, 4½, 5, 5½)"
(11, 11, 11.5, 12.5, 14) cm

(4¾, 5½, 6, 6, 6¼)"
(12, 14, 15, 15, 16) cm

(13, 14, 15, 16, 17)"
(33, 35.5, 38, 40.5, 43) cm

(6½, 7, 7½, 8, 8½)"
(16.5, 18, 19, 20.5, 21.5) cm

2"
6.5 cm

(5, 5½, 6, 6, 6)"
(12.5, 14, 15, 15, 15) cm

Front(s) & Back

(12½, 14, 15½, 17, 18)"
(31.5, 35.5, 39.5, 43, 45.5) cm

Sleeve

(7½, 9, 10½, 12, 13½)"
(19, 23, 26.5, 30.5, 34.5) cm

(6½, 7, 7½, 8, 8½)"
(16.5, 18, 19, 20.5, 21.5) cm

(1½, 1½, 1½, 2, 2)"
(3.8, 3.8, 3.8, 5, 5) cm

Note: Left half of front shows crewneck shaping, right half shows V-neck shaping.

(13, 14, 15, 16, 17)"
(33, 35.5, 38, 40.5, 43) cm

(6, 6½, 7, 7½, 8)"
(15, 16.5, 18, 19, 20.5) cm

child sizes 26"–34" (66 cm–86.5cm)

quick**tips** for tidy edges

- For a snug lower edge, cast on ten to twenty percent fewer stitches and work a ribbed edging for the desired length, increasing to the designated number of stitches on the last row of ribbing.

- If the ribbing or edging around a sleeve cuff or waist band isn't as snug as you'd like, sew a few rows of elastic thread around the inside of the edging.

- If you are unsure about what type of lower edging you want, use a provisional method of casting on (see Glossary), then come back later and work the edging downward from the cast-on row.

- To avoid binding off too tightly, bind off using a needle a couple of sizes larger than that used for the main knitting. You can also try a sewn or suspended bind-off (see Glossary).

- To avoid casting on too tightly, cast on using two needles held together or onto needles a couple of sizes larger than you plan to use for the rest of the sweater.

- When you're picking up stitches for neck or front edgings, pick up and knit one stitch for each bound-off stitch along horizontal edges, and about two stitches for every three rows, or three stitches for every four rows, along vertical or slanted edges. After working a few rows of the edging, evaluate how it looks. If the edging flares and ripples, you have too many stitches; if the body puckers and bubbles, you have too few stitches. Don't be afraid to rip out edging and try again. Even experienced designers may make two or three attempts before getting the look they want.

sizing adult

Finished Bust/Chest Circumference

36	38	40	42	44	46	48	50	52	54"
91.5	96.5	101.5	106.5	112	117	122	127	132	137 cm

Yarn Requirements

GAUGE											
3	610	660	720	780	870	900	960	1000	1050	1100 yd
	558	604	658	713	796	823	878	914	960	1006 m
4	860	930	1020	1100	1230	1270	1360	1420	1490	1560
	786	850	933	1006	1125	1161	1244	1298	1362	1426
5	1090	1180	1280	1390	1550	1600	1710	1790	1880	1970
	997	1079	1170	1271	1417	1463	1564	1637	1719	1801
6	1540	1660	1810	1960	2190	2270	2420	2530	2660	2780
	1408	1518	1655	1792	2003	2076	2213	2313	2432	2542
7	1690	1830	2000	2160	2410	2500	2670	2790	2930	3070
	1545	1673	1829	1975	2204	2286	2441	2551	2679	2807

Pullover Back
CO:

GAUGE										
3	54	58	60	64	66	70	72	76	78	82 sts.
4	72	76	80	84	88	92	96	100	104	108
5	90	94	100	106	110	116	120	126	130	136
6	108	114	120	126	132	138	144	150	156	162
7	126	134	140	148	154	162	168	176	182	190

Work edging of choice (see pages 35–37), then cont even until piece measures desired length to armhole, or about:

13½	13½	14	14½	15	15	15	15	15	15"
34.5	34.5	35.5	37	38	38	38	38	38	38 cm

Mark Armholes
Mark each edge of the last row for base of armhole. Cont even until armholes measure:

9	9½	10	10½	11	11½	12	12½	13	13½"
23	24	25.5	26.5	28	29	30.5	31.5	33	34.5 cm

Shape Shoulders and Neck
BO all sts, marking first and last:

GAUGE										
3	17	19	20	22	23	24	24	26	26	28 sts
4	23	25	27	28	30	31	32	34	35	37
5	29	31	34	36	37	39	40	42	44	46
6	35	37	40	43	45	47	48	51	52	55
7	40	44	47	50	52	54	56	59	61	64

Finished Bust/Chest Circumference									
36	38	40	42	44	46	48	50	52	54"
91.5	96.5	101.5	106.5	112	117	122	127	132	137 cm

for each shoulder and rem sts for back neck:

3	20	20	20	20	20	22	24	24	26	26 sts.
4	26	26	26	28	28	30	32	32	34	34
5	32	32	32	34	36	38	40	42	42	44
6	38	40	40	40	42	44	48	48	52	52
7	46	46	46	48	50	54	56	58	60	62

Pullover Front with Crewneck

(For V-neck option, see page 22.) Work as for back, ending with a WS row, until armholes measure:

6½	7	7½	8	8½	8½	9	9½	10	10½"
16.5	18	19	20.5	21.5	21.5	23	24	25.5	26.5 cm

Shape Crewneck

With RS facing, work across:

3	22	24	25	27	27	29	30	32	32	34 sts,
4	29	31	33	35	36	38	40	42	43	45
5	37	39	42	45	45	48	50	53	54	57
6	44	47	50	53	54	57	60	63	65	68
7	51	55	58	62	63	67	70	74	76	80

join new yarn and BO for front neck:

3	10	10	10	10	12	12	12	12	14	14 sts,
4	14	14	14	14	16	16	16	16	18	18
5	16	16	16	16	20	20	20	20	22	22
6	20	20	20	20	24	24	24	24	26	26
7	24	24	24	24	28	28	28	28	30	30

work to end. There will be the following number of sts at each side:

3	22	24	25	27	27	29	30	32	32	34 sts.
4	29	31	33	35	36	38	40	42	43	45
5	37	39	42	45	45	48	50	53	54	57
6	44	47	50	53	54	57	60	63	65	68
7	51	55	58	62	63	67	70	74	76	80

Working each side separately, at each neck edge BO 3 sts (if number is zero, omit these rows):

3	0	0	0	0	0	0	0	0	0	0 time(s).
4	0	0	0	1	0	1	1	1	1	1
5	1	1	1	1	1	1	1	2	1	2
6	1	1	1	1	1	1	2	2	2	2
7	2	2	2	2	2	2	2	2	2	2

Finished Bust/Chest Circumference

36	38	40	42	44	46	48	50	52	54"
91.5	96.5	101.5	106.5	112	117	122	127	132	137 cm

Then BO 2 sts:

	36	38	40	42	44	46	48	50	52	54"
3	1	1	1	1	1	1	2	2	2	2 time(s).
4	2	2	2	1	2	1	1	1	1	1
5	1	1	1	2	1	2	2	1	2	1
6	2	2	2	2	2	2	2	2	2	2
7	1	1	1	2	1	2	3	3	3	3

Then dec 1 st every RS row:

	36	38	40	42	44	46	48	50	52	54"
3	3	3	3	3	2	3	2	2	2	2 times.
4	2	2	2	2	2	2	3	3	3	3
5	3	3	3	2	3	2	3	3	3	3
6	2	3	3	3	2	3	2	2	3	3
7	3	3	3	2	3	3	2	3	3	4

There will be the following number of sts at each side:

	36	38	40	42	44	46	48	50	52	54"
3	17	19	20	22	23	24	24	26	26	28 sts.
4	23	25	27	28	30	31	32	34	35	37
5	29	31	34	36	37	39	40	42	44	46
6	35	37	40	43	45	47	48	51	52	55
7	40	44	47	50	52	54	56	59	61	64

Work even until armholes measure same as back to shoulder.

Shape Shoulders
BO all sts.

Pullover Front with V-Neck
Work as for back until armholes measure (ending with a WS row):

3	3	3½	3¾	4¼	4½	5	5¼	5½	6"
7.5	7.5	9	9.5	11	11.5	12.5	13.5	14	15 cm

With RS facing, work to center of row. Turn and work these sts only to shoulder (place rem sts on a holder to work later). Dec 1 st at neck edge every RS row:

	36	38	40	42	44	46	48	50	52	54"
3	6	5	5	5	5	6	8	7	9	9 times.
4	9	8	8	9	9	10	12	12	13	13
5	12	11	11	12	14	15	17	18	17	19
6	15	16	16	14	16	17	21	20	23	23
7	20	19	19	19	21	24	26	27	28	30

Finished Bust/Chest Circumference

	36	38	40	42	44	46	48	50	52	54"
	91.5	96.5	101.5	106.5	112	117	122	127	132	137 cm

Then dec 1 st at neck edge every 4 rows:

3	4	5	5	5	5	5	4	5	4	4 time(s).
4	4	5	5	5	5	5	4	4	4	4
5	4	5	5	5	4	4	3	3	4	3
6	4	4	4	6	5	5	3	4	3	3
7	3	4	4	5	4	3	2	2	2	1

There will remain:

3	17	19	20	22	23	24	24	26	26	28 sts.
4	23	25	27	28	30	31	32	34	35	37
5	29	31	34	36	37	39	40	42	44	46
6	35	37	40	43	45	47	48	51	52	55
7	40	44	47	50	52	54	56	59	61	64

Work even until armhole measures same as back to shoulder. BO all sts. Rejoin yarn at neck edge of held sts and work as for first half, reversing neck and shoulder shaping.

Sleeves

CO:

3	28	28	30	30	30	30	32	32	34	34 sts.
4	38	38	40	40	40	44	44	44	46	46
5	46	46	50	50	50	54	54	56	58	58
6	56	56	60	60	60	66	66	66	68	68
7	66	66	70	70	70	76	76	76	80	80

Work edging of choice until piece measures desired length or about:

	2½	2½	2½	2½	2½	2½	2½	2½	2½	2½"
	6.5	6.5	6.5	6.5	6.5	6.5	6.5	6.5	6.5	6.5 cm

Change to St st and inc 1 st each end of needle every 2 rows (if number is zero, omit these rows):

3	0	0	0	0	0	0	0	0	0	4 times.
4	0	0	0	0	0	0	0	4	6	10
5	0	0	0	0	0	0	3	7	11	16
6	0	0	0	0	2	0	6	14	18	26
7	0	0	0	0	5	3	11	19	23	31

Finished Bust/Chest Circumference

36	38	40	42	44	46	48	50	52	54"
91.5	96.5	101.5	106.5	112	117	122	127	132	137 cm

Then inc I st each end of needle every 4 rows (if number is zero, omit these rows):

3	0	5	4	5	10	12	15	19	22	19 times.
4	5	9	10	15	19	18	24	24	23	21
5	12	16	18	21	29	27	30	27	25	22
6	16	23	24	31	34	36	33	28	26	21
7	20	27	31	38	37	39	35	30	28	23

Then inc I st each end of needle every 6 rows (if number is zero, omit these rows):

3	13	10	11	11	8	7	5	2	0	0 time(s).
4	12	10	10	7	5	6	2	0	0	0
5	10	8	7	6	1	3	0	0	0	0
6	10	6	6	2	0	0	0	0	0	0
7	10	6	4	0	0	0	0	0	0	0

There will be:

3	54	58	60	62	66	68	72	74	78	80 sts.
4	72	76	80	84	88	92	96	100	104	108
5	90	94	100	104	110	114	120	124	130	134
6	108	114	120	126	132	138	144	150	156	162
7	126	132	140	146	154	160	168	174	182	188

Work even if necessary until piece measures:

19	19½	20	20½	21	21½	22	22	22	22"
48.5	49.5	51	52	53.5	54.5	56	56	56	56 cm

BO all sts.

Finishing

Block pieces to measurements. With yarn threaded on a tapestry needle, sew one shoulder seam.

Neckband: Choose a crewneck finish on pages 66–67 or a V-neck finish on pages 68–69. With smaller needles, RS facing, and beg at other shoulder, pick up and knit I st for each BO st and about 3 sts for every 4 rows along sloped edges around neck opening. Adjust st count if necessary to achieve a full multiple of the edging patt you've chosen, plus 2 extra "seam" sts. Work in chosen pattern until neckband measures I" (2.5 cm), or desired length. BO all sts in patt.

Seams: Sew rem shoulder and neckband seam. Measure down (9, 9½, 10, 10½, 11, 11½, 12, 12½, 13, 13½)" (23 [24, 25.5, 26.5, 28, 29, 30.5, 31.5, 33, 34.5] cm) from shoulder seam and mark front and back for sleeve placement. Lay garment flat with RS facing upward. Fold sleeve in half lengthwise to locate shoulder point (center of BO edge), and pin RS of sleeve to body

Finished Bust/Chest Circumference

36	38	40	42	44	46	48	50	52	54"
91.5	96.5	101.5	106.5	112	117	122	127	132	137 cm

without stretching or easing the fabric, matching shoulder points, and making sure that front and back armholes are the same length. With yarn threaded on a tapestry needle and beginning at the shoulder point (leave sufficient yarn at the beginning of the seam to be used later to work the other half), sew sleeve to back armhole to the underarm. Repeat for front half of armhole. Sew sleeve and side seams in a continuous line.
Weave in loose ends. Block again, if desired.

Cardigan Back
Work as for pullover version.

Cardigan Left Front with Crewneck
CO:

3	27	29	30	32	33	35	36	38	39	41 sts.
4	36	38	40	42	44	46	48	50	52	54
5	45	47	50	53	55	58	60	63	65	68
6	54	57	60	63	66	69	72	75	78	81
7	63	67	70	74	77	81	84	88	91	95

Work edging of choice (as for back), then cont even until piece measures same length as back to armhole. Mark beg of RS row for armhole placement. Cont even until armhole measures (ending with a RS row):

6½	7	7½	8	8½	8½	9	9½	10	10½"
16.5	18	19	20.5	21.5	21.5	23	24	25.5	26.5 cm

Shape Crewneck
At beg of next WS row BO:

3	5	5	5	5	6	6	6	6	7	7 sts,
4	7	7	7	7	8	8	8	8	9	9
5	8	8	8	8	10	10	10	10	11	11
6	10	10	10	10	12	12	12	12	13	13
7	12	12	12	12	14	14	14	14	15	15

work to end. At neck edge BO 3 sts (if number is zero, omit these rows):

3	0	0	0	0	0	0	0	0	0	0 time(s).
4	0	0	0	1	0	1	1	1	1	1
5	1	1	1	1	1	1	1	2	1	2
6	1	1	1	1	1	1	2	2	2	2
7	2	2	2	2	2	2	2	2	2	2

Finished Bust/Chest Circumference

36	38	40	42	44	46	48	50	52	54"
91.5	96.5	101.5	106.5	112	117	122	127	132	137 cm

Then BO 2 sts:

3	1	1	1	1	1	1	2	2	2	2 time(s).
4	2	2	2	1	2	1	1	1	1	1
5	1	1	1	2	1	2	2	1	2	1
6	2	2	2	2	2	2	2	2	2	2
7	1	1	1	2	1	2	3	3	3	3

Then dec 1 st at neck edge every RS row:

3	3	3	3	3	2	3	2	2	2	2 times.
4	2	2	2	2	2	2	3	3	3	3
5	3	3	3	2	3	2	3	3	3	3
6	2	3	3	3	2	3	2	2	3	3
7	3	3	3	2	3	3	2	3	3	4

There will remain:

3	17	19	20	22	23	24	24	26	26	28 sts.
4	23	25	27	28	30	31	32	34	35	37
5	29	31	34	36	37	39	40	42	44	46
6	35	37	40	43	45	47	48	51	52	55
7	40	44	47	50	52	54	56	59	61	64

Cont even until piece measures same as back to shoulder.

Shape Shoulder
With RS facing, BO all sts.

Cardigan Right Front with Crewneck
Work as for left front but reverse shaping (i.e., shape neck at beg of RS rows; BO for shoulder at beg of WS row).

Cardigan Left Front with V-Neck
Work as for crewneck version until armholes measure (ending with a WS row):

3	3	3½	3¾	4¼	4½	5	5¼	5½	6"
7.5	7.5	9	9.5	11	11.5	12.5	13.5	14	15 cm

Finished Bust/Chest Circumference

36	38	40	42	44	46	48	50	52	54"
91.5	96.5	101.5	106.5	112	117	122	127	132	137 cm

Dec 1 st at neck edge (end of RS rows) every RS row:

3	6	5	5	5	5	6	8	7	9	9 times.
4	9	8	8	9	9	10	12	12	13	13
5	12	11	11	12	14	15	17	18	17	19
6	15	16	16	14	16	17	21	20	23	23
7	20	19	19	19	21	24	26	27	28	30

Then dec 1 st at neck edge every 4 rows:

3	4	5	5	5	5	5	4	5	4	4 time(s).
4	4	5	5	5	5	5	4	4	4	4
5	4	5	5	5	4	4	3	3	4	3
6	4	4	4	6	5	5	3	4	3	3
7	3	4	4	5	4	3	2	2	2	1

There will remain:

3	17	19	20	22	23	24	24	26	26	28 sts.
4	23	25	27	28	30	31	32	34	35	37
5	29	31	34	36	37	39	40	42	44	46
6	35	37	40	43	45	47	48	51	52	55
7	40	44	47	50	52	54	56	59	61	64

Work even until piece measures same as back to shoulder. Shape shoulder as for back.

Cardigan Right Front with V-Neck

Work as for left front with V-neck but reverse neck and shoulder shaping (i.e., shape neck at beg of RS rows and BO for shoulder at beg of WS row).

Finishing

Block pieces to measurements. With yarn threaded on a tapestry needle, sew shoulder seams. *Neckband*: With smaller needles, RS facing, and beg at center front, pick up and knit 1 st for every BO st and about 3 sts for every 4 rows along sloped edges around neck opening for a crewneck version. (Combine the neckband with the button and buttonhole bands for a V-neck version.) Adjust st count if necessary to achieve a full multiple of the edging pattern you've chosen. Work in chosen pattern until band measures 1" (2.5 cm) or desired length. BO all sts in patt. *Seams*: Measure down (9, 9½, 10, 10½, 11, 11½, 12, 12½, 13, 13½)" (23 [24, 25.5, 26.5, 28, 29, 30.5, 31.5, 33, 34.5] cm) from shoulder seam and mark front and back for sleeve placement. Lay the garment flat with the RS facing upward. Fold the sleeve in half lengthwise to find the shoulder point (center of the BO edge), and pin the right side of the sleeve against the body without stretching or easing of the fabric, matching the shoulder points and making sure that the front and back armholes are the same length. With yarn threaded on a tapestry needle and beginning at the shoulder point (leave sufficient yarn at the beginning of the seam to be used later to work the other half), sew the sleeve to armhole to the underarm. Repeat for the other half of the armhole. Sew the sleeve and side seams in a continuous line.

Button band: (on left front for females; right front for males) With RS facing, pick up and knit about 3 sts for every 4 rows along center front edge. Adjust st count if necessary to achieve a full multiple of the edging pattern chosen. Work in chosen pattern until band measures ¾" (2 cm). BO all sts in patt. Mark placement of 7 to 9 buttons, one ½" (1.3 cm) up from CO edge, one at beg of neck shaping, and the others evenly spaced in between.

Buttonhole band: (on right front for females; left front for males) Work as for button band, working one-row buttonholes (see Glossary) opposite markers when band measures between ¼" and ½" (.6 and 1.3 cm). BO all sts in patt.

Weave in loose ends. Sew buttons to button band opposite buttonholes. Block again, if desired.

quick**tips** for general success

- Alter sweater length as you wish—from a cropped top to an ankle-length tunic—by adjusting the number of rows you knit before you start the armhole shaping. Remember that altering the length will affect the amount of yarn you'll need.

- For a snug-fitting sweater with a retro look, follow the instructions that give you one or two inches of ease around the chest/bust. For an oversized sweater, follow the instructions that give you six or more inches of ease around the chest/bust. In either case, follow the length measurements for the size that gives you three to four inches of ease.

- To ensure a sweater that fits the way you like, measure a similar sweater that fits planned wearer well; use the measurements from that sweater in choosing the size to make.

- Always check dyelots to make sure all of your balls or skeins will match when knitted up. Make a note of the dyelot number so that if you want more yarn, you'll be more likely to match what you have.

- For the most inconspicuous yarn joins, introduce the new yarn at the end of a row, not in the middle where a slight difference in texture or gauge may be noticeable.

- Taper the shoulders on drop-shoulder and modified drop-shoulder sweaters by binding off the shoulder stitches in three steps (on three rows); bind off one third of the stitches in each step.

- When you're shaping armholes and neck, use directional decreases for a clean finish—ssk for a left-slanting decrease at one edge and k2tog for a right-slanting decrease at the other edge.

- Knit with yarn that you really like. You'll enjoy what you're doing.

- If possible, don't put knitting down in the middle of a row. The stitches can stretch and become distorted by the time you pick up your knitting again.

- Keep a notebook or journal of your knitting projects so you can easily refer to them when it's time to knit another garment of the same yarn or for the same person.

- Make a photocopy of the chart you plan to use and circle or highlight the numbers that apply to your size and gauge before you begin knitting. That way, you will avoid accidentally following the wrong instructions.

- Sew a couple of yards of extra yarn into the side seams of a sweater to have yarn for darning holes later.

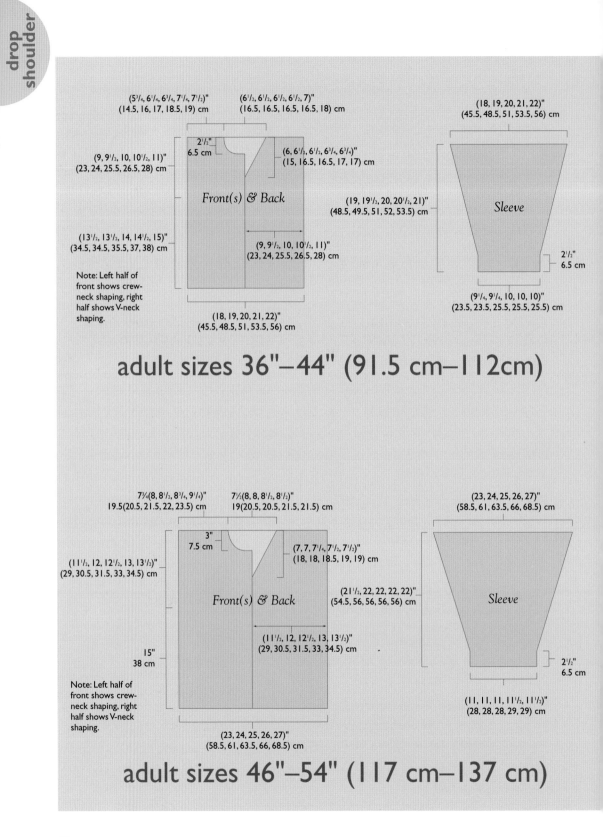

(5³/₄, 6¹/₄, 6³/₄, 7¹/₄, 7¹/₂)"
(14.5, 16, 17, 18.5, 19) cm

(6¹/₂, 6¹/₂, 6¹/₂, 6¹/₂, 7)"
(16.5, 16.5, 16.5, 16.5, 18) cm

(18, 19, 20, 21, 22)"
(45.5, 48.5, 51, 53.5, 56) cm

2¹/₂"
6.5 cm

(9, 9¹/₂, 10, 10¹/₂, 11)"
(23, 24, 25.5, 26.5, 28) cm

(6, 6¹/₂, 6¹/₂, 6³/₄, 6³/₄)"
(15, 16.5, 16.5, 17, 17) cm

Front(s) & Back

(19, 19¹/₂, 20, 20¹/₂, 21)"
(48.5, 49.5, 51, 52, 53.5) cm

Sleeve

(13¹/₂, 13¹/₂, 14, 14¹/₂, 15)"
(34.5, 34.5, 35.5, 37, 38) cm

(9, 9¹/₂, 10, 10¹/₂, 11)"
(23, 24, 25.5, 26.5, 28) cm

Note: Left half of
front shows crew-
neck shaping, right
half shows V-neck
shaping.

2¹/₂"
6.5 cm

(9¹/₄, 9¹/₄, 10, 10, 10)"
(23.5, 23.5, 25.5, 25.5, 25.5) cm

(18, 19, 20, 21, 22)"
(45.5, 48.5, 51, 53.5, 56) cm

adult sizes 36"–44" (91.5 cm–112cm)

7³/₄(8, 8¹/₂, 8³/₄, 9¹/₄)"
19.5(20.5, 21.5, 22, 23.5) cm

7¹/₂(8, 8, 8¹/₂, 8¹/₂)"
19(20.5, 20.5, 21.5, 21.5) cm

(23, 24, 25, 26, 27)"
(58.5, 61, 63.5, 66, 68.5) cm

3"
7.5 cm

(11¹/₂, 12, 12¹/₂, 13, 13¹/₂)"
(29, 30.5, 31.5, 33, 34.5) cm

(7, 7, 7¹/₄, 7¹/₂, 7¹/₂)"
(18, 18, 18.5, 19, 19) cm

Front(s) & Back

(21¹/₂, 22, 22, 22, 22)"
(54.5, 56, 56, 56, 56) cm

Sleeve

15"
38 cm

(11¹/₂, 12, 12¹/₂, 13, 13¹/₂)"
(29, 30.5, 31.5, 33, 34.5) cm

Note: Left half of
front shows crew-
neck shaping, right
half shows V-neck
shaping.

2¹/₂"
6.5 cm

(11, 11, 11, 11¹/₂, 11¹/₂)"
(28, 28, 28, 29, 29) cm

(23, 24, 25, 26, 27)"
(58.5, 61, 63.5, 66, 68.5) cm

adult sizes 46"–54" (117 cm–137 cm)

Chunky Drop-Shoulder Turtleneck

This loose-fitting pullover follows the instructions for the crewneck version of the drop-shoulder sweater. To prevent the lower body and sleeve ribbing from pulling in too much, they are worked on the same size needle as the main body. Because the yarn is thick and the gauge is large—3 stitches to the inch—one extra "seam" stitch is added at each selvedge so that excess width isn't lost in the seams. The lower half of the turtleneck is worked on needles one size smaller than the body; the upper half is worked on larger needles to allow it to fold over nicely.

Finished Size: 32" (81.5 cm) chest circumference.

Yarn: Muench Via Mala (100% wool; 73 yd [67 m]/50 g): #22 chartreuse, 8 balls.

Needles: Body and sleeves—Size 11 (8 mm): straight and set of 4 double-pointed (dpn). Neck—Size 10½ (6.5 mm): set of 4 dpn. Adjust needle size if necessary to obtain the correct gauge.

Notions: Markers (m); tapestry needle.

Gauge: 3 sts and 5 rows = 1" (2.5 cm) in stockinette stitch on size 11 (8-mm) needles.

Back

With larger needles, CO 50 sts (48 sts + 2 edge sts). *Set-up row*: P1, *P2, k2; rep from *, end p1. Cont in rib as established until piece measures 1½" (3.8 cm) from beg, ending with a WS row. Change to St st and cont even until piece measures 12" (30.5 cm) from beg. Mark each edge of last row for base of armholes. Cont even until armholes measure 8" (20.5 cm), ending with a WS row. BO all sts, marking first and last 16 sts (15 sts + 1 edge st) for shoulders, and center 18 sts for back neck.

Front

Work as for back until armholes measure 6" (15 cm), ending with a WS row. *Shape crewneck*: (RS) K20, join new yarn and BO center 10 sts, knit to end—20 sts each side. Working each side separately, at each neck edge, BO 2 sts once, then BO 1 st 2 times—16 sts rem each side. Cont even until piece measures same as back to shoulder. BO all sts.

Sleeves

With larger needles, CO 24 sts (22 sts + 2 edge sts). Work k2, p2 rib for 7 rows. Change to St st and inc 1 st each end of needle every 4 rows 5 times, then every 6 rows 8 times—50 sts. Cont even until piece measures 17" (43 cm) from beg. BO all sts.

Finishing

Block pieces to measurements. With yarn threaded on a tapestry needle, sew shoulder seams. Sew sleeve tops to front and back between armhole markers. Sew sleeve and side seams. *Turtleneck:* With smaller dpn, RS facing, and beg at right shoulder seam, pick up and knit 18 sts across back neck, 10 sts along side front neck, 10 sts across front neck, and 10 sts along other side front neck—48 sts total. Place marker (pm) and join into a rnd. Work k2, p2 rib until neck measures 3" (7.5 cm). Change to larger dpn and cont in rib for 3" (7.5 cm) more. BO all sts in patt. Weave in loose ends. Block again if desired.

Mistake Rib Cardigan

This lightweight crewneck cardigan demonstrates how easy it is to add a stitch pattern to the basic charted instructions. The mistake rib stitch is a multiple of four stitches that just happens to match the number of stitches for a 40" (101.5 cm) finished circumference at a gauge of 5 stitches per inch. To allow for seams that don't interrupt the stitch pattern, one extra "seam" stitch is added to the side edges of the fronts and back. The

---

Finished Size: 40" (101.5 cm) bust/chest circumference, buttoned.
Yarn: GGH Soft Kid (70% kid mohair, 25% nylon, 5% wool; 151 yd [138 m]/25 g): #19 maroon, 9 balls. Yarn distributed by GGH/Muench.
Needles: Size 8 (5 mm). Adjust needle size if necessary to obtain the correct gauge.
Notions: Tapestry needle; nine ¾" (2-cm) buttons.
Gauge: 5 sts and 7 rows = 1" (2.5 cm) in mistake rib on size 8 (5-mm) needles; 4½ sts and 6 rows = 1" (2.5 cm) in stockinette stitch on size 8 (5-mm) needles.

---

lower body and sleeves are trimmed with a bit of k2, p2 rib that flows gracefully into the mistake rib stitch of the main body. The button and buttonhole bands are picked up and knitted sideways from the center fronts.

Mistake Rib
(multiple of 4 sts)
Row 1: *K2, p2; rep from *.
Row 2: *P1, k2, p1; rep from *.
Repeat Rows 1 and 2 for pattern.

Back
CO 102 sts (100 sts + 2 sts to balance rib). Work k2, p2 rib until piece measures 1" (2.5 cm) from beg. Work all sts in mistake rib until piece measures 14" (35.5 cm) from beg. Mark each edge of last row for base of armholes. Cont as established until armholes measure 10" (25.5 cm), ending with a WS row. BO all sts, marking first and last 35 sts for shoulders and center 32 sts for back neck.

Left Front
CO 51 sts (50 sts + 1 edge st). K1 (edge st; work in St st throughout), *k2, p2; rep from *, ending k2. Cont as established until piece measures 1" (2.5 cm) from beg, ending with a WS row. Keeping edge st in St st as established and working last 2 sts of RS rows as k2, work rem 48 sts in mistake rib until piece measures 14" (35.5 cm) from beg. Mark beg of RS row for base of armhole. Cont as established until armhole measures 7½" (19 cm), ending with a RS row. *Shape crewneck*: (WS) BO 8 sts at beg of row, work in patt to end—43 sts rem. At neck edge, BO 3 sts once, then BO 2 sts once, then dec 1 st every RS row 3 times—

35 sts rem (34 patt sts + I edge st). Cont even until piece measures same as back to shoulder. BO all sts.

Right Front

Work as for left front but reverse shaping (BO and shape neck at beg of RS rows; BO for shoulder at beg of WS rows).

Sleeves

CO 50 sts. Work k2, p2 rib until piece measures I" (2.5 cm) from beg, ending with a WS row. Next row: K1 (edge st; work in St st throughout), work 48 sts in mistake rib, k1 (edge st; work in St st throughout). Working edge sts in St st, cont as established, inc I st each end of needle every 4 rows 18 times, then every 6 rows 7 times, working new sts into patt—100 sts. Cont even in patt until piece measures 20" (51 cm) from beg. BO all sts.

Finishing

Block pieces to measurements. With yarn threaded on a tapestry needle, sew shoulder seams. Sew sleeve tops to front and back between armhole markers. Sew sleeve and side seams. **Neckband:** With RS facing and beg at right front neck, pick up and knit 3 sts for every 4 rows and I st for every BO st around neck opening—76 sts; each end of band has a purl edge st followed by k2 as viewed from RS. Adjust sts if necessary to balance k2, p2 rib. Work k2, p2 rib until band measures I" (2.5 cm). BO all sts. **Button band:** With RS facing, pick up and knit about 3 sts for every 4 rows along left front edge—110 sts; band begs and ends with k2 on RS. Work k2, p2 rib until band measures ¾" (2 cm). BO all sts. On but-

ton band, mark placement of 9 buttons, one ½" (1.3 cm) up from CO edge, one at center of neckband, and the others evenly spaced in between. **Buttonhole band:** With RS facing, pick up and knit 110 sts along right front edge as for button band. Work as for button band, working 2-st one-row buttonholes (see Glossary) opposite markers when band measures between ¼" (0.6 cm) and ½" (1.3 cm). BO all sts. Weave in loose ends. Sew buttons to button band opposite buttonholes. Block again if desired.

Tweed V-Neck Pullover

This unisex pullover follows the basic drop-shoulder chart with V-neck shaping. Instead ribbing, the edges have short hems that are punctuated at the turning point with a garter ridge.

Finished Size: 44" (112 cm) bust/chest circumference.

Yarn: Horstia Tweed (55% wool, 27% acrylic, 18% viscose; 109 yd [100 m]/50 g): #2 turquoise, 14 balls. Yarn distributed by GGH/Muench.

Needles: Body and sleeves—Size 8 (5 mm): straight and 16" (40-cm) circular (cir). Adjust needle size if necessary to obtain the correct gauge.

Notions: Tapestry needle; markers (m).

Gauge: 5 sts and 7 rows = I" (2.5 cm) in stockinette stitch on size 8 (5-mm) needles.

The directional decreases for the V-neck are worked one stitch in from the edge to form a prominent line (called full-fashioning) that outlines and accentuates the neck opening.

Back

With straight needles, CO 110 sts. Purl 1 row. Knit 1 row. Purl 3 rows for turning ridge. Cont in St st until piece measures 15" (38 cm) from turning ridge. Mark each edge of last row for base of armholes. Cont even until armholes measure 11" (28 cm), ending with a WS row. BO all sts, marking first and last 37 sts for shoulders, and center 36 sts for back neck.

Front

Work as for back until armholes measure 4¼" (11 cm), ending with a WS row. **Shape V-neck**: (RS) K52, k2tog, k1, join new yarn, k1, ssk, knit to end—54 sts rem each side. Working each side separately, dec 1 st at neck edge every RS row 13 more times, then every 4 rows 4 times—37 sts rem each side. Work even until piece measures same as back to shoulder. BO all sts.

Sleeves

With straight needles, CO 50 sts. Purl 1 row. Knit 1 row. Purl 3 rows. Cont in St st until piece measures 2½" (6.5 cm) from turning ridge, ending with a WS row. Inc 1 st each end on needle every 4 rows 29 times, then every 6 rows once—110 sts. Cont even until piece measures 21" (53.5 cm) from turning ridge, ending with a WS row. BO all sts.

Finishing

Block pieces to measurements. With yarn threaded on a tapestry needle, sew shoulder seams. Sew sleeve tops to front and back between armhole markers. Sew sleeve and side seams. **Neckband**: With cir needle, RS facing, and beg at right shoulder seam, pick up and knit 100 sts evenly spaced around neck opening, placing a marker at base of V. Join for working in the rnd. Work St st, and *at the same time* dec 1 st each side of marker as foll: Knit to 2 sts before m, k2tog, slip m, ssk, knit to end—94 sts rem after 3 rnds have been worked. Purl 1 rnd. Knit 3 more rnds, and *at the same time* inc 1 st each side of marker every rnd as foll: Knit to 1 st before m, M1 (see Glossary), k1, slip m, k1, M1, knit to end—100 sts after 3 rnds have been worked. BO all sts. Turn facings to WS along fold lines and sew in place. Weave in loose ends. Block again if desired.

personal**touches** edgings

To prevent curling, hide uneven edge stitches, and conceal stair-step notches along shaped armholes and necklines, most garments are worked with some type of edging stitch. Depending on the type of edging used, a sweater can take on a casual or elegant look. Here are some of the most common edging stitches/techniques.

Garter Stitch
Worked by knitting every stitch in every row, a garter-stitch edging forms horizontal bands of "bumps" that are identical on the right and wrong sides of the work. Garter stitch can be worked on any number of stitches.

The Cabled Yoke Pullover on page 196 has garter-stitch edgings.

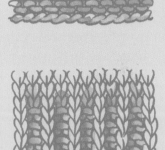

Ribbing
Because it alternates columns of knit and purl stitches, ribbing tends to pull in and narrow the width of a piece. You can use a variety of ribbings, the most common of which are single rib (alternating one knit stitch with one purl stitch) and double rib (alternating two knit stitches with two purl stitches). Single rib is worked on a multiple of two stitches, double rib on a multiple of four. You'll find dozens of other ribbing options in books of stitch patterns.

Single rib

The Child's Fair Isle Pullover on page 192 has single rib edgings, the Striped Crewneck Pullover on page 169 has double rib edgings.

Double rib

Cable Ribbing
You can add interest to a ribbed edging by introducing cables in some of the columns of knit stitches. Because there are purl stitches between the cables, this ribbing does not curl, but it does draw in like a double rib. The width of the cables and the number of purl stitches in the purl column between them dictates the number of stitches in the pattern repeat.

The Cable Panel Pullover on page 59 has cable ribbing.

personal**touches** edgings

I-Cord

I-cord makes a tidy, rounded edge that is sophisticated in its simplicity. It is worked on two double-pointed needles in such a way that a small tube is formed (see Glossary). As an edging, it can be worked separately and sewn in place, or attached 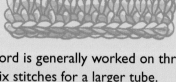 directly to the edge of the piece as it is knitted. I-cord is generally worked on three stitches, but you can work it on four, five, or even six stitches for a larger tube.

The Zip-Front Jacket on page 133 has I-cord edgings.

Rolled Edging

A rolled edging appears to be a cross between a garter edging and an I-cord edging. It is formed by the natural tendency of knitted fabric to curl. A rolled edging can be worked on any number of stockinette stitches for the desired length of roll. To control the amount of roll, work a row of reverse stockinette stitch or a few rows of single 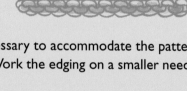 or double rib (adjusting the stitch number if necessary to accommodate the pattern repeat) between the roll and the garment body. Work the edging on a smaller needle for a tighter roll.

The Diamond Cable Pullover on page 136 has a rolled edging at the neck.

Hemmed Edging

A hem gives a clean, straight line without interruption to the garment body. Begin by knitting a facing on needles a size smaller than you use to get the main gauge. Work stockinette stitch for the length of the facing, then work a turning row (purl one right-side row, or knit one wrong-side row). Change to the larger needles and work stockinette stitch for the same length as the facing, ending with a wrong-side row. Join the facing to the body on the next right-side row as follows: Fold the facing to the inside and knit each stitch on the needle together with the edge loop of the corresponding stitch of the cast-on row.

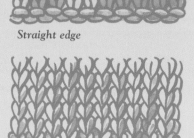

Straight edge

Picot edge

Alternatively, you can stitch the facing in place after completing the knitting. You can work a hemmed edging on any number of stitches. For a delicate variation, work a picot turning row on an odd number of stitches as follows: *Knit two stitches together, yarnover; repeat from *.

The Tweed V-Neck Pullover on page 33 has a hemmed edging. The button and buttonhole bands on the Lace-Edged Cardigan on page 61 have picot-hemmed edgings.

Lace Edging

There are hundreds of stitch patterns in which yarnovers are paired with decreases to create lacy patterns that can be used to trim the sleeve, neck, and lower body edges of a garment. Look to the many reference books of stitch patterns to find suitable candidates. Shown here is the Feather Lace edging. Remember, you may have to adjust your stitch count to accommodate full pattern repeats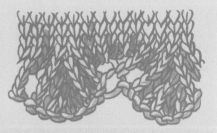

of the edging pattern you choose. Unless your pattern has nearly the same number of knit stitches as purl stitches, it will tend to curl and may require firm blocking.

The Lace-Edged Cardigan on page 61 has a feather lace edging.

Single Crochet

Sometimes you may want an inconspicuous edging that will control curling and even out the edge stitches, but not add length or disrupt the pattern in the body. Single crochet can be ideal for these situations. Worked with a crochet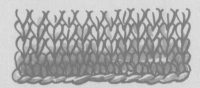

hook, a single crochet edging has a neat appearance and can be worked on any number of stitches. Because it is worked independently of the knitted stitches, you have the freedom to add and skip stitches as desired to get the results you want. Because single crochet won't completely eliminate curling, it works best on knitted fabrics that contain a mixture of knit and purl stitches—such fabrics are less prone to curling than stockinette stitch—and on nonelastic fibers such as cotton, silk, and some man-made fibers. Instructions for working single crochet are provided in the Glossary.

The Chenille Yoke Cardigan on page 193 has a single crochet edging.

modified drop-shoulder sweaters

The modified drop shoulder (also called indented sleeve or square armhole) makes a slightly more fitted version of the drop-shoulder sweater (see page 10) without compromising easy execution. The front and back rectangles are notched at the armholes (achieved by binding off several stitches), which brings the top of the sleeve closer to the shoulder, thus eliminating some of the excess fabric at the armholes. Like the drop-shoulder sleeve, the top of the sleeve is straight; there is no sleeve cap shaping. The sleeves are worked a bit longer than their drop-shoulder counterparts to fill in the armhole notch.

It's no wonder that modified drop-shoulder sweaters are enormously popular. The knitting is straightforward, the seaming is uncomplicated, the sleeves are easy to place in the notched upper body, and there is little shaping to interrupt a texture or color pattern. Although the fit is more refined than in a drop-shoulder sweater, modified drop-shoulder sweaters maintain the casual, boxy look.

Three sweater variations following the modified drop-shoulder chart. Top to bottom: Lace-Edged Cardigan at 34" (86.5 cm) circumference and 6 stitches/inch, Cable Panel Pullover at 42" (106.5 cm) circumference and 5 stitches/inch, and Shawl-Collar Pullover at 30" (76 cm) circumference and 4 stitches/inch. Step-by-step instructions for these sweaters begin on page 59.

basic anatomy

The following modified drop-shoulder sweaters are worked in pieces—back, front(s), and sleeves—from the lower edges upward. The back is worked straight to the armholes at which point a few stitches are bound off for the armholes, then the piece continues straight to the shoulders. The shoulders and back neck are bound off in a single step—there is no shoulder shaping. For the pullover version, the front is worked the same as the back up to the point where stitches are bound off and/or decreased to shape a crew- or V-neck. For the cardigan version, the front consists of two pieces—each with half the number of stitches used for the back. The sleeves are widened for the upper arm by paired increases worked at specific intervals until the desired width is achieved. The upper sleeve is worked straight for the depth of the armhole notch in the body, then all of the sleeve stitches are bound off at once. After the pieces are blocked, they are sewn together and the neck is finished off with the desired edging. The seaming is easy in this sweater as long as the upper sleeve width matches the space allotted between the notches—check your gauge and measure carefully to make sure that they match.

To use the following chart to make a modified drop-shoulder sweater, you need to choose yarn, determine your gauge (see page 6), and pick a size based on the desired finished bust/chest circumference. You'll also need straight needles in the size necessary to obtain the desired gauge (and needles one or two sizes smaller for edgings, if appropriate), a tapestry needle, and buttons for cardigan versions: 5 to 7 for child sizes, 7 to 9 for adult sizes. Gauge runs vertically along the left side of the chart; finished bust/chest circumference is listed horizontally across the top. The chart for children's sizes begins on page 41; schematics are on page 46. The chart for adult sizes begins on page 47; schematics are on page 58.

sizing child

Finished Chest Circumference

26	28	30	32	34"
66	71	76	81.5	86.5 cm

26	28	30	32	34"
66	71	76	81.5	86.5 cm

G A U G E

Yarn Requirements

3	270	340	410	490	550 yd
	247	311	375	448	503 m
4	390	480	580	690	780
	357	439	530	631	713
5	490	610	730	870	990
	448	558	667	796	905
6	690	860	1030	1230	1400
	631	786	942	1125	1280
7	760	950	1140	1350	1540
	695	869	1042	1234	1408

Pullover Back
CO:

3	40	42	46	48	52 sts.
4	52	56	60	64	68
5	64	70	74	80	86
6	78	84	90	96	102
7	90	98	106	112	120

Work edging of choice (see pages 35–37), then cont even until piece measures desired length to armhole, or about:

7½	9	10½	12	13½"
19	23	26.5	30.5	34.5 cm

Shape Armholes
At beg of next 2 rows BO:

3	3	3	3	3	4 sts.
4	4	4	4	4	5
5	5	5	5	5	6
6	5	5	6	6	7
7	6	6	7	7	8

There will remain:

3	34	36	40	42	44 sts.
4	44	48	52	56	58
5	54	60	64	70	74
6	68	74	78	84	88
7	78	86	92	98	104

Cont even until armholes measure:

6½	7	7½	8	8½"
16.5	18	19	20.5	21.5 cm

Shape Shoulders and Neck
BO all sts, marking first and last:

3	10	10	11	12	13 sts
4	12	13	14	16	17
5	15	17	17	20	21
6	19	21	21	24	26
7	21	24	24	28	30

for each shoulder, and rem sts for back neck:

3	14	16	18	18	18 sts.
4	20	22	24	24	24
5	24	26	30	30	32
6	30	32	36	36	36
7	36	38	44	42	44

Pullover Front with Crewneck
(For V-neck option, see page 42.) Work as for back until armholes measure (ending with a WS row):

4½	5	5½	6	6½"
11.5	12.5	14	15	16.5 cm

Shape Crewneck
With RS facing, work across:

3	14	14	15	16	17 sts,
4	18	19	19	21	22
5	22	23	24	27	29
6	28	29	29	32	34
7	32	33	34	37	40

41

Finished Chest Circumference

26	28	30	32	34"		26	28	30	32	34"
66	71	76	81.5	86.5 cm		66	71	76	81.5	86.5 cm

join new yarn and BO for front neck:

	26	28	30	32	34"
3	6	8	10	10	10 sts,
4	8	10	14	14	14
5	10	14	16	16	16
6	12	16	20	20	20
7	14	20	24	24	24

work to end. There will be the foll number of sts at each side:

	26	28	30	32	34"
3	14	14	15	16	17 sts.
4	18	19	19	21	22
5	22	23	24	27	29
6	28	29	29	32	34
7	32	33	34	37	40

Working each side separately, at each neck edge BO 3 sts (if number is zero, omit these rows):

	26	28	30	32	34"
3	0	0	0	0	0 time(s).
4	0	0	0	0	0
5	1	1	1	1	1
6	1	1	1	1	1
7	2	1	1	1	1

Then BO 2 sts:

	26	28	30	32	34"
3	1	1	1	1	1 time(s).
4	2	2	1	1	1
5	1	1	1	1	1
6	2	1	1	1	1
7	1	2	2	2	2

Then dec 1 st at neck edge every RS row:

	26	28	30	32	34"
3	2	2	2	2	2 time(s).
4	2	2	3	3	3
5	2	1	2	2	3
6	2	3	3	3	3
7	3	2	3	2	3

There will rem the foll number of sts at each side:

	26	28	30	32	34"
3	10	10	11	12	13 sts.
4	12	13	14	16	17
5	15	17	17	20	21
6	19	21	21	24	26
7	21	24	24	28	30

Work even until armholes measure same as back to shoulder. BO all sts.

Pullover Front with V-Neck

Work as for back until armholes measure (ending with a WS row):

1½	1½	1½	2	2½"
3.8	3.8	3.8	5	6.5 cm

With RS facing, work to center of row. Turn and work these sts only (place rem sts on a holder to work later). Dec 1 st at neck edge every RS row:

	26	28	30	32	34"
3	3	3	4	4	4 times.
4	6	6	7	7	7
5	8	8	10	10	12
6	11	11	13	13	13
7	15	15	18	16	18

Then dec 1 st at neck edge every 4 rows:

	26	28	30	32	34"
3	4	5	5	5	5 times.
4	4	5	5	5	5
5	4	5	5	5	4
6	4	5	5	5	5
7	3	4	4	5	4

There will remain:

	26	28	30	32	34"
3	10	10	11	12	13 sts.
4	12	13	14	16	17
5	15	17	17	20	21
6	19	21	21	24	26
7	21	24	24	28	30

Finished Chest Circumference

26	28	30	32	34"
66	71	76	81.5	86.5 cm

26	28	30	32	34"
66	71	76	81.5	86.5 cm

Work even until armhole measures same as back to shoulder. BO all sts. Rejoin yarn at neck edge of held sts and work as for first half, reversing neck shaping.

Sleeves
CO:

	26	28	30	32	34"
3	18	20	22	22	24 sts.
4	24	26	28	30	32
5	30	32	36	38	40
6	36	40	42	46	48
7	42	46	48	52	56

Work edging of choice until piece measures:

1½	1½	1½	2	2"
3.8	3.8	3.8	5	5 cm

Change to St st and inc 1 st each end of needle every 2 rows (if number is zero, omit these rows):

3	0	0	0	0	0 times.
4	0	0	0	0	0
5	2	0	0	0	0
6	3	0	0	0	0
7	6	2	0	0	0

Then inc 1 st each end of needle every 4 rows:

3	9	5	6	5	6 times.
4	14	11	11	11	11
5	16	19	17	16	18
6	18	21	22	21	23
7	19	24	29	29	29

Then inc 1 st each end of needle every 6 rows (if number is zero, omit these rows):

3	2	6	6	8	8 time(s).
4	0	4	5	6	7
5	0	0	3	5	5
6	0	1	2	4	4
7	0	0	0	1	3

There will be:

3	40	42	46	48	52 sts.
4	52	56	60	64	68
5	66	70	76	80	86
6	78	84	90	96	102
7	92	98	106	112	120

Work even if necessary until piece measures desired length to armhole, or about:

12½	14	15½	17	18"
31.5	35.5	39.5	43	45.5 cm

Mark Armhole
Mark each end of row for armhole placement. Cont even for:

¾	¾	1	1	1¼"
2	2	2.5	2.5	3.2 cm

BO all sts.

Finishing
Block pieces to measurements. With yarn threaded on a tapestry needle, sew left shoulder seam.
Neckband: Choose a crewneck finish on pages 66–67 or a V-neck finish on pages 68–69. With smaller needles, RS facing, and beg at right shoulder, pick up and knit 1 st for each BO st and about 3 sts for every 4 rows along sloped edges around neck opening. Adjust st count if necessary to achieve a full multiple of the edging patt you've chosen, plus 2 extra "seam" sts. Work in chosen pattern until neckband measures ¾" (2 cm), or desired length. BO all sts in patt.
Seams: Sew rem shoulder and neckband seam. Sew sleeve tops to front and back armholes. Sew sleeve and side seams.
Weave in loose ends. Block again, if desired.

Cardigan Back
Work as for pullover version.

Finished Chest Circumference

26	28	30	32	34"
66	71	76	81.5	86.5 cm

26	28	30	32	34"
66	71	76	81.5	86.5 cm

Cardigan Left Front with Crewneck

(See page 45 for V-neck option.) CO:

3	20	21	23	24	26 sts.
4	26	28	30	32	34
5	33	35	38	40	43
6	39	42	45	48	51
7	46	49	53	56	60

Work edging of choice (as for back), then cont even until piece measures same as back to armhole, ending with a WS row.

Shape Armhole

At beg of next RS row BO:

3	3	3	3	3	4 sts.
4	4	4	4	4	5
5	5	5	5	5	6
6	5	5	6	6	7
7	6	6	7	7	8

There will remain:

3	17	18	20	21	22 sts.
4	22	24	26	28	29
5	28	30	33	35	37
6	34	37	39	42	44
7	40	43	46	49	52

Cont even until armhole measures (ending with a RS row):

4½	5	5½	6	6½"
11.5	12.5	14	15	16.5 cm

Shape Crewneck

At beg of next WS row, BO:

3	3	4	5	5	5 sts,
4	4	5	7	7	7
5	5	7	8	8	8
6	6	8	10	10	10
7	7	10	12	12	12

work to end. At neck edge, BO 3 sts (if number is zero, omit these rows):

3	0	0	0	0	0 time(s).
4	0	0	0	0	0
5	1	1	1	1	1
6	1	1	1	1	1
7	1	1	1	1	1

Then BO 2 sts (if number is zero, omit these rows):

3	1	1	1	1	1 time(s).
4	2	2	1	1	1
5	2	0	1	1	1
6	2	1	0	1	0
7	3	2	2	1	1

Then dec 1 st at neck edge every RS row:

3	2	2	2	2	2 time(s).
4	2	2	3	3	3
5	1	3	3	2	3
6	2	3	5	3	5
7	3	2	3	4	5

There will remain:

3	10	10	11	12	13 sts.
4	12	13	14	16	17
5	15	17	17	20	21
6	19	21	21	24	26
7	21	24	24	28	30

Cont even until piece measures same as back to shoulder. BO all sts.

Cardigan Right Front with Crewneck

Work as for left front with crewneck but reverse shaping (i.e., BO for armhole and shoulder at beg of WS rows; shape neck at beg of RS rows).

Cardigan Left Front with V-Neck

Work as for crewneck version until armhole measures (ending with WS row):

1½	1½	1½	2	2½"
3.8	3.8	3.8	5	6.5 cm

Dec 1 st at neck edge (end of RS rows) every RS row:

3	3	3	4	4	4 times.
4	6	6	7	7	7
5	8	8	10	10	12
6	11	11	13	13	13
7	15	15	18	16	18

Then dec 1 st at neck edge every 4 rows:

3	4	5	5	5	5 times.
4	4	5	5	5	5
5	4	5	5	5	4
6	4	5	5	5	5
7	3	4	4	5	4

There will remain:

3	10	10	11	12	13 sts.
4	12	13	14	16	17
5	15	17	17	20	21
6	19	21	21	24	26
7	21	24	24	28	30

Work even until armhole measures same as back to shoulder. Shape shoulder as for back.

Cardigan Right Front with V-Neck

Work as for left front with V-neck but reverse shaping (i.e., BO for armhole and shoulder at beg of WS rows; shape neck at beg of RS rows).

Finishing

Block pieces to measurements. With yarn threaded on a tapestry needle, sew shoulder seams.

Neckband: Choose a crewneck finish on pages 66–67 or a V-neck finish on pages 68–69. With smaller needles, RS facing, and beg at center front, pick up and knit 1 st for every BO st and about 3 sts for every 4 rows along sloped edges around neck opening for crewneck. (Combine neckband with button and buttonhole bands for a V-neck version.) Adjust st count if necessary to achieve a full multiple of the edging pattern you've chosen. Work in chosen edging pattern until neckband measures ¾" (2 cm), or desired length. BO all sts in patt.

Button band: (on left front for females; right front for males) With smaller needles and RS facing, pick up and knit about 3 sts for every 4 rows along center front edge. Adjust stitch count if necessary to achieve a full multiple of the edging pattern you've chosen. Work in chosen pattern until band measures ¾" (2 cm). BO all sts in patt. Mark placement of 5 buttons, one ½" (1.3 cm) up from CO edge, one at beg of neck shaping, and the others evenly spaced in between.

Buttonhole band: (on right front for females; left front for males) Work as for button band, working one-row buttonholes (see Glossary) opposite markers when band measures between ¼" and ½" (.6 and 1.3 cm). BO all sts in patt.

Seams: Sew tops of sleeves to front and back armholes. Sew sleeve and side seams.

Weave in loose ends. Sew buttons to button band opposite buttonholes. Block again, if desired.

modified drop

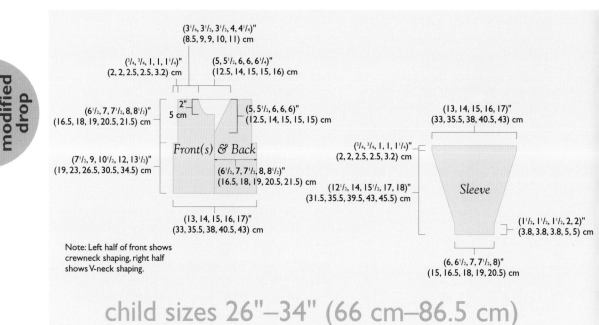

(3¼, 3½, 3½, 4, 4¼)"
(8.5, 9, 9, 10, 11) cm

(¾, ¾, 1, 1, 1¼)"
(2, 2, 2.5, 2.5, 3.2) cm

(5, 5½, 6, 6, 6¼)"
(12.5, 14, 15, 15, 16) cm

(6½, 7, 7½, 8, 8½)"
(16.5, 18, 19, 20.5, 21.5) cm

2"
5 cm

(5, 5½, 6, 6, 6)"
(12.5, 14, 15, 15, 15) cm

(13, 14, 15, 16, 17)"
(33, 35.5, 38, 40.5, 43) cm

Front(s) & Back

(¾, ¾, 1, 1, 1¼)"
(2, 2, 2.5, 2.5, 3.2) cm

(7½, 9, 10½, 12, 13½)"
(19, 23, 26.5, 30.5, 34.5) cm

(6½, 7, 7½, 8, 8½)"
(16.5, 18, 19, 20.5, 21.5) cm

(12½, 14, 15½, 17, 18)"
(31.5, 35.5, 39.5, 43, 45.5) cm

Sleeve

(13, 14, 15, 16, 17)"
(33, 35.5, 38, 40.5, 43) cm

(1½, 1½, 1½, 2, 2)"
(3.8, 3.8, 3.8, 5, 5) cm

Note: Left half of front shows
crewneck shaping, right half
shows V-neck shaping.

(6, 6½, 7, 7½, 8)"
(15, 16.5, 18, 19, 20.5) cm

child sizes 26"–34" (66 cm–86.5 cm)

quick**tips** for consistent gauge

- To ensure that you're getting the gauge you expect, recheck the gauge (and the width-wise dimensions of your piece) several times as you knit. Repeated checking is especially important if your mood changes drastically during a project (many of us knit tighter when we're angry or tense).

- Take a break and wash your hands if they tend to get sweaty as you knit (particularly in the warm summer months); otherwise, your tension—and gauge—may become undesirably tight.

- To compensate for the gauge tightening during isolated stranded colorwork patterns (such as the yoke of a sweater in which the lower body and sleeves are worked in a single color), work the colorwork patterns on needles a size larger than those used to achieve gauge in a solid color.

- Try knitting your gauge swatch on different types of needles. Some yarns, such as chenille, are easier to knit on metal needles. Other yarns, such as wool, can be easier to work on wooden needles.

- If you knit tighter than you purl, or vice versa, try using two different-sized needles. Use the smaller needle for rows that you tend to work looser and the larger needle for rows that you tend to work tighter.

sizing adult

Finished Bust/Chest Circumference

36	38	40	42	44	46	48	50	52	54"
91.5	96.5	101.5	106.5	112	117	122	127	132	137 cm

Yarn Requirements

GAUGE											
3	610	660	720	780	870	900	960	1000	1050	1100 yd
	558	604	658	713	796	823	878	914	960	1006 m
4	860	930	1020	1100	1230	1270	1360	1420	1490	1560
	786	850	933	1006	1125	1161	1244	1298	1362	1426
5	1090	1180	1280	1390	1550	1600	1710	1790	1880	1970
	997	1079	1170	1271	1417	1463	1564	1637	1719	1801
6	1540	1660	1810	1960	2190	2270	2420	2530	2660	2780
	1408	1518	1655	1792	2003	2076	2213	2313	2432	2542
7	1690	1830	2000	2160	2410	2500	2670	2790	2930	3070
	1545	1673	1829	1975	2204	2286	2441	2551	2679	2807

Pullover Back

CO:

GAUGE										
3	54	58	60	64	66	70	72	76	78	82 sts.
4	72	76	80	84	88	92	96	100	104	108
5	90	94	100	106	110	116	120	126	130	136
6	108	114	120	126	132	138	144	150	156	162
7	126	134	140	148	154	162	168	176	182	190

Work edging of choice (see pages 35–37), then cont even until piece measures desired length to armhole, or about:

13½	13½	14	14½	15	15	15	15	15	15"
34.5	34.5	35.5	37	38	38	38	38	38	38 cm

Shape Armholes

At beg of next 2 rows BO:

GAUGE										
3	4	5	5	6	6	6	6	7	7	8 sts.
4	5	7	7	8	8	8	9	9	10	10
5	6	8	8	10	10	10	11	11	12	13
6	8	10	10	12	12	12	14	14	15	15
7	9	12	12	14	14	14	15	16	17	18

Finished Bust/Chest Circumference

	36	38	40	42	44	46	48	50	52	54"
	91.5	96.5	101.5	106.5	112	117	122	127	132	137 cm

There will remain:

3	46	48	50	52	54	58	60	62	64	66 sts.
4	62	62	66	68	72	76	78	82	84	88
5	78	78	84	86	90	96	98	104	106	110
6	92	94	100	102	108	114	116	122	126	132
7	108	110	116	120	126	134	138	144	148	154

Cont even until armholes measure:

	9	9½	10	10½	11	11½	12	12½	13	13½"
	23	24	25.5	26.5	28	29	30.5	31.5	33	34.5 cm

Shape shoulders and back neck

BO all sts, marking first and last:

3	13	14	15	16	17	18	18	19	19	20 sts
4	18	18	20	20	22	23	23	25	25	27
5	23	23	26	26	27	29	29	31	32	33
6	27	27	30	31	33	35	34	37	37	40
7	31	32	35	36	38	40	41	43	44	46

for each shoulder and rem sts for back neck:

3	20	20	20	20	20	22	24	24	26	26 sts.
4	26	26	26	28	28	30	32	32	34	34
5	32	32	32	34	36	38	40	42	42	44
6	38	40	40	40	42	44	48	48	52	52
7	46	46	46	48	50	54	56	58	60	62

Pullover Front with Crewneck

(See page 51 for V-neck option.) Work as for back until armholes measure (ending with a WS row):

	6½	7	7½	8	8½	8½	9	9½	10	10½"
	16.5	18	19	20.5	21.5	21.5	23	24	25.5	26.5 cm

Shape Crewneck

With RS facing, work across:

3	18	19	20	21	21	23	24	25	25	26 sts,
4	24	24	26	27	28	30	31	33	33	35
5	31	31	34	35	35	38	39	42	42	44
6	36	37	40	41	42	45	46	49	50	53
7	42	43	46	48	49	53	55	58	59	62

Finished Bust/Chest Circumference									
36	38	40	42	44	46	48	50	52	54"
91.5	96.5	101.5	106.5	112	117	122	127	132	137 cm

join new yarn and BO for front neck:

3	10	10	10	10	12	12	12	12	14	14 sts,
4	14	14	14	14	16	16	16	16	18	18
5	16	16	16	16	20	20	20	20	22	22
6	20	20	20	20	24	24	24	24	26	26
7	24	24	24	24	28	28	28	28	30	30

work to end. There will be the foll number of sts at each side:

3	18	19	20	21	21	23	24	25	25	26 sts.
4	24	24	26	27	28	30	31	33	33	35
5	31	31	34	35	35	38	39	42	42	44
6	36	37	40	41	42	45	46	49	50	53
7	42	43	46	48	49	53	55	58	59	62

Working each side separately, at each neck edge BO 3 sts (if number is zero, omit these rows):

3	0	0	0	0	0	0	0	0	0	0 time(s).
4	0	0	0	0	0	0	1	1	1	1
5	1	1	1	1	1	1	1	2	1	2
6	1	1	1	1	1	1	2	2	2	2
7	1	1	1	2	1	2	2	2	2	3

Then BO 2 sts:

3	1	1	1	1	1	1	2	2	2	2 time(s).
4	2	2	2	2	2	2	1	1	1	1
5	1	1	1	2	1	2	2	1	2	1
6	2	2	2	2	2	2	2	2	2	2
7	3	3	3	2	3	2	3	3	3	2

Then dec 1 st at each neck edge every RS row:

3	3	3	3	3	2	3	2	2	2	2 times.
4	2	2	2	3	2	3	3	3	3	3
5	3	3	3	2	3	2	3	3	3	3
6	2	3	3	3	2	3	2	2	3	3
7	2	2	2	2	2	3	2	3	3	3

Finished Bust/Chest Circumference

36	38	40	42	44	46	48	50	52	54"
91.5	96.5	101.5	106.5	112	117	122	127	132	137 cm

There will rem the foll number of sts at each side:

3	13	14	15	16	17	18	18	19	19	20 sts.
4	18	18	20	20	22	23	23	25	25	27
5	23	23	26	26	27	29	29	31	32	33
6	27	27	30	31	33	35	34	37	37	40
7	31	32	35	36	38	40	41	43	44	46

Work even until armholes measure same as back to shoulders. BO all sts.

Pullover Front with V-Neck

Work as for back until armholes measure (ending with a WS row):

3	3	3½	3¾	4¼	4½	5	5¼	5½	6"	
7.5	7.5	9	9.5	11	11.5	12.5	13.5	14	15 cm	

With RS facing, work to center of row. Turn and work these sts only to shoulder (place rem sts on a holder to work later). Dec 1 st at neck edge every RS row:

3	6	5	5	5	5	6	8	7	9	9 times.
4	9	8	8	9	9	10	12	12	13	13
5	12	11	11	12	14	15	17	18	17	19
6	15	16	16	14	16	17	21	20	23	23
7	20	19	19	19	21	24	26	27	28	30

Then dec 1 st at neck edge every 4 rows (if number is zero, omit these rows):

3	4	5	5	5	5	5	4	5	4	4 time(s).
4	4	5	5	5	5	5	4	4	4	4
5	4	5	5	5	4	4	3	3	4	3
6	4	4	4	6	5	5	3	4	3	3
7	3	4	4	5	4	3	2	2	2	1

There will remain:

3	13	14	15	16	17	18	18	19	19	20 sts.
4	18	18	20	20	22	23	23	25	25	27
5	23	23	26	26	27	29	29	31	32	33
6	27	27	30	31	33	35	34	37	37	40
7	31	32	35	36	38	40	41	43	44	46

Work even until armhole measures same as back to shoulder. BO all sts. Rejoin yarn at neck edge of held sts and work as for first half, reversing neck shaping.

Finished Bust/Chest Circumference

36	38	40	42	44	46	48	50	52	54"
91.5	96.5	101.5	106.5	112	117	122	127	132	137 cm

Sleeves

CO:

3	28	28	30	30	30	30	32	32	34	34 sts.
4	38	38	40	40	40	44	44	44	46	46
5	46	46	50	50	50	54	54	56	58	58
6	56	56	60	60	60	66	66	66	68	68
7	66	66	70	70	70	76	76	76	80	80

Work edging of choice until piece measures:

2½	2½	2½	2½	2½	2½	2½	2½	2½	2½"
6.5	6.5	6.5	6.5	6.5	6.5	6.5	6.5	6.5	6.5 cm

Change to St st and inc 1 st each end of needle every 2 rows (if number is zero, omit these rows):

3	0	0	0	0	0	0	0	0	0	4 times.
4	0	0	0	0	0	0	0	4	6	10
5	0	0	0	0	0	0	3	7	11	16
6	0	0	0	0	2	0	6	14	18	26
7	0	0	0	0	6	3	11	19	23	31

Then inc 1 st each end of needle every 4 rows (if number is zero, omit these rows):

3	0	5	4	5	10	12	15	19	22	19 times.
4	5	9	10	15	19	18	24	24	23	21
5	12	16	18	21	29	27	30	27	25	22
6	16	23	24	31	34	36	33	28	26	21
7	20	27	31	38	36	39	35	30	28	23

Then inc 1 st each end of needle every 6 rows (if number is zero, omit these rows):

3	13	10	11	11	8	7	5	2	0	0 time(s).
4	12	10	10	7	5	6	2	0	0	0
5	10	8	7	6	1	3	0	0	0	0
6	10	6	6	2	0	0	0	0	0	0
7	10	6	4	0	0	0	0	0	0	0

There will be:

3	54	58	60	62	66	68	72	74	78	80 sts.
4	72	76	80	84	88	92	96	100	104	108
5	90	94	100	104	110	114	120	124	130	134

modified drop

Finished Bust/Chest Circumference

36	38	40	42	44	46	48	50	52	54"
91.5	96.5	101.5	106.5	112	117	122	127	132	137 cm

6	108	114	120	126	132	138	144	150	156	162
7	126	132	140	146	154	160	168	174	182	188

Work even if necessary until piece measures desired length to armhole, or about:

19	19½	20	20½	21	21½	22	22	22	22"
48.5	49.5	51	52	53.5	54.5	56	56	56	56 cm

Mark Armhole
Mark each end of next row for armhole placement. Cont even for:

1¼	1¾	1¾	2	2	2	2¼	2¼	2½	2½"
3.2	4.5	4.5	5	5	5	5.5	5.5	6.5	6.5 cm

BO all sts.

Finishing
Block pieces to measurements. With yarn threaded on a tapestry needle, sew left shoulder seam.

Neckband: Choose a crewneck finish on pages 66–67 or a V-neck finish on pages 68–69. With smaller needles, RS facing, and beg at right shoulder, pick up and knit 1 st for each BO st and about 3 sts for every 4 rows along sloped edges around neck opening. Adjust st count if necessary to achieve a full multiple of the edging pattern you've chosen, plus 2 extra "seam" sts. Work in chosen pattern until neckband measures 1" (2.5 cm), or desired length. BO all sts in patt.

Seams: Sew rem shoulder and neckband seam. Sew sleeve tops to front and back armholes. Sew sleeve and side seams.

Weave in loose ends. Block again, if desired.

Cardigan Back
Work as for pullover version.

Cardigan Left Front with Crewneck
(See page 55 for V-neck option.) CO:

3	27	29	30	32	33	35	36	38	39	41 sts.
4	36	38	40	42	44	46	48	50	52	54
5	45	47	50	53	55	58	60	63	65	68
6	54	57	60	63	66	69	72	75	78	81
7	63	67	70	74	77	81	84	88	91	95

Work edging of choice (as for back), then cont even until piece measures same as back to armhole, ending with a WS row.

Finished Bust/Chest Circumference

36	38	40	42	44	46	48	50	52	54"
91.5	96.5	101.5	106.5	112	117	122	127	132	137 cm

Shape Armhole
At beg of next RS row BO:

3	4	5	5	6	6	6	6	7	7	8 sts.
4	5	7	7	8	8	8	9	9	10	10
5	6	8	8	10	10	10	11	11	12	13
6	8	10	10	12	12	12	14	14	15	15
7	9	12	12	14	14	14	15	16	17	18

There will remain:

3	23	24	25	26	27	29	30	31	32	33 sts.
4	31	31	33	34	36	38	39	41	42	44
5	39	39	42	43	45	48	49	52	53	55
6	46	47	50	51	54	57	58	61	63	66
7	54	55	58	60	63	67	69	72	74	77

Cont even until armhole measures (ending with a RS row):

6½	7	7½	8	8½	8½	9	9½	10	10½"
16.5	18	19	20.5	21.5	21.5	23	24	25.5	26.5 cm

Shape Crewneck
At beg of next WS row BO:

3	5	5	5	5	6	6	6	6	7	7 sts,
4	7	7	7	7	8	8	8	8	9	9
5	8	8	8	8	10	10	10	10	11	11
6	10	10	10	10	12	12	12	12	13	13
7	12	12	12	12	14	14	14	14	15	15

work to end. At neck edge BO 3 sts (if number is zero, omit these rows):

3	0	0	0	0	0	0	0	0	0	0 time(s).
4	0	0	0	1	0	1	1	1	1	1
5	1	1	1	1	1	1	1	2	1	2
6	1	1	1	1	1	1	2	2	2	2
7	2	2	2	2	2	2	2	2	2	3

Then BO 2 sts:

3	1	1	1	1	1	1	2	2	2	2 time(s).
4	2	2	2	1	2	1	1	1	1	1
5	1	1	1	2	1	2	2	1	2	1

Finished Bust/Chest Circumference

	36	38	40	42	44	46	48	50	52	54"
	91.5	96.5	101.5	106.5	112	117	122	127	132	137 cm
6	2	2	2	2	2	2	2	2	2	2
7	1	1	1	2	1	2	3	3	3	2

Then dec 1 st at neck edge every RS row:

3	3	3	3	3	2	3	2	2	2	2 times.
4	2	2	2	2	2	2	3	3	3	3
5	3	3	3	2	3	2	3	3	3	3
6	2	3	3	3	2	3	2	2	3	3
7	3	3	3	2	3	3	2	3	3	3

There will remain:

3	13	14	15	16	17	18	18	19	19	20 sts.
4	18	18	20	20	22	23	23	25	25	27
5	23	23	26	26	27	29	29	31	32	33
6	27	27	30	31	33	35	34	37	37	40
7	31	32	35	36	38	40	41	43	44	46

Cont even until piece measures same as back to shoulder. BO all sts.

Cardigan Right Front with Crewneck

Work as for left front with crewneck but reverse shaping (i.e., BO for armhole and shoulder at beg of WS rows; shape neck at beg of RS rows).

Cardigan Left Front with V-Neck

Work as for crewneck version until armhole measures (ending with a WS row):

	3	3	3½	3¾	4¼	4½	5	5¼	5½	6"
	7.5	7.5	9	9.5	11	11.5	12.5	13.5	14	15 cm

Dec 1 st at neck edge (end of RS rows) every RS row:

3	6	5	5	5	5	6	8	7	9	9 times.
4	9	8	8	9	9	10	12	12	13	13
5	12	11	11	12	14	15	17	18	17	19
6	15	16	16	14	16	17	21	20	23	23
7	20	19	19	19	21	24	26	27	28	30

Finished Bust/Chest Circumference

36	38	40	42	44	46	48	50	52	54"
91.5	96.5	101.5	106.5	112	117	122	127	132	137 cm

Then dec I st at neck edge every 4 rows:

3	4	5	5	5	5	5	4	5	4	4 time(s).
4	4	5	5	5	5	5	4	4	4	4
5	4	5	5	5	4	4	3	3	4	3
6	4	4	4	6	5	5	3	4	3	3
7	3	4	4	5	4	3	2	2	2	I

There will remain:

3	13	14	15	16	17	18	18	19	19	20 sts.
4	18	18	20	20	22	23	23	25	25	27
5	23	23	26	26	27	29	29	31	32	33
6	27	27	30	31	33	35	34	37	37	40
7	31	32	35	36	38	40	41	43	44	46

Work even until armhole measures same as back to shoulder. Shape shoulder as for back.

Cardigan Right Front with V-Neck
Work as for left front with V-neck but reverse shaping (i.e., BO for armhole and shoulder at beg of WS rows; shape neck at beg of RS rows).

Finishing
Block pieces to measurements. With yarn threaded on a tapestry needle, sew shoulder seams.
Neckband: Choose a crewneck finish on pages 66–67 or a V-neck finish on pages 68–69. With smaller needles, RS facing, and beg at center front, pick up and knit I st for every BO st and about 3 sts for every 4 rows along sloped edges around neck opening for a crewneck. (Combine neckband with button and buttonhole bands for a V-neck version.) Adjust st count if necessary to achieve a full multiple of the edging pattern you've chosen. Work in chosen pattern until band measures I" (2.5 cm) or desired length. BO all sts in patt.
Button band: (on left front for females; right front for males) With smaller needles and RS facing, pick up and knit about 3 sts for every 4 rows along center front edge. Adjust st count if necessary to achieve a full multiple of the edging pattern chosen. Work in chosen pattern until band measures about ¾" (2 cm). BO all sts in patt. Mark placement of 7 to 9 buttons, one ½" (1.3 cm) up from CO edge, one at beg of neck shaping, and the others evenly spaced in between.
Buttonhole band: (on right front for females; left front for males) Work as for button band, working one-row buttonholes (see Glossary) opposite markers when band measures between ¼" and ½" and (.6 and 1.3 cm). BO all sts in patt.
Seams: Sew sleeve tops to front and back armholes. Sew sleeve and side seams.
Weave in loose ends. Sew buttons to button band opposite buttonholes. Block again, if desired.

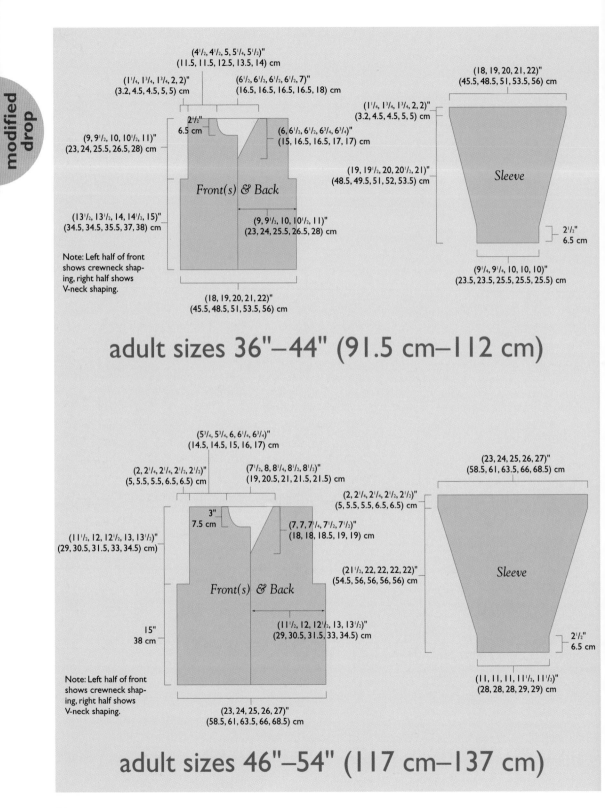

(4½, 4½, 5, 5¼, 5½)"
(11.5, 11.5, 12.5, 13.5, 14) cm

(1¼, 1¾, 1¾, 2, 2)"
(3.2, 4.5, 4.5, 5, 5) cm

(6½, 6½, 6½, 6½, 7)"
(16.5, 16.5, 16.5, 16.5, 18) cm

(18, 19, 20, 21, 22)"
(45.5, 48.5, 51, 53.5, 56) cm

2½"
6.5 cm

(9, 9½, 10, 10½, 11)"
(23, 24, 25.5, 26.5, 28) cm

(6, 6½, 6½, 6¾, 6¾)"
(15, 16.5, 16.5, 17, 17) cm

(1¼, 1¾, 1¾, 2, 2)"
(3.2, 4.5, 4.5, 5, 5) cm

(19, 19½, 20, 20½, 21)"
(48.5, 49.5, 51, 52, 53.5) cm

Sleeve

Front(s) & Back

(13½, 13½, 14, 14½, 15)"
(34.5, 34.5, 35.5, 37, 38) cm

(9, 9½, 10, 10½, 11)"
(23, 24, 25.5, 26.5, 28) cm

2½"
6.5 cm

Note: Left half of front
shows crewneck shap-
ing, right half shows
V-neck shaping.

(9¼, 9¼, 10, 10, 10)"
(23.5, 23.5, 25.5, 25.5, 25.5) cm

(18, 19, 20, 21, 22)"
(45.5, 48.5, 51, 53.5, 56) cm

adult sizes 36"–44" (91.5 cm–112 cm)

(5¾, 5¾, 6, 6¼, 6¾)"
(14.5, 14.5, 15, 16, 17) cm

(2, 2¼, 2¼, 2½, 2½)"
(5, 5.5, 5.5, 6.5, 6.5) cm

(7½, 8, 8¼, 8½, 8½)"
(19, 20.5, 21, 21.5, 21.5) cm

(23, 24, 25, 26, 27)"
(58.5, 61, 63.5, 66, 68.5) cm

3"
7.5 cm

(2, 2¼, 2¼, 2½, 2½)"
(5, 5.5, 5.5, 6.5, 6.5) cm

(11½, 12, 12½, 13, 13½)"
(29, 30.5, 31.5, 33, 34.5) cm)

(7, 7, 7¼, 7½, 7½)"
(18, 18, 18.5, 19, 19) cm

(21½, 22, 22, 22, 22)"
(54.5, 56, 56, 56, 56) cm

Sleeve

Front(s) & Back

15"
38 cm

(11½, 12, 12½, 13, 13½)"
(29, 30.5, 31.5, 33, 34.5) cm

2½"
6.5 cm

Note: Left half of front
shows crewneck shap-
ing, right half shows
V-neck shaping.

(11, 11, 11, 11½, 11½)"
(28, 28, 28, 29, 29) cm

(23, 24, 25, 26, 27)"
(58.5, 61, 63.5, 66, 68.5) cm

adult sizes 46"–54" (117 cm–137 cm)

Cable Panel Pullover

A panel of three sizes of right-twist cables extends from the lower body to the top of the neck on the front of this modified drop-shoulder pullover. To compensate for the natural tendency of the cables to draw in the fabric (and cause the front to be narrower than the back), extra stitches are increased at the base of each of the three center cables. When it is time to shape the front crewneck, the center stitches are placed onto a holder instead of being bound off, then they are worked seamlessly into the stand-up neck. Small cables in the ribbings bring unity to the design.

Finished Size: 42" (106.5 cm) bust/chest circumference.
Yarn: Baabajoes WoolPak 10-Ply (100% wool; 430 yd [393 m]/250 g): #28 brownstone, 4 skeins.
Needles: Size 7 (4.5 mm): straight and 16" (40-cm) circular (cir). Adjust needle size if necessary to obtain the correct gauge.
Notions: Markers (m); cable needle (cn); stitch holder, tapestry needle.
Gauge: 5 sts and 7 rows = 1" (2.5 cm) in stockinette stitch on size 7 (4.5-mm) needles.

Back

With straight needles, CO 112 sts (110 sts + 2 sts to balance patt). With WS facing, work set-up row of Cable Rib chart (page 60). Rep Rows 1 and 2 of chart 6 times, then work Row 1 once more—7 cable crossing rows. *Next row:* (WS) Purl, dec 6 sts evenly spaced—106 sts rem. Work even in St st until piece measures 14½" (37 cm) from beg, ending with a WS row. **Shape armholes:** BO 10 sts at beg of next 2 rows–86 sts rem. Cont even until armholes measure 10½" (26.5 cm), ending with a WS row. **Shape shoulders:** BO all sts, marking first and last 26 sts for shoulders, and center 34 sts for back neck.

Front

With straight needles, CO 110 sts (106 sts + 4 sts to balance patt). With WS facing, work set-up row of Cable Panel chart. *Next row:* (RS; Row 1 of chart) Work 42 sts in cable rib as shown on chart, place marker (pm), p2, k2, pick up and knit 2 sts behind the 2 sts just worked (2 sts inc'd), p2, k3, pick up and knit 3 sts behind the 3 sts just worked (3 sts inc'd), p2, k4, pick up and knit 4 sts behind the 4 sts just worked (4 sts inc'd), p2, k3, pick up and knit 3 sts behind the 3 sts just worked (3 sts inc'd), p2, k2, pick up and knit 2 sts behind the 2 sts just worked (2 sts inc'd), pm, work 42 sts in cable rib as shown to end—124 sts. Cont through Row 13 of chart. *Next row:* (WS) P42, work 40 sts of center cable panel according to Row 14 of chart, p42. Working first and last 42 sts in St st, cont to work center cable panel through Row 33. Cont working St st at each side, rep Rows 2–33 *only* for center cable panel (do not repeat the set-up row or Row 1) until piece measures same as back to armholes, ending with a WS row. **Shape armholes:** BO 10 sts at beg of next 2 rows—104 sts rem. Cont even as established until armholes

copy**cats**

Neck

Cable Rib

28 sts front cable panel

2 reps (20 sts)

5 reps (50 sts)

set-up row

Cable Panel

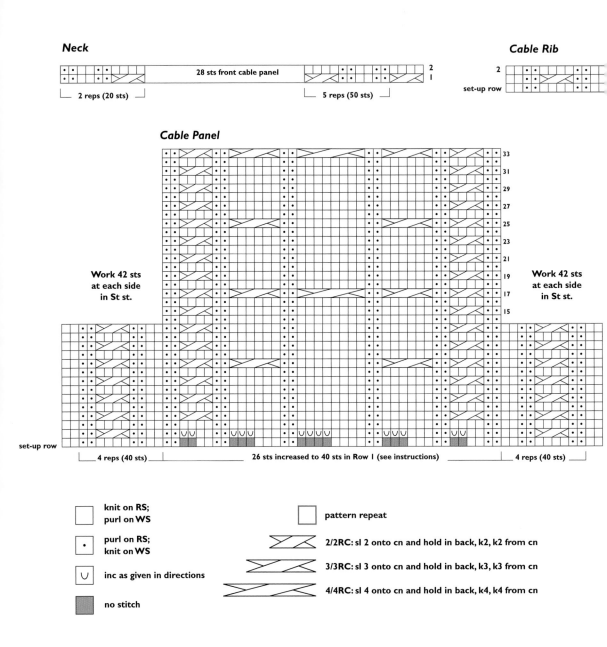

Work 42 sts
at each side
in St st.

Work 42 sts
at each side
in St st.

33
31
29
27
25
23
21
19
17
15

set-up row

4 reps (40 sts)

26 sts increased to 40 sts in Row 1 (see instructions)

4 reps (40 sts)

knit on RS;
purl on WS

purl on RS;
knit on WS

inc as given in directions

no stitch

pattern repeat

2/2RC: sl 2 onto cn and hold in back, k2, k2 from cn

3/3RC: sl 3 onto cn and hold in back, k3, k3 from cn

4/4RC: sl 4 onto cn and hold in back, k4, k4 from cn

measure 8" (20.5 cm), ending with a WS row. **Shape crewneck**: (RS) Keeping in patt, work 38 sts, place center 28 sts on holder, join new yarn, and work to end—38 sts each side. Make a note of the last row worked for center cable panel so you can resume the cable pattern for the neckband at the correct row. Working each side separately and treating the 4-st cables at each side of center front as 2 sts by working k2tog twice for cable when you come to bind off, BO 3 sts once, then BO 2 sts 2 times, then dec 1 st every RS row 3 times—26 sts rem each side (2 dec'd from top of 4-st cables; 10 regular sts BO). Cont even until armholes measure same as back to shoulders. BO all sts.

Sleeves

With straight needles, CO 52 sts (50 sts + 2 sts to balance patt). With WS facing, work set-up row of Cable Rib chart. Rep Rows 1 and 2 of chart 6 times, then work Row 1 once more—7 cable crossing rows. *Next row*: (WS) Purl all sts. Change to St st and work even until piece measures 2½" (6.5 cm) from beg. Inc 1 st each end of needle every 4 rows 21 times, then every 6 rows 5 times (one less dec worked than specified by chart because 2 extra sts were CO to balance cable patt)—104 sts. Cont even until piece measures 20½" (52 cm) from beg. Mark each end of row for armhole placement. Cont even until piece measures 2" (5 cm) from markers. BO all sts.

Finishing

Block pieces to measurements. With yarn threaded on a tapestry needle, sew shoulder seams. Sew sleeves into armholes, matching markers to BO on body. Sew sleeve and side seams. **Funnel neck**: With cir needle, RS facing, and beg at right shoulder, pick up and knit 34 sts across back neck to left shoulder, 20 sts along left front neck, work 28 held front neck sts in patt, pick up and knit 20 sts along right front neck—102 sts total. Place m and join for working in the rnd. Working 28 sts of center front panel as established, rep Rnds 1 and 2 of Neck chart until neck measures about 4" (10 cm), ending with Row 17 or 33 of front cable panel. BO all sts loosely in patt. Weave in loose ends. Block again if desired.

Lace-Edged Cardigan

A simple lace edging, dainty collar, and picot-edged front bands bring femininity to the boxy silhouette of this modified drop-shoulder cardigan. The body and sleeves, worked from the lower edge upward, begin with the appropriate number of stitches to accommodate full repeats of the lace edging. At the end of the edging, stitches are decreased to match the numbers provided in the basic chart. The collar is picked up and worked from the crewneck opening; the lace edging is worked in the opposite direction to make it match the lower body and sleeves. Increases are worked on the collar, concentrated over the shoulder seams, so that it will fold over gracefully.

copy**cats**

Finished Size: 34" (86.5 cm) bust/chest circumference, buttoned.
Yarn: Baabajoes WoolPak Yarn 8-Ply (100% wool; 525 yd [480 m]/250 g): #35 aubergine, 3 skeins.
Needles: Body and sleeves—Size 4 (3.5 mm). Front bands and collar—Size 3 (3.25 mm). Adjust needle size if necessary to obtain the correct gauge.
Notions: Tapestry needle; seven ¾" (2-cm) buttons.
Gauge: 6 sts and 7½ rows = 1" (2.5 cm) in stockinette stitch on size 4 (3.5-mm) needles.

Feather Lace

(multiple of 9 sts + 4)
Row 1: (RS) K3, *yo, k2, ssk, k2tog, k2, yo, k1; rep from *, end last rep k2.
Rows 2 and 4: Purl.
Row 3: K2, *yo, k2, ssk, k2tog, k2, yo, k1; rep from *, end last rep k3.
Repeat Rows 1–4 for pattern.

Back

With larger needles, CO 103 sts (102 sts + 1 st to balance patt). Work Rows 1–4 of feather lace 2 times, dec 1 st on last row—102 sts rem. Change to St st and work even until piece measures 13½" (34.5 cm) from beg, ending with a WS row. **Shape armholes**: BO 7 sts at beg of next 2 rows—88 sts rem. Cont even until armholes measure 8½" (21.5 cm), ending with a WS row. **Shape shoulders**: BO all sts, marking first and last 26 sts for shoulders and center 36 sts for back neck.

Left Front

With larger needles, CO 49 sts (52 sts - 2 sts to balance patt). Work Rows 1–4 of feather lace 2 times, inc 2 sts on last row—51 sts. Change to St st and work even until piece measures 13½" (34.5 cm) from beg, ending with a WS row. **Shape armhole**: (RS) BO 7 sts at beg of row, knit to end—44 sts rem. Cont even until armhole measures 6½" (16.5 cm), ending with a RS row. **Shape crewneck**: (WS) BO 10 sts at beg of row, knit to end—34 sts rem. At neck edge (beg of WS rows), BO 3 sts once, then dec 1 st every RS row 5 times—26 sts rem. Cont even until armhole measures same as back to shoulder. BO all sts.

Right Front

Work as left front but reverse shaping (BO for armhole and shoulder at beg of WS rows; shape neck at beg of RS rows).

Sleeves

With larger needles, CO 49 sts (48 sts + 1 st to balance patt). Work Rows 1–4 of feather lace 2 times, dec 1 st on last row—48 sts rem. Change to St st and work even until piece measures 2" (5 cm) from beg. Inc 1 st each end of needle every 4 rows 23 times, then every 6 rows 4 times—102 sts. Cont even until piece measures 18" (45.5 cm) from beg. Mark each end of row for armhole placement. Cont even until piece measures 1¼" (3.2 cm) from markers. BO all sts.

Finishing

Block pieces to measurements. With yarn threaded on a tapestry needle, sew shoulder seams. Sew sleeve tops into armholes, matching markers to BO on body. Sew sleeve and side seams. **Button band**: With smaller needles, RS facing, and beg at neck edge of left front, pick up and knit about 5 sts for every 6 rows along center front edge. Work St st for 5 rows, ending with a WS row. *Next row*: (RS) Form turning ridge as foll: *P2tog, yo; rep from *. Cont in St st for 5 more rows. BO all sts. Mark placement of 7 buttons on button band as foll: One ½" (1.3 cm) up from lower edge, one ½" (1.3 cm) down from neck edge, and the others evenly spaced in between. **Buttonhole band**: With smaller needles, RS facing, and beg at lower edge of right front, pick up and knit sts as for button band. Purl 1 row. Knit 1 row. Purl next row and at the same time, work a buttonhole opposite each button marker as foll: yo, p2tog. Knit 1 row. Purl 1 row. Work turning ridge as for button band. Work St st for 2 rows, rep buttonhole row, work St st for 2 more rows. BO all sts. Fold band to WS along turning ridge and sew in place. **Collar**: With smaller needles, RS facing, and beg at center front neck, pick up and knit 93 sts around neck opening. Knit the next row, and *at the same time* inc 5 sts centered over each shoulder seam by working k1f&b 5 times at each shoulder—103 sts. Purl 1 row. Knit 1 row, inc 5 sts centered over one shoulder seam as before and 4 sts centered over the other shoulder seam—112 sts (multiple of 9 sts + 4). Cont in St st until piece measures about 1½" (3.8 cm) from pick up, ending with a purl row. *Next row*: (RS) Working pattern in reverse order (from Row 4 to Row 1), work feather lace for a total of 6 rows. Loosely BO all sts purlwise. Weave in loose ends. Block collar, pinning out

scallops on lace edgings. Weave in loose ends. Sew buttons to button band opposite buttonholes. Block again if desired.

Shawl-Collar Pullover

This child's sweater follows the basic instructions for a modified-drop shoulder with a V-neck and the addition of a textured stitch pattern. Because the stitch pattern calls for an odd number of stitches, one stitch is added to each garment piece. On the back, this extra stitch is included in the neck stitches; on the front it is put on a holder at the base of the V-neck, then later worked into the shawl collar. The shawl collar

> **Finished Size:** 30" (76 cm) chest circumference.
> **Yarn:** Baabajoes NZ WoolPak 14-Ply (100% wool; 310 yd [283 m]/250 g): #33 bluebell, 3 skeins.
> **Needles:** Body and sleeves—Size 10½ (6.5 mm): 24" (60-cm) circular (cir). Ribbing—Size 9 (5.5 mm): straight. Adjust needle size if necessary to obtain the correct gauge.
> **Notions:** Stitch holder; markers (m); tapestry needle.
> **Gauge:** 4 sts and 6.75 rows = 1" (2.5 cm) in textured rib on size 10½ (6.5-mm) needles; 3½ sts and 4¾ rows = 1" (2.5 cm) in stockinette stitch on size 10 (6-mm) needles.

is shaped with short rows and is worked on the larger body needles to provide the ease necessary for it to fold over. The ribbing along the lower body and cuffs is worked on needles two sizes smaller than used for the main body, which causes them to pull in and fit snuggly.

Textured Rib:

(multiple of 4 sts + 1)
Rows 1 and 3: (RS) Knit.
Row 2: P1, *k3, p1; rep from *.
Row 4: P1, *k1, p1; rep from *.
Repeat Rows 1–4 for pattern.

Back

With smaller needles, CO 60 sts. Work k1, p1 rib until piece measures 1½" (3.8 cm) from beg, ending with RS row. *Next row:* Change to larger needle and work in patt, inc 1 st—61 sts (60 sts + 1 st to balance patt). Cont even in textured rib until piece measures 10½" (26.5 cm) from beg, ending with a WS row. *Shape armholes:* BO 4 sts at beg of next 2 rows—53 sts rem (52 sts + 1 st to balance patt). Cont even in patt until armholes measure 7½" (19 cm), ending with

a WS row. *Shape shoulders:* BO all sts, marking first and last 14 sts for shoulders, and center 25 sts for back neck.

Front

Work as back until armholes measure 1½" (3.8 cm), ending with a WS row—53 sts. *Shape V-neck:* (RS) Keeping in patt, work to 3 sts before center st, k2tog, k1, place center st on holder, join new yarn, k1, ssk, work to end—25 sts rem each side. Working each side separately, dec 1 st at neck edge every RS row 6 more times, then every 4 rows 5 times—14 sts rem each side. Cont even until armholes measure the same as back to shoulders. BO all sts.

Sleeves

With smaller needles, CO 29 sts (28 sts + 1 st to balance patt). Work k1, p1 rib until piece measures 1½" (3.8 cm) from beg, ending with a WS row. Change to larger needle and textured rib. Inc 1 st each end of needle every 4 rows 11 times, then every 6 rows 5 times, working new sts into patt—61 sts. Cont even until piece measures 15½" (39.5 cm) from beg. Mark each end of row for base of armholes.

Cont even until piece measures 1" (2.5 cm) from markers. BO all sts.

Finishing
Block pieces to measurements. With yarn threaded on a tapestry needle, sew shoulder seams. Sew sleeves into armholes, matching markers to BO on body. Sew sleeve and side seams. **Shawl collar:** With cir needle, RS facing, and beg at center front, place held center front st on needle, join yarn and pick up and knit 35 sts along side front to shoulder seam, 25 sts across back

neck, and 35 sts down other side front—96 sts. Do not join. With WS facing, work k1, p1 rib to 4 sts past shoulder seam, wrap next st (see Glossary) and turn, work to 4 sts past other shoulder seam, wrap next st and turn, *work to 1 st beyond previous wrapped st (2 sts past previous turn), wrap next st and turn; rep from * until 6 sts rem unworked at each side. **Work to wrapped st (1 st past previous turn), work st tog with its wrap, and turn; rep from ** until all sts have been worked. BO all sts in rib. Weave in loose ends. Block again if desired.

quicktips for professional seams

- Consider purchasing a set of blocking wires if you want to block pieces without telltale scallops from pins.

- To facilitate seaming, block individual pieces before sewing them together.

- If you use a novelty or mohair yarn, sew the seams with a smooth yarn of similar weight and color. If you use a heavy or bulky yarn, use just one or two of the plies for seaming.

- To make seaming easier, add a selvedge stitch (an extra stitch used just for sewing seams) at the edge of each piece, and work the selvedge stitches in garter stitch (knit every row). It will be easy to match the two pieces row for row when you're sewing them together.

- To make sure that the front and back are the same length and that their seams will match perfectly, count the number of rows between the lower edging and the first armhole bind-off and make sure the numbers are the same for all body pieces. To facilitate counting, mark twenty-row intervals with coilless markers as you go.

- Use plastic hair-roller pins (the kind that come with old-fashioned brush rollers) to pin pieces of knitting together in preparation for seaming. Roller pins are longer and thicker than straight pins, and much less sharp.

personal**touches** crewneck finishes

There are a number of ways to finish off a crewneck opening on a pullover or cardigan. In general, stitches are picked up around the neck opening, usually with the right side facing. For a cardigan, stitches are picked up from one center-front neck edge to the other. For a pullover, stitch pick-up usually begins at a shoulder or near the edge of the back neck. A common problem with a crewneck is that the stitches are bound off so tightly that they make the neck opening too snug to get over the head comfortably. If you have this problem, try binding off with larger needles or try using the sewn bind-off (see Glossary).

Basic Crewneck

For a basic crewneck, work the desired edging for an inch or so. The most common edgings are single rib, double rib, and hemmed. Also found are stockinette stitch, single crochet, and I-cord.

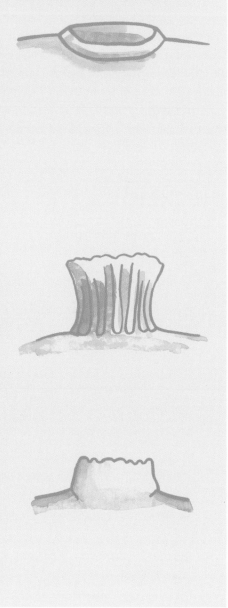

The Striped Crewneck Pullover on page 169 has a basic crewneck finish. So do the Lace-Edged Cardigan (page 61), Floating Cables Pullover (page 97), and Zip-Front Jacket (page 133).

Turtleneck

Work a turtleneck by picking up stitches as for a regular crewneck and working these stitches for the necessary number of inches so that the edging can fold back on itself. Many knitters change to larger needles when they get to the foldline so that the outer layer (the one that folds over to the outside) is slightly larger in circumference. This technique prevents the neck from becoming too tight.

The Chunky Drop-Shoulder Turtleneck on page 31 has a turtleneck.

Funnel Neck

Funnel necks are basic crewnecks that incorporate continuations of the same stitch pattern as the front and/or back. Stitches are picked up just like a regular crewneck sweater, but they are usually worked in stockinette stitch (perhaps with the continuation of a cable or color pattern from the center front and/or back). A funnel neck is usually worked for more rows than a crewneck, but not as many as a turtleneck.

The Cable Panel Pullover on page 59 has a funnel neck.

Basic Collar
A collar is very easy to work on either cardigans or pullovers. Simply pick up the desired number of stitches, beginning and ending where you want the split in the collar to be. Do not join the stitches, but work them back and forth in rows. To prevent the edges of the collar from curling, work it in a ribbed or other non-curling stitch. Or work just the stitches along the edges of the collar in a rib.

The Gatsby Cardigan on page 167 has a basic collar.

Collar with Side Split
This type of collar positions the split at the shoulder seam. It therefore isn't practical for cardigans (unless the front opening is offset to one side). Starting and ending at the shoulder edge, pick up and knit stitches around the neck edge. Then work back and forth in the desired edging stitch for the desired length. To create additional splay at the outer edge of the collar, and to make the outer layer lie gracefully against the front of the garment, change to larger needles at the folding point.

The Diagonal Eyelet Pullover on page 101 has a collar with a side split.

Collar with Front Split
A simple variation on the turtleneck/funnel neck is to leave a split at the front neck. The split makes for a comfortable fit because the neckline isn't constricting.

The Ribbed-Sleeve Pullover on page 166 has a stand-up collar with a front split.

personal**touches** v-neck finishes

The challenge with the V-neck opening is to work a neckband that is shaped into the base of the V. To do so, you must decrease stitches at the center of the V. If you are working with an odd number of stitches, place the center front stitch at the bottom of the V on a holder while you work the rest of the neck shaping. Then when it's time to work the edging, continue this center stitch, usually as a knit stitch on the right side. Decrease one stitch on each side of this center stitch every row of ribbing to create a mitered corner at the base of the V. If you have an even number of stitches, work the center two stitches as knit stitches and decrease one stitch on each side of this pair for a prominent center line on the V. For a less conspicuous look, mark the center point (the space between the center two stitches) and work directional decreases (see Glossary) on either side of the marker.

Basic V-Neck

Pick up and knit the desired number of stitches around the neck opening. Then work the desired edging, while at the same time, decreasing one stitch on each side of the center point every row until the edging measures the desired length. For a hemmed variation, work stockinette stitch for the desired length, working decreases at the base of the V, work a garter or picot turning row (see pages 36–37), then work stockinette stitch for the facing, working increases to mirror the decreases worked previously.

The Tweed V-Neck Pullover on page 33 has a basic hemmed edging with a garter turning row.

Shawl Collar

For a shawl collar, use a circular needle to pick up knit stitches around the entire neck opening, beginning and ending at the center front. Do not join into a round. Work the edging (usually a single or double rib) to the shoulder and across the back neck to the other shoulder. Work short rows (see Glossary) back and forth from shoulder to shoulder, always working one or two more stitches at the end of the needle until all the stitches have been worked. Work all stitches for a couple of rows, if desired, then bind off all stitches and block the collar in place.

The Shawl-Collar Pullover on page 63 has a shawl collar.

Crossover V-Neck

Beginning at the center front point of the V, pick up and knit stitches around the entire neck opening. Working back and forth in rows, work the edging for the desired length, then bind off all stitches. Tack the selvedges of the edging to the garment in line with the V shape.

The Cartridge Rib Pullover on page 132 has a crossover V-neck collar.

set-in sleeve sweaters

Sweaters with set-in sleeves have the most fitted silhouette. Because they are shaped to follow the contour of the body where the upper arm meets the shoulder, they require more detailed shaping. About an inch of stitches is bound off at the base of the armhole, then additional stitches are gradually decreased at each side edge until the width of the front and back above the armholes extends exactly from shoulder bone to shoulder bone. This type of shaping eliminates all of the excess fabric at the armholes, and results in a refined fit. It also necessitates more detailed shaping of the tops of the sleeves (the caps) to create the rounded shape necessary to fit into the armhole perfectly. To mimic the natural slope of the shoulders and enhance the fit of the sweater, the shoulder stitches are bound off in a series of steps.

Sweaters with set-in sleeves have a timeless, classic quality. Because there is no excess fabric at the armholes, this type of sweater style is particularly well suited for close-fitting variations (see waist shapings on pages 104–105). However, this requires that the edge of the armhole and top of the sleeve fall at the edge of the shoulder line, and that the pieces must fit together perfectly. There isn't much

Three sweater variations following the set-in sleeve chart. Top to bottom: Floating Cables Pullover at 42" (106.5 cm) circumference and 6 stitches/inch, Diagonal Eyelet Pullover at 38" (96.5 cm) circumference and 5 stitches/inch, and Cropped Cardigan at 36" (91.5 cm) circumference and 6 stitches/inch. Step-by-step instructions for these sweaters begin on page 97.

leeway in how the cap fits into the armhole; if the seam is not sewn in just right, the sleeve cap may pull or pucker. It is not uncommon for even accomplished designers to rip out and resew a sleeve to the body several times before being satisfied.

basic anatomy

The following set-in sleeve sweaters are worked in pieces—back, front(s), and sleeves—from the lower edges upward. The back is worked straight to the armhole (with waist shaping if desired), a few stitches are bound off at each side edge at once, followed by a series of decreases to create a smooth curve until the armhole is in line with the shoulder bone, then the piece is worked straight to the desired armhole depth. The shoulders are bound off in a series of steps to form a slope. For the pullover version, the front is worked the same as the back up to the point where stitches are bound off and/or decreased to shape the crew- or V-neck. For the cardigan version, the front consists of two pieces—each with half the number of stitches used for the back. The sleeves are widened for the upper arm by paired increases worked at specific intervals until the desired width is achieved. At the underarm, the sleeve cap is shaped by binding off about an inch of stitches followed by a series of decreases worked at different rates to create the rounded shape necessary to fit exactly into the armhole. After the pieces are blocked, they are sewn together—first the shoulders are joined, then the sleeves are sewn into the armholes, and then the sleeve and side seams are joined in a continuous line. Finally, the neck is finished off with the desired edging.

To use the following chart to make a set-in sleeve sweater, you need to choose yarn, determine your gauge (see page 6), and pick a size based on the desired finished bust/chest circumference. You'll also need straight needles in the size necessary to obtain the desired gauge (and needles one or two sizes smaller for edgings, if appropriate), a tapestry needle, and buttons for cardigan versions: 5 to 7 for child sizes, 7 to 9 for adult sizes. Gauge runs vertically along the left side of the chart; finished bust/chest circumference is listed horizontally across the top. The chart for children's sizes begins on page 73; schematics are on page 80. The chart for adult sizes begins on page 81; schematics are on page 96.

sizing child

Finished Chest Circumference									
26	28	30	32	34"	26	28	30	32	34"
66	71	76	81.5	86.5 cm	66	71	76	81.5	86.5 cm

GAUGE

Yarn Requirements

3	250	310	380	450	510 yd
	229	283	347	411	466 m
4	350	440	530	630	730
	320	402	485	576	668
5	440	560	670	800	920
	402	512	613	732	841
6	620	790	950	1130	1290
	567	722	869	1033	1180
7	690	870	1050	1240	1420
	631	796	960	1134	1298

Pullover Back
CO:

3	40	42	46	48	52 sts.
4	52	56	60	64	68
5	64	70	74	80	86
6	78	84	90	96	102
7	90	98	106	112	120

Work edging of choice (see pages 35–37), then cont even until piece measures desired length to armhole, or about:

7¾	8¾	10¼	11¾	13¼"
19.5	22	26	30	33.5 cm

Shape Armholes
At beg of next 2 rows BO:

3	2	2	2	2	3 sts.
4	3	3	3	3	3
5	4	4	4	4	4
6	5	5	5	5	5
7	5	5	5	5	6

At beg of foll 2 rows BO:

3	2	2	2	2	2 sts.
4	3	3	3	3	3

set-in sleeve

5	3	3	3	3	3
6	4	4	4	4	4
7	4	4	4	4	4

Dec 1 st each end of needle every RS row

3	1	1	1	2	2 time(s).
4	1	1	1	2	2
5	1	1	1	3	2
6	1	1	1	2	2
7	2	2	2	3	3

There will remain:

3	30	32	36	36	38 sts.
4	38	42	46	48	52
5	48	54	58	60	68
6	58	64	70	74	80
7	68	76	84	88	94

Cont even until armholes measure:

5½	6½	7	7½	8"
14	16.5	18	19	20.5 cm

Shape Shoulders
At beg of next 2 rows BO:

3	4	4	5	5	5 sts.
4	5	5	6	6	7
5	6	7	7	8	9
6	5	6	6	7	8
7	6	7	7	8	9

At beg of foll 2 rows BO:

3	4	4	4	4	5 sts.
4	4	5	5	6	7
5	6	7	7	7	9
6	5	5	6	6	7
7	5	6	7	8	8

Finished Chest Circumference

	26	28	30	32	34"
	66	71	76	81.5	86.5 cm

At beg of foll 2 rows BO (if number is zero, omit these rows):

	26	28	30	32	34"
3	0	0	0	0	0 sts.
4	0	0	0	0	0
5	0	0	0	0	0
6	4	5	5	6	7
7	5	6	6	7	8

BO rem sts for back neck:

	26	28	30	32	34"
3	14	16	18	18	18 sts.
4	20	22	24	24	24
5	24	26	30	30	32
6	30	32	36	36	36
7	36	38	44	42	44

Pullover Front with Crewneck

(See page 75 for V-neck option.) Work as for back until armholes measure (ending with a WS row):

4	5	5½	6	6½"
10	13	14	15	16.5 cm

There will be:

	26	28	30	32	34"
3	30	32	36	36	38 sts.
4	38	42	46	48	52
5	48	54	58	60	68
6	58	64	70	74	80
7	68	76	84	88	94

Shape Crewneck

With RS facing, work across:

	26	28	30	32	34"
3	12	12	13	13	14 sts,
4	15	16	16	17	19
5	19	20	21	22	26
6	23	24	25	27	30
7	27	28	30	32	35

join new yarn and BO for front neck:

	26	28	30	32	34"
3	6	8	10	10	10 sts,
4	8	10	14	14	14
5	10	14	16	16	16
6	12	16	20	20	20
7	14	20	24	24	24

work to end. There will be the foll number of sts at each side:

	26	28	30	32	34"
3	12	12	13	13	14 sts.
4	15	16	16	17	19
5	19	20	21	22	26
6	23	24	25	27	30
7	27	28	30	32	35

Working each side separately, at each neck edge BO 3 sts (if number is zero, omit these rows):

	26	28	30	32	34"
3	0	0	0	0	0 time(s).
4	0	0	0	0	0
5	1	1	1	1	1
6	1	1	1	1	1
7	2	1	1	1	1

Then BO 2 sts:

	26	28	30	32	34"
3	1	1	1	1	1 time(s).
4	2	2	1	1	1
5	1	1	1	1	2
6	2	1	1	1	1
7	1	2	2	2	2

Then dec 1 st at neck edge every RS row:

	26	28	30	32	34"
3	2	2	2	2	2 time(s).
4	2	2	3	3	3
5	2	1	2	2	1
6	2	3	3	3	3
7	3	2	3	2	3

There will rem the foll number of sts at each side:

	26	28	30	32	34"
3	8	8	9	9	10 sts.
4	9	10	11	12	14
5	12	14	14	15	18

Finished Chest Circumference

26	28	30	32	34"
66	71	76	81.5	86.5 cm

	26	28	30	32	34"
	66	71	76	81.5	86.5 cm

6	14	16	17	19	22
7	16	19	20	23	25

Work even until armholes measure same as back to shoulder.

Shape Shoulders

At each armhole edge, BO:

3	4	4	5	5	5 sts
4	5	5	6	6	7
5	6	7	7	8	9
6	5	6	6	7	8
7	6	7	7	8	9

once, then BO:

3	4	4	4	4	5 sts
4	4	5	5	6	7
5	6	7	7	7	9
6	5	5	6	6	7
7	5	6	7	8	8

once, then BO rem (if number is zero, omit this row):

3	0	0	0	0	0 sts
4	0	0	0	0	0
5	0	0	0	0	0
6	4	5	5	6	7
7	5	6	6	7	8

Pullover Front with V-Neck

Work as for back until armholes measure (ending with a WS row):

1¼	1¾	1¾	2¼	2¾"
3.2	4.5	4.5	5.5	7 cm

With RS facing, work to center of row. Turn and work these sts only (place rem sts on a holder to work later). Cont to work armhole shaping as for back, if necessary, and

at the same time dec 1 st at neck edge every RS row:

3	4	4	5	5	5 times.
4	7	8	8	8	8
5	9	10	12	12	14
6	13	13	15	15	15
7	17	17	20	18	20

Then dec 1 st at neck edge every 4 rows:

3	3	4	4	4	4 time(s).
4	3	3	4	4	4
5	3	3	3	3	2
6	2	3	3	3	3
7	1	2	2	3	2

There will remain:

3	8	8	9	9	10 sts.
4	9	10	11	12	14
5	12	14	14	15	18
6	14	16	17	19	22
7	16	19	20	23	25

Work even until armhole measures same as back to shoulder. Shape shoulder as for crewneck version. Rejoin yarn at neck edge of held sts and work as for first half, reversing neck and shoulder shaping.

Sleeves

CO:

3	18	20	22	22	24 sts.
4	24	26	28	30	32
5	30	32	36	38	40
6	36	40	42	46	48
7	42	46	48	52	56

Work edging of choice for desired length or until piece measures about:

1½	1½	1½	2	2"
3.8	3.8	3.8	5	5 cm

Finished Chest Circumference

	26	28	30	32	34"
	66	71	76	81.5	86.5 cm

Change to St st and inc 1 st each end of needle every 4 rows (if number is zero, omit these rows):

	26	28	30	32	34"
3	0	0	0	0	0 time(s).
4	0	4	3	3	4
5	0	8	4	6	8
6	1	10	11	10	14
7	0	12	15	13	17

Then inc 1 st each end of needle every 6 rows:

3	5	7	8	9	10 times.
4	7	6	8	9	9
5	9	5	9	9	8
6	10	5	6	8	6
7	12	5	5	8	6

There will be:

3	28	34	38	40	44 sts.
4	38	46	50	54	58
5	48	58	62	68	72
6	58	70	76	82	88
7	66	80	88	94	102

Work even if necessary until piece measures desired length to armhole, or about:

11	11¾	13	14½	15"
28	30	33	37	38 cm

Shape Cap

At beg of next 2 rows BO:

3	2	2	2	2	3 sts.
4	3	3	3	3	3
5	4	4	4	4	4
6	5	5	5	5	5
7	5	5	5	5	6

At beg of foll 2 rows BO:

3	2	2	2	2	2 sts.
4	3	3	3	3	3
5	3	3	3	3	3

	26	28	30	32	34"
	66	71	76	81.5	86.5 cm

6	4	4	4	4	4
7	4	4	4	4	4

Dec 1 st each end of needle every RS row

3	1	1	1	2	2 time(s).
4	1	1	1	2	2
5	1	1	1	3	2
6	1	1	1	2	2
7	2	2	2	3	3

There will remain:

3	18	24	28	28	30 sts.
4	24	32	36	38	42
5	32	42	46	48	54
6	38	50	56	60	66
7	44	58	66	70	76

Dec 1 st each end of needle every 4 rows (if number is zero, omit these rows):

3	0	2	1	2	1 time(s).
4	1	0	0	0	1
5	1	1	0	0	0
6	0	0	0	0	0
7	1	0	0	0	0

Then dec 1 st each end of needle every 2 rows:

3	4	2	5	3	5 times.
4	3	7	9	9	6
5	4	6	10	8	9
6	7	8	10	9	9
7	6	10	11	9	9

Then BO 2 sts at beg of next (if number is zero, omit these rows):

3	0	0	0	0	0 rows.
4	0	0	0	0	4
5	0	2	0	2	4
6	0	4	4	6	8
7	0	2	4	8	10

Finished Chest Circumference

	26	28	30	32	34"
	66	71	76	81.5	86.5 cm

Then BO:

3	2	4	4	4	4 sts
4	4	4	4	4	4
5	3	3	3	3	3
6	3	3	3	3	3
7	4	4	4	4	4

at beg of next:

3	2	2	2	2	2 rows.
4	2	2	2	2	2
5	4	4	4	4	4
6	4	4	4	4	4
7	4	4	4	4	4

There will remain:

3	6	8	8	10	10 sts.
4	8	10	10	12	12
5	10	12	14	16	16
6	12	14	16	18	20
7	14	18	20	20	22

BO all sts.

Finishing

Block pieces to measurements. With yarn threaded on a tapestry needle, sew left shoulder seam.

Neckband: Choose a crewneck finish on pages 66–67 or a V-neck finish on pages 68–69. With smaller needles, RS facing, and beg at right shoulder, pick up and knit 1 st for each BO st and about 3 sts for every 4 rows along sloped edges around neck opening. Adjust st count if necessary to achieve a full multiple of the edging patt you've chosen plus 2 extra "seam" sts. Work in chosen pattern until neckband measures ¾" (2 cm), or desired length. BO all sts in patt. *Seams*: Sew

Finished Chest Circumference

	26	28	30	32	34"
	66	71	76	81.5	86.5 cm

rem shoulder and neckband seam. Lay garment flat with RS facing upward. Fold sleeve in half lengthwise to locate shoulder point (center of BO edge), and pin RS of sleeve to body without stretching or easing the fabric and matching shoulder points. With yarn threaded on a tapestry needle and beg at shoulder point (leave sufficient yarn at beg of seam to be used later for other half), sew sleeve to back armhole to the underarm. Repeat for front half of armhole. Sew sleeve and side seams in a continuous line. Weave in loose ends. Block again, if desired.

Cardigan Back

Work as for pullover version.

Cardigan Left Front with Crewneck

(See page 79 for V-neck option.) CO:

3	20	21	23	24	26 sts.
4	26	28	30	32	34
5	32	35	37	40	43
6	39	42	45	48	51
7	45	49	53	56	60

Work edging of choice (as for back), then cont even until piece measures same as back to armhole, ending with a WS row.

Shape Armhole

At beg of next RS row BO:

3	2	2	2	2	3 sts.
4	3	3	3	3	3
5	4	4	4	4	4
6	5	5	5	5	5
7	5	5	5	5	6

set-in sleeve

	26	28	30	32	34"		26	28	30	32	34"
	66	71	76	81.5	86.5 cm		66	71	76	81.5	86.5 cm

set-in sleeve

At beg of foll RS row BO:

3	2	2	2	2	2 sts.
4	3	3	3	3	3
5	3	3	3	3	3
6	4	4	4	4	4
7	4	4	4	4	4

Dec 1 st at beg of needle every RS row:

3	1	1	1	2	2 time(s).
4	1	1	1	2	2
5	1	1	1	3	2
6	1	1	1	2	2
7	2	2	2	3	3

There will remain:

3	15	16	18	18	19 sts.
4	19	21	23	24	26
5	24	27	29	30	34
6	29	32	35	37	40
7	34	38	42	44	47

Cont even until armhole measures (ending with a WS row):

	4	5	5½	6	6½"
	10	13	14	15	16.5 cm

Shape Crewneck

At beg of next WS row, BO:

3	3	4	5	5	5 sts,
4	4	5	7	7	7
5	5	7	8	8	8
6	6	8	10	10	10
7	7	10	12	12	12

work to end. At neck edge, BO 3 sts (if number is zero, omit these rows):

3	0	0	0	0	0 time(s).
4	0	0	0	0	0
5	1	1	1	1	1
6	1	1	1	1	1
7	2	1	1	1	1

Then BO 2 sts:

3	1	1	1	1	1 time(s).
4	2	2	1	1	1
5	1	1	1	1	2
6	2	1	1	1	1
7	1	2	2	2	2

Then dec 1 st at neck edge every RS row:

3	2	2	2	2	2 time(s).
4	2	2	3	3	3
5	2	1	2	2	1
6	2	3	3	3	3
7	3	2	3	2	3

There will remain:

3	8	8	9	9	10 sts.
4	9	10	11	12	14
5	12	14	14	15	18
6	14	16	17	19	22
7	16	19	20	23	25

Cont even until piece measures same as back to shoulder, ending with a WS row.

Shape Shoulder

At armhole edge (beg of RS row), BO:

3	4	4	5	5	5 sts.
4	5	5	6	6	7
5	6	7	7	8	9
6	5	6	6	7	8
7	6	7	7	8	9

At beg of next RS row, BO:

3	4	4	4	4	5 sts.
4	4	5	5	6	7
5	6	7	7	7	9
6	5	5	6	6	7
7	5	6	7	8	8

Finished Chest Circumference

26	28	30	32	34"
66	71	76	81.5	86.5 cm

At beg of foll RS row, BO (if number is zero, omit this row):

3	0	0	0	0	0 sts.
4	0	0	0	0	0
5	0	0	0	0	0
6	4	5	5	6	7
7	5	6	6	7	8

Cardigan Right Front with Crewneck

Work as for left front with crewneck, but reverse shaping (i.e., BO for armhole and shoulder at beg of WS rows; shape neck at beg of RS rows).

Cardigan Left Front with V-Neck

Work as for crewneck option until armhole measures (ending with a WS row):

1¼	1¾	1¾	2¼	2¾"
3.2	4.5	4.5	5.5	7 cm

Cont to work armhole shaping as for back, if necessary, and *at the same time* dec 1 st at neck edge (end of RS row) every RS row:

3	4	4	5	5	5 times.
4	7	8	8	8	8
5	9	10	12	12	14
6	13	13	15	15	15
7	17	17	20	18	20

Then dec 1 st at neck edge every 4 rows:

3	3	4	4	4	4 time(s).
4	3	3	4	4	4
5	3	3	3	3	2
6	2	3	3	3	3
7	1	2	2	3	2

There will remain:

3	8	8	9	9	10 sts.
4	9	10	11	12	14
5	12	14	14	15	18

6	14	16	17	19	22
7	16	19	20	23	25

Work even until armhole measures same as back to shoulder. Shape shoulder as for crewneck version.

Cardigan Right Front with V-Neck

Work as for left front with V-neck but reverse shaping (i.e., BO for armhole and shoulder at beg of WS rows; shape neck at beg of RS rows).

Finishing

Block pieces to measurements. With yarn threaded on a tapestry needle, sew shoulder seams.

Neckband: Choose a crewneck finish on pages 66–67 or a V-neck finish on pages 68–69. With smaller needles, RS facing, and beg at center front, pick up and knit 1 st for every BO st and about 3 sts for every 4 rows along sloped edges around neck opening for a crewneck. (Combine neckband with button and buttonhole bands for a V-neck version.) Adjust st count if necessary to achieve a full multiple of the edging pattern you've chosen. Work in chosen patt until neckband measures ¾" (2 cm), or desired length. BO all sts in patt.

Button band: (on left front for females; right front for males) With smaller needles and RS facing, pick up and knit about 3 sts for every 4 rows along center front edge. Adjust st count if necessary to achieve a full multiple of the edging pattern you've chosen. Work in chosen pattern until band measures ¾" (2 cm). BO all sts in patt. Mark placement of 5 buttons, one ½" (1.3 cm) up from CO edge, one at beg of neck shaping, and the others evenly spaced in between.

Buttonhole band: (on right front for females; left front for males) Work as for button band, working one-row buttonholes (see Glossary) opposite markers when band measures between ¼" and ½" (.6 and 1.3 cm). BO all sts in patt.

Seams: Lay garment flat with RS facing upward. Fold sleeve in half lengthwise to locate shoulder point (center of BO edge), and pin RS of sleeve to body without stretching or easing the fabric and matching shoulder points. With yarn threaded on a tapestry needle and beg at shoulder point (leave sufficient yarn at beg of seam to be used later to work other half), sew sleeve to back armhole to the underarm. Repeat for front armhole. Sew sleeve and side seams in a continuous line.

Weave in loose ends. Sew buttons to button band opposite buttonholes. Block again, if desired.

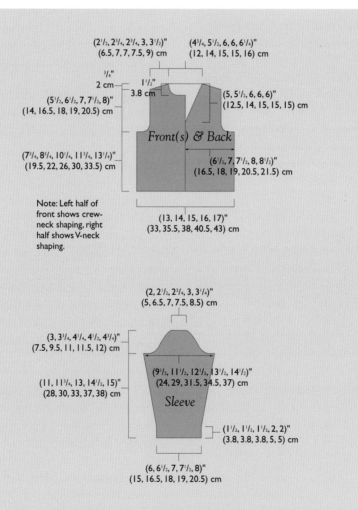

(2½, 2¾, 2¾, 3, 3½)"
(6.5, 7, 7, 7.5, 9) cm

(4¾, 5½, 6, 6, 6¼)"
(12, 14, 15, 15, 16) cm

¾"
2 cm

1½"
3.8 cm

(5½, 6½, 7, 7½, 8)"
(14, 16.5, 18, 19, 20.5) cm

(5, 5½, 6, 6, 6)"
(12.5, 14, 15, 15, 15) cm

Front(s) & Back

(7¾, 8¾, 10¼, 11¾, 13¼)"
(19.5, 22, 26, 30, 33.5) cm

(6½, 7, 7½, 8, 8½)"
(16.5, 18, 19, 20.5, 21.5) cm

Note: Left half of front shows crew-neck shaping, right half shows V-neck shaping.

(13, 14, 15, 16, 17)"
(33, 35.5, 38, 40.5, 43) cm

(2, 2½, 2¾, 3, 3¼)"
(5, 6.5, 7, 7.5, 8.5) cm

(3, 3¾, 4¼, 4½, 4¾)"
(7.5, 9.5, 11, 11.5, 12) cm

(9½, 11½, 12½, 13½, 14½)"
(24, 29, 31.5, 34.5, 37) cm

(11, 11¾, 13, 14½, 15)"
(28, 30, 33, 37, 38) cm

Sleeve

(1½, 1½, 1½, 2, 2)"
(3.8, 3.8, 3.8, 5, 5) cm

(6, 6½, 7, 7½, 8)"
(15, 16.5, 18, 19, 20.5) cm

child sizes 26"–34" (66 cm–86.5 cm)

sizing adult

Finished Bust/Chest Circumference

36	38	40	42	44	46	48	50	52	54"
91.5	96.5	101.5	106.5	112	117	122	127	132	137 cm

Yarn Requirements

	36	38	40	42	44	46	48	50	52	54"
3	570	620	680	730	780	830	870	900	940	980 yd
	521	567	622	668	713	759	796	823	860	896 m
4	810	870	960	1040	1110	1180	1230	1280	1330	1380
	741	796	878	951	1015	1079	1125	1170	1216	1262
5	1020	1100	1210	1310	1400	1480	1550	1610	1680	1740
	933	1006	1106	1198	1280	1353	1417	1472	1536	1591
6	1440	1560	1710	1850	1970	2100	2190	2280	2380	2470
	1317	1426	1564	1692	1801	1920	2003	2085	2176	1591
7	1590	1710	1880	2030	2170	2310	2420	2510	2620	2710
	1454	1564	1719	1856	1984	2112	2213	2295	2396	2478

Pullover Back
CO:

	36	38	40	42	44	46	48	50	52	54"
3	54	58	60	64	66	70	72	76	78	82 sts.
4	72	76	80	84	88	92	96	100	104	108
5	90	94	100	106	110	116	120	126	130	136
6	108	114	120	126	132	138	144	150	156	162
7	126	134	140	148	154	162	168	176	182	190

Work edging of choice (see pages 35–37), then cont even until piece measures desired length to armhole, or about:

13	13	13½	14¼	15	15¼	15½	15¾	16	16¼"
33	33	34.5	36	38	38.5	39.5	40	40.5	41.5 cm

Shape Armholes
At beg of next 2 rows BO:

	36	38	40	42	44	46	48	50	52	54"
3	3	3	3	3	3	3	3	4	4	5 sts.
4	4	4	4	4	4	4	5	5	5	6
5	5	5	5	5	5	5	6	6	6	7
6	6	6	6	6	6	6	7	7	7	8
7	7	7	7	7	7	7	8	9	9	10

Finished Bust/Chest Circumference

	36	38	40	42	44	46	48	50	52	54"
	91.5	96.5	101.5	106.5	112	117	122	127	132	137 cm

At beg of foll 2 rows BO:

	36	38	40	42	44	46	48	50	52	54"
3	2	2	2	2	2	2	2	2	2	2 sts.
4	3	3	3	3	3	3	3	3	3	3
5	3	3	3	3	3	3	3	3	3	3
6	4	4	4	4	4	4	4	4	4	4
7	4	4	4	4	4	4	4	4	4	4

Dec I st each end of needle every RS row:

	36	38	40	42	44	46	48	50	52	54"
3	2	3	3	3	4	4	4	5	5	5 times.
4	3	3	4	4	4	5	5	6	7	7
5	3	4	5	5	5	6	6	8	9	9
6	4	5	6	6	6	7	8	9	11	11
7	5	5	7	7	7	9	9	10	12	12

There will remain:

	36	38	40	42	44	46	48	50	52	54"
3	40	42	44	48	48	52	54	54	56	58 sts.
4	52	56	58	62	66	68	70	72	74	76
5	68	70	74	80	84	88	90	92	94	98
6	80	84	88	94	100	104	106	110	112	116
7	94	102	104	112	118	122	126	130	132	138

Cont even until armholes measure:

	36	38	40	42	44	46	48	50	52	54"
	8½	9	9½	9¾	10	10¼	10½	10¾	11	11¼"
	21.5	23	24	25	25.5	26	26.5	27.5	28	28.5 cm

Shape Shoulders

At beg of next 2 rows BO:

	36	38	40	42	44	46	48	50	52	54"
3	5	6	6	7	7	5	5	5	5	6 sts.
4	7	8	8	9	10	7	7	7	7	7
5	6	7	7	8	8	9	9	9	9	9
6	7	8	8	9	10	10	10	11	10	11
7	8	10	10	11	12	12	12	12	12	13

At beg of foll 2 rows BO:

	36	38	40	42	44	46	48	50	52	54"
3	5	5	6	7	7	5	5	5	5	5 sts.
4	6	7	8	8	9	6	6	7	7	7
5	6	6	7	8	8	8	8	8	9	9
6	7	7	8	9	10	10	10	10	10	11
7	8	9	10	11	11	11	12	12	12	13

Finished Bust/Chest Circumference

	36	38	40	42	44	46	48	50	52	54"
	91.5	96.5	101.5	106.5	112	117	122	127	132	137 cm

At beg of foll 2 rows BO (if number is zero, omit these rows):

3	0	0	0	0	0	5	5	5	5	5 sts.
4	0	0	0	0	0	6	6	6	6	7
5	6	6	7	7	8	8	8	8	8	9
6	7	7	8	9	9	10	9	10	10	10
7	8	9	9	10	11	11	11	12	12	12

BO rem sts for back neck:

3	20	20	20	20	20	22	24	24	26	26 sts.
4	26	26	26	28	28	30	32	32	34	34
5	32	32	32	34	36	38	40	42	42	44
6	38	40	40	40	42	44	48	48	52	52
7	46	46	46	48	50	54	56	58	60	62

Pullover Front with Crewneck

(See page 86 for V-neck option.) Work as for back until armholes measure (ending with a WS row):

	7	7½	8	8¼	8½	8¼	8½	8¾	9	9¼"
	18	19	20.5	21	21.5	21	21.5	22	23	23.5 cm

There will be:

3	40	42	44	48	48	52	54	54	56	58 sts.
4	52	56	58	62	66	68	70	72	74	76
5	68	70	74	80	84	88	90	92	94	98
6	80	84	88	94	100	104	106	110	112	116
7	94	102	104	112	118	122	126	130	132	138

Shape Crewneck

With RS facing, work across:

3	15	16	17	19	18	20	21	21	21	22 sts,
4	19	21	22	24	25	26	27	28	28	29
5	26	27	29	32	32	34	35	36	36	38
6	30	32	34	37	38	40	41	43	43	45
7	35	39	40	44	45	47	49	51	51	54

join new yarn and BO for front neck:

3	10	10	10	10	12	12	12	12	14	14 sts,
4	14	14	14	14	16	16	16	16	18	18
5	16	16	16	16	20	20	20	20	22	22

Finished Bust/Chest Circumference									
36	38	40	42	44	46	48	50	52	54"
91.5	96.5	101.5	106.5	112	117	122	127	132	137 cm

6	20	20	20	20	24	24	24	24	26	26
7	24	24	24	24	28	28	28	28	30	30

work to end. There will be the foll number of sts at each side:

3	15	16	17	19	18	20	21	21	21	22 sts.
4	19	21	22	24	25	26	27	28	28	29
5	26	27	29	32	32	34	35	36	36	38
6	30	32	34	37	38	40	41	43	43	45
7	35	39	40	44	45	47	49	51	51	54

Working each side separately, at each neck edge BO 3 sts (if number is zero, omit these rows):

3	0	0	0	0	0	0	0	0	0	0 time(s).
4	0	0	0	1	0	1	1	1	1	1
5	1	1	1	1	1	1	1	2	1	2
6	1	1	1	1	1	1	2	2	2	2
7	2	2	2	2	2	2	2	2	2	2

Then BO 2 sts:

3	1	1	1	1	1	1	2	2	2	2 time(s).
4	2	2	2	1	2	1	1	1	1	1
5	1	1	1	2	1	2	2	1	2	1
6	2	2	2	2	2	2	2	2	2	2
7	1	1	1	2	1	2	3	3	3	4

Then dec 1 st at neck edge every RS row:

3	3	3	3	3	2	3	2	2	2	2 times.
4	2	2	2	2	2	2	3	3	3	3
5	3	3	3	2	3	2	3	3	3	3
6	2	3	3	3	2	3	2	2	3	3
7	3	3	3	2	3	3	2	3	3	2

There will rem the foll number of sts at each side:

3	10	11	12	14	14	15	15	15	15	16 sts.
4	13	15	16	17	19	19	19	20	20	21
5	18	19	21	23	24	25	25	25	26	27
6	21	22	24	27	29	30	29	31	30	32
7	24	28	29	32	34	34	35	36	36	38

Work even until armholes measure same as back to shoulder.

Finished Bust/Chest Circumference									
36	38	40	42	44	46	48	50	52	54"
91.5	96.5	101.5	106.5	112	117	122	127	132	137 cm

Shape Shoulders

At each armhole edge, BO:

3	5	6	6	7	7	5	5	5	5	6 sts
4	7	8	8	9	10	7	7	7	7	7
5	6	7	7	8	8	9	9	9	9	9
6	7	8	8	9	10	10	10	11	10	11
7	8	10	10	11	12	12	12	12	12	13

once, then BO:

3	5	5	6	7	7	5	5	5	5	5 sts
4	6	7	8	8	9	6	6	7	7	7
5	6	6	7	8	8	8	8	8	9	9
6	7	7	8	9	10	10	10	10	10	11
7	8	9	10	11	11	11	12	12	12	13

once, then BO rem (if number is zero, omit this row):

3	0	0	0	0	0	5	5	5	5	5 sts.
4	0	0	0	0	0	6	6	6	6	7
5	6	6	7	7	8	8	8	8	8	9
6	7	7	8	9	9	10	9	10	10	10
7	8	9	9	10	11	11	11	12	12	12

Pullover Front with V-Neck

Work as for back until armholes measure (ending with a WS row):

	3½	3½	4	4	4¼	4¼	4½	4½	4½	4¾"
	9	9	10	10	11	11	11.5	11.5	11.5	12 cm

With RS facing, work to center of row. Turn and work these sts only (place rem sts on a holder to work later). Cont to work armhole shaping as for back, if necessary, and *at the same time* dec 1 st at neck edge every RS row:

3	8	7	7	6	6	7	9	9	10	10 times.
4	11	10	10	11	11	12	14	13	15	15
5	15	13	13	14	16	17	19	20	19	21
6	18	18	18	17	19	20	24	23	26	26
7	23	22	22	22	24	27	28	29	30	31

Finished Bust/Chest Circumference									
36	38	40	42	44	46	48	50	52	54"
91.5	96.5	101.5	106.5	112	117	122	127	132	137 cm

Then dec I st at neck edge every 4 rows (if number is zero, omit these rows):

3	2	3	3	4	4	4	3	3	3	3 time(s).
4	2	3	3	3	3	3	2	3	2	2
5	1	3	3	3	2	2	1	1	2	1
6	1	2	2	3	2	2	0	0	0	0
7	0	1	1	2	1	0	0	0	0	0

There will remain:

3	10	11	12	14	14	15	15	15	15	16 sts.
4	13	15	16	17	19	19	19	20	20	21
5	18	19	21	23	24	25	25	25	26	27
6	21	22	24	27	29	30	29	31	30	32
7	24	28	29	32	34	34	35	36	36	38

Work even until armhole measures same as back to shoulder. Shape shoulder as for crew-neck version. Rejoin yarn at neck edge of held sts and work as for first half, reversing neck and shoulder shaping.

Sleeves

CO:

3	28	28	30	30	30	32	32	32	34	34 sts.
4	38	38	40	40	40	44	44	44	46	46
5	46	46	50	50	50	54	54	56	58	58
6	56	56	60	60	60	66	66	66	68	68
7	66	66	70	70	70	76	76	76	80	80

Work edging of choice for desired length or until piece measures about:

2½	2½	2½	2½	2½	2½	2½	2½	2½	2½"
6.5	6.5	6.5	6.5	6.5	6.5	6.5	6.5	6.5	6.5 cm

Change to St st and inc I st each end of needle every 2 rows (if number is zero, omit these rows):

3	0	0	0	0	0	0	0	0	0	0 time(s).
4	0	0	0	0	0	0	0	0	0	0
5	0	0	0	0	0	0	0	0	0	0
6	0	0	0	0	0	0	0	0	1	4
7	0	6	4	10	13	0	0	2	2	7

Finished Bust/Chest Circumference

36	38	40	42	44	46	48	50	52	54"
91.5	96.5	101.5	106.5	112	117	122	127	132	137 cm

set-in sleeve

Then inc 1 st each end of needle every 4 rows (if number is zero, omit these rows):

3	0	2	1	3	5	5	5	8	8	11 time(s).
4	0	4	7	9	10	7	10	13	13	16
5	6	10	12	14	16	15	18	18	18	24
6	9	16	18	20	24	17	23	26	27	25
7	9	7	13	5	3	25	28	30	30	27

Then inc 1 st each end of needle every 6 rows (if number is zero, omit these rows):

3	9	9	10	9	8	8	8	6	6	4 time(s).
4	12	10	8	7	7	9	7	5	5	3
5	10	8	7	6	5	6	4	4	4	0
6	10	6	5	4	2	7	3	1	0	0
7	12	12	9	13	14	4	2	0	0	0

There will be:

3	46	50	52	54	56	58	58	60	62	64 sts.
4	62	66	70	72	74	76	78	80	82	84
5	78	82	88	90	92	96	98	100	102	106
6	94	100	106	108	112	114	118	120	124	126
7	108	116	122	126	130	134	136	140	144	148

Work even if necessary until piece measures desired length to armhole, or about:

16	16½	16¾	17	17½	17¾	18¼	18¾	18¾	18½"
40.5	42	42.5	43	44.5	45	46.5	47.5	47.5	47 cm

Shape Cap

At beg of next 2 rows BO:

3	3	3	3	3	3	3	3	4	4	5 sts.
4	4	4	4	4	4	4	5	5	5	6
5	5	5	5	5	5	5	6	6	6	7
6	6	6	6	6	6	6	7	7	7	8
7	7	7	7	7	7	7	8	9	9	10

At beg of foll 2 rows BO:

3	2	2	2	2	2	2	2	2	2	2 sts.
4	3	3	3	3	3	3	3	3	3	3
5	3	3	3	3	3	3	3	3	3	3
6	4	4	4	4	4	4	4	4	4	4
7	4	4	4	4	4	4	4	4	4	4

Finished Bust/Chest Circumference

	36	38	40	42	44	46	48	50	52	54"
	91.5	96.5	101.5	106.5	112	117	122	127	132	137 cm

Dec 1 st each end of needle every RS row

3	2	3	3	3	4	4	4	4	5	5 times.
4	3	3	4	4	4	5	5	6	7	7
5	3	4	5	5	5	6	6	8	9	9
6	4	5	6	6	6	7	8	9	11	11
7	5	5	7	7	7	9	9	10	12	12

There will remain:

3	32	34	36	38	38	40	40	40	40	40 sts.
4	42	46	48	50	52	52	52	52	52	52
5	56	58	62	64	66	68	68	66	66	68
6	66	70	74	76	80	80	80	80	80	80
7	76	84	86	90	94	94	94	94	94	96

Dec 1 st each end of needle every 4 rows (if number is zero, omit these rows):

3	1	1	1	1	1	1	3	3	3	3 time(s).
4	0	0	0	1	0	2	3	4	1	2
5	0	0	0	0	0	4	4	2	4	3
6	0	0	0	1	0	4	4	3	3	4
7	0	0	0	0	0	4	4	4	4	5

Then dec 1 st each end of needle every RS row (if number is zero, omit these rows):

3	6	6	7	8	7	6	2	2	1	3 time(s).
4	10	11	10	8	11	5	4	0	7	6
5	9	8	9	9	10	1	3	4	1	3
6	10	8	9	8	9	1	2	3	2	1
7	12	11	11	12	11	0	0	0	1	0

Then BO 2 sts at beg of next (if number is zero, omit these rows):

3	0	0	0	0	0	2	4	4	4	2 rows.
4	0	0	2	4	2	0	0	0	4	4
5	4	6	6	6	6	0	0	0	0	0
6	6	10	10	10	12	4	2	2	2	2
7	6	10	10	10	12	10	18	12	4	2

Finished Bust/Chest Circumference									
36	38	40	42	44	46	48	50	52	54"
91.5	96.5	101.5	106.5	112	117	122	127	132	137 cm

Then BO 3 sts at beg of next (if number is zero, omit these rows):

3	0	0	0	0	0	0	0	0	0	0 rows.
4	0	0	0	0	0	4	4	6	0	0
5	4	4	4	4	4	12	10	10	10	10
6	4	4	4	4	4	12	12	12	12	12
7	0	0	0	0	0	6	0	4	8	10

Then BO 4 sts at beg of next (if number is zero, omit these rows):

3	2	2	2	2	2	2	2	2	2	2 rows.
4	2	2	2	2	2	2	2	2	2	2
5	0	0	0	0	0	0	0	0	0	0
6	0	0	0	0	0	0	0	0	0	0
7	4	4	4	4	4	4	4	4	4	4

There will remain:

3	10	12	12	12	14	14	14	14	16	16 sts.
4	14	16	16	16	18	18	18	18	20	20
5	18	18	20	22	22	22	24	24	26	26
6	22	22	24	26	26	26	28	28	30	30
7	24	26	28	30	32	32	34	34	36	36

BO all sts.

Finishing
Block pieces to measurements. With yarn threaded on a tapestry needle, sew left shoulder seam.

Neckband: Choose a crewneck finish on pages 66–67 or a V-neck finish on pages 68–69. With smaller needles, RS facing, and beg at right shoulder, pick up and knit 1 st for each BO st and about 3 sts for every 4 rows along sloped edges around neck opening. Adjust st count if necessary to achieve a full multiple of the edging patt you've chosen, plus 2 extra "seam" sts. Work in chosen patt until neckband measures 1" (2.5 cm), or desired length. BO all sts in patt.

Seams: Sew rem shoulder and neckband seam. Lay garment flat with RS facing upward. Fold sleeve in half lengthwise to locate shoulder point (center of BO edge), and pin RS of sleeve to body without stretching or easing the fabric and matching shoulder points. With yarn threaded on a tapestry needle and beg at shoulder point (leave sufficient yarn at beg of seam to be used later to work the other half), sew sleeve to back armhole to the underarm. Repeat for front half of armhole. Sew sleeve and side seams in a continuous line.

Weave in loose ends. Block again, if desired.

Finished Bust/Chest Circumference

36	38	40	42	44	46	48	50	52	54"
91.5	96.5	101.5	106.5	112	117	122	127	132	137 cm

Cardigan Back
Work as for pullover version.

Cardigan Left Front with Crewneck
(See page 93 for V-neck option.) CO:

3	27	29	30	32	33	35	36	38	39	41 sts.
4	36	38	40	42	44	46	48	50	52	54
5	45	47	50	53	55	58	60	63	65	68
6	54	57	60	63	66	69	72	75	78	81
7	63	67	70	74	77	81	84	88	91	95

Work edging of choice (as for back), then cont even until piece measures same as back to armhole, ending with a WS row.

Shape Armhole
At beg of next RS row BO:

3	3	3	3	3	3	3	3	4	4	5 sts.
4	4	4	4	4	4	4	5	5	5	6
5	5	5	5	5	5	5	6	6	6	7
6	6	6	6	6	6	6	7	7	7	8
7	7	7	7	7	7	7	8	9	9	10

At beg of foll RS row BO:

3	2	2	2	2	2	2	2	2	2	2 sts.
4	3	3	3	3	3	3	3	3	3	3
5	3	3	3	3	3	3	3	3	3	3
6	4	4	4	4	4	4	4	4	4	4
7	4	4	4	4	4	4	4	4	4	4

Dec 1 st at beg of needle every RS row:

3	2	3	3	3	4	4	4	5	5	5 times.
4	3	3	4	4	4	5	5	6	7	7
5	3	4	5	5	5	6	6	8	9	9
6	4	5	6	6	6	7	8	9	11	11
7	5	5	7	7	7	9	9	10	12	12

Finished Bust/Chest Circumference

36	38	40	42	44	46	48	50	52	54"
91.5	96.5	101.5	106.5	112	117	122	127	132	137 cm

There will remain:

3	20	21	22	24	24	26	27	27	28	29 sts.
4	26	28	29	31	33	34	35	36	37	38
5	34	35	37	40	42	44	45	46	47	49
6	40	42	44	47	50	52	53	55	56	58
7	47	51	52	56	59	61	63	65	66	69

Cont even until armhole measures (ending with a WS row):

7	7½	8	8¼	8½	8¼	8½	8¾	9	9¼"
18	19	20.5	21	21.5	21	21.5	22	23	23.5 cm

Shape Crewneck

At beg of next WS row, BO:

3	5	5	5	5	6	6	6	6	7	7 sts,
4	7	7	7	7	8	8	8	8	9	9
5	8	8	8	8	10	10	10	10	11	11
6	10	10	10	10	12	12	12	12	13	13
7	12	12	12	12	14	14	14	14	15	15

work to end. At neck edge, BO 3 sts (if number is zero, omit these rows):

3	0	0	0	0	0	0	0	0	0	0 time(s).
4	0	0	0	1	0	1	1	1	1	1
5	1	1	1	1	1	1	1	2	1	2
6	1	1	1	1	1	1	2	2	2	2
7	2	2	2	2	2	2	2	2	2	2

Then BO 2 sts:

3	1	1	1	1	1	1	2	2	2	2 time(s).
4	2	2	2	1	2	1	1	1	1	1
5	1	1	1	2	1	2	2	1	2	1
6	2	2	2	2	2	2	2	2	2	2
7	1	1	1	2	1	2	3	3	3	4

Then dec 1 st at neck edge every RS row:

3	3	3	3	3	2	3	2	2	2	2 times.
4	2	2	2	2	2	2	3	3	3	3
5	3	3	3	2	3	2	3	3	3	3
6	2	3	3	3	2	3	2	2	3	3
7	3	3	3	2	3	3	2	3	3	2

Finished Bust/Chest Circumference									
36	38	40	42	44	46	48	50	52	54"
91.5	96.5	101.5	106.5	112	117	122	127	132	137 cm

There will remain:

3	10	11	12	14	14	15	15	15	15	16 sts.
4	13	15	16	17	19	19	19	20	20	21
5	18	19	21	23	24	25	25	25	26	27
6	21	22	24	27	29	30	29	31	30	32
7	24	28	29	32	34	34	35	36	36	38

Cont even until piece measures same as back to shoulder, ending with a WS row.

Shape Shoulder
At armhole edge (beg of RS row), BO:

3	5	6	6	7	7	5	5	5	5	6 sts.
4	7	8	8	9	10	7	7	7	7	7
5	6	7	7	8	8	9	9	9	9	9
6	7	8	8	9	10	10	10	11	10	11
7	8	10	10	11	12	12	12	12	12	13

At beg of foll RS row, BO:

3	5	5	6	7	7	5	5	5	5	5 sts.
4	6	7	8	8	9	6	6	7	7	7
5	6	6	7	8	8	8	8	8	9	9
6	7	7	8	9	10	10	10	10	10	11
7	8	9	10	11	11	11	12	12	12	13

At beg of foll RS row, BO (if number is zero, omit this row):

3	0	0	0	0	0	5	5	5	5	5 sts.
4	0	0	0	0	0	6	6	6	6	7
5	6	6	7	7	8	8	8	8	8	9
6	7	7	8	9	9	10	9	10	10	10
7	8	9	9	10	11	11	11	12	12	12

Cardigan Right Front with Crewneck
Work as for left front with crewneck, but reverse shaping (i.e., BO for armhole and shoulder at beg of WS rows; shape neck at beg of RS rows).

Cardigan Left Front with V-Neck
Work front as for crewneck option until armhole measures (ending with a WS row):

3½	3½	4	4	4¼	4¼	4½	4½	4½	4¾"
9	9	10	10	11	11	11.5	11.5	11.5	12 cm

Finished Bust/Chest Circumference									
36	38	40	42	44	46	48	50	52	54"
91.5	96.5	101.5	106.5	112	117	122	127	132	137 cm

Cont to work armhole shaping as for back, if necessary, and *at the same time* dec 1 st at neck edge (end of RS row) every RS row:

3	8	7	7	6	6	7	9	9	10	10 times.
4	11	10	10	11	11	12	14	13	15	15
5	15	13	13	14	16	17	19	20	19	21
6	18	18	18	17	19	20	24	23	26	26
7	23	22	22	12	24	27	28	29	30	31

Then dec 1 st at neck edge every 4 rows (if number is zero, omit these rows):

3	2	3	3	4	4	4	3	3	3	3 time(s).
4	2	3	3	3	3	3	2	3	2	2
5	1	3	3	3	2	2	1	1	2	1
6	1	2	2	3	2	2	0	1	0	0
7	0	1	1	2	1	0	0	0	0	0

There will remain:

3	10	11	12	14	14	15	15	15	15	16 sts.
4	13	15	16	17	19	19	19	20	20	21
5	18	19	21	23	24	25	25	25	26	27
6	21	22	24	27	29	30	29	31	30	32
7	24	28	29	32	34	34	35	36	36	38

Work even until armhole measures same as back to shoulder. Shape shoulder as for back.

Cardigan Right Front with V-Neck

Work as for left front with V-neck but reverse shaping (i.e., BO for armhole and shoulder at beg of WS rows; shape neck at beg of RS rows).

Finishing

Block pieces to measurements. With yarn threaded on a tapestry needle, sew shoulder seams. *Neckband*: Choose a crewneck finish on pages 66–67 or a V-neck finish on pages 68–69. With smaller needles, RS facing, and beg at center front, pick up and knit 1 st for every BO st and about 3 sts for every 4 rows along sloped edges around neck opening for a crewneck. (Combine neckband with button and buttonhole bands for a V-neck version.) Adjust st count if necessary to achieve a full multiple of the edging patt you've chosen. Work chosen patt until neckband measures 1" (2.5 cm) or desired length. BO all sts in patt.

Button band: (on left front for females; right front for males) With smaller needles and RS facing, pick up and knit about 3 sts for every 4 rows along center front edge. Adjust st count if necessary to achieve a full multiple of the edging pattern you've chosen. Work in chosen pattern until band measures 1" (2.5 cm). BO all sts in patt. Mark placement of desired number of buttons, one ½" (1.3 cm) up from CO edge, one at beg of neck shaping, and the others evenly spaced in between.

Buttonhole band: (on right front for females; left front for males) Work as for button band, working one-row buttonholes (see Glossary) opposite markers when band measures between ¼" and ½" (.6 and 1.3 cm). BO all sts in patt.

Seams: Lay garment flat with RS facing upward. Fold sleeve in half lengthwise to find shoulder point (center of BO edge), and pin RS of sleeve to body without stretching or easing fabric and matching shoulder points. With yarn threaded on a tapestry needle and beg at shoulder point (leave sufficient yarn at beg of seam to be used later to work the other half), sew sleeve to back armhole to the underarm. Repeat for front half of armhole. Sew sleeve and side seams in a continuous line.

Weave in loose ends. Sew buttons to button band opposite buttonholes. Block again, if desired.

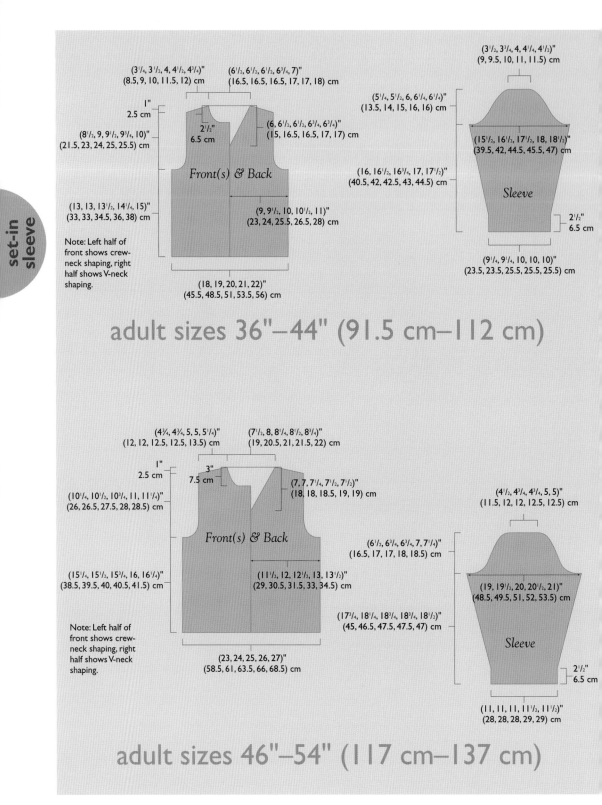

(3¼, 3½, 4, 4½, 4¾)"
(8.5, 9, 10, 11.5, 12) cm

(6½, 6½, 6½, 6¾, 7)"
(16.5, 16.5, 16.5, 17, 17, 18) cm

(3½, 3¾, 4, 4¼, 4½)"
(9, 9.5, 10, 11, 11.5) cm

1"
2.5 cm

2½"
6.5 cm

(6, 6½, 6½, 6¾, 6¾)"
(15, 16.5, 16.5, 17, 17) cm

(5¼, 5½, 6, 6¼, 6¼)"
(13.5, 14, 15, 16, 16) cm

(8½, 9, 9½, 9¾, 10)"
(21.5, 23, 24, 25, 25.5) cm

(15½, 16½, 17½, 18, 18½)"
(39.5, 42, 44.5, 45.5, 47) cm

Front(s) & Back

(16, 16½, 16¾, 17, 17½)"
(40.5, 42, 42.5, 43, 44.5) cm

Sleeve

(13, 13, 13½, 14¼, 15)"
(33, 33, 34.5, 36, 38) cm

(9, 9½, 10, 10½, 11)"
(23, 24, 25.5, 26.5, 28) cm

2½"
6.5 cm

Note: Left half of
front shows crew-
neck shaping, right
half shows V-neck
shaping.

(18, 19, 20, 21, 22)"
(45.5, 48.5, 51, 53.5, 56) cm

(9¼, 9¼, 10, 10, 10)"
(23.5, 23.5, 25.5, 25.5, 25.5) cm

adult sizes 36"–44" (91.5 cm–112 cm)

(4¾, 4¾, 5, 5, 5¼)"
(12, 12, 12.5, 12.5, 13.5) cm

(7½, 8, 8¼, 8½, 8¾)"
(19, 20.5, 21, 21.5, 22) cm

1"
2.5 cm

3"
7.5 cm

(7, 7, 7¼, 7½, 7½)"
(18, 18, 18.5, 19, 19) cm

(4½, 4¾, 4¾, 5, 5)"
(11.5, 12, 12, 12.5, 12.5) cm

(10¼, 10½, 10¾, 11, 11¼)"
(26, 26.5, 27.5, 28, 28.5) cm

Front(s) & Back

(6½, 6¾, 6¾, 7, 7¼)"
(16.5, 17, 17, 18, 18.5) cm

(15¼, 15½, 15¾, 16, 16¼)"
(38.5, 39.5, 40, 40.5, 41.5) cm

(11½, 12, 12½, 13, 13½)"
(29, 30.5, 31.5, 33, 34.5) cm

(19, 19½, 20, 20½, 21)"
(48.5, 49.5, 51, 52, 53.5) cm

(17¾, 18¼, 18¾, 18¾, 18½)"
(45, 46.5, 47.5, 47.5, 47) cm

Sleeve

Note: Left half of
front shows crew-
neck shaping, right
half shows V-neck
shaping.

2½"
6.5 cm

(23, 24, 25, 26, 27)"
(58.5, 61, 63.5, 66, 68.5) cm

(11, 11, 11, 11½, 11½)"
(28, 28, 28, 29, 29) cm

adult sizes 46"–54" (117 cm–137 cm)

Floating Cables Pullover

Six-stitch cables floating on a moss stitch background form an allover texture pattern on this set-in sleeve pullover. Although the yarn used here knits up at five stitches to the inch in stockinette stitch, the texture pattern tightens the overall gauge to six stitches per inch. To maintain the integrity of the moss stitch pattern along the armhole, neck, and sleeve cap shaping, the decreases are worked at the very edges of the pieces. The edges are trimmed with single rib, which is worked on the same size needles as the body so that it prevents curling but doesn't draw in too much.

Finished Size: 42" (106.5 cm) bust/chest circumference.
Yarn: Plymouth Silk-Merino (70% merino, 30% mulberry silk; 109 yd [100 m]/50 g): #285 red, 17 balls.
Needles: Size 8 (5 mm): straight and 16" (40-cm) circular (cir). Adjust needle size if necessary to obtain the correct gauge.
Notions: Markers (m); tapestry needle.
Gauge: 6 sts and 8 rows = 1" (2.5 cm) in cable moss stitch on size 8 (5-mm) needles; 5 sts and 7 rows = 1" (2.5 cm) in stockinette stitch on size 8 (5-mm) needles.

Back

With straight needles, CO 126 sts. Work k1, p1 rib until piece measures 2" (5 cm) from beg, ending with a WS row. With RS facing, and beg with Row 1 as indicated on chart, work Floating Cables chart (page 98) until piece measures 14¼" (36 cm) from beg, ending with a WS row (place markers between cable motifs, if necessary, to keep them properly aligned). Make note of chart row just completed so front can match. *Shape armholes*: BO 6 sts at beg of next 2 rows, then BO 4 sts at beg of foll 2 rows—106 sts rem. Dec 1 st each end of needle (work decs on the 2 edge sts to maintain the integrity of the moss st patt) every RS row 6 times—94 sts rem. Cont even until armholes measure 9¾" (25 cm), ending with a WS row. Make note of chart row just completed. *Shape shoulders*: BO 9 sts at beg of next 6 rows—40 sts rem. BO all sts.

Front

Work as back until armholes measure 8¼" (21 cm), taking care to beg armhole shaping on same chart row as for back—94 sts rem. *Shape crewneck*: Keeping in patt, work 37 sts, join new yarn and BO 20 sts, work to end—37 sts each side. Working each side separately, at each neck edge BO 3 sts once, then BO 2 sts 2 times, then dec 1 st every RS row 3 times (work decs on the 2 edge sts as for armholes)—27 sts rem. Cont even if necessary until armholes measure same as back to shoulder, ending with the same chart row as for back. Shape shoulders as for back.

Sleeves

With straight needles, CO 60 sts. Work k1, p1 rib until piece measures 2" (5 cm) from beg, ending with a WS row. With RS facing, and beg with Row 1 as indicated on chart, work Floating Cables chart, and *at the same time* inc 1 st each end of needle every 4 rows 20 times, then every 6 rows 4 times, working new sts into patt—108 sts. Cont even until piece measures 17" (43 cm), ending with a WS row. **Shape armholes**: BO 6 sts at beg of next 2 rows, then BO 4 sts at beg of foll 2 rows, then dec 1 st each end of needle (work decs on the 2 edge sts) every RS row 6 times—76 sts rem. Dec 1

st each end of needle every 4 rows once, then every RS row 8 times—58 sts rem. BO 2 sts at beg of next 10 rows, then BO 3 sts at beg of next 4 rows—26 sts rem. BO all sts.

Finishing

Block pieces to measurements. With yarn threaded on a tapestry needle, sew shoulder seams. Sew sleeve caps into armholes. Sew sleeve and side seams. **Neckband**: With cir needle, RS facing, and beg at right shoulder

Floating Cables

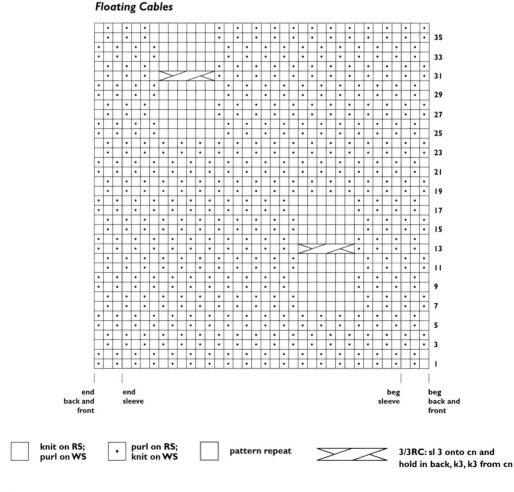

knit on RS; purl on WS	purl on RS; knit on WS	pattern repeat

3/3RC: sl 3 onto cn and hold in back, k3, k3 from cn

seam, pick up and knit 40 sts across back neck, 18 sts along left side neck, 20 sts across front neck, and 18 sts along right side neck—96 sts total. Place marker and join. Work k1, p1 rib until neckband measures 1" (2.5 cm). BO all sts in rib. Block again if desired.

Cropped Cardigan

This cardigan demonstrates how easy it is to adjust the body and sleeve lengths provided in the charted instructions. The body is 2" (5 cm) shorter than specified and the three-quarter length sleeves are 3" (7.5 cm) shorter. To account for the wider circumference of the forearm than the cuff, more

---

Finished Size: 36" (91.5 cm) bust/chest circumference, buttoned.
Yarn: Le Fibre Nobili Taj Mahal (70% wool, 22% silk, 8% cashmere; 187 yd [170 m]/ 50 g): #1425 olive (MC), 7 balls; #1424 lime (CC), 1 ball. Yarn distributed by Plymouth Yarn.
Needles: Body and sleeves—Size 5 (3.75 mm). Ribbing—Size 4 (3.5 mm). Adjust needle size if necessary to obtain the correct gauge.
Notions: Marker (m); stitch holders; tapestry needle; twelve ⅜" (1-cm) buttons.
Gauge: 6 sts and 8 rows = 1" (2.5 cm) in stockinette stitch on size 5 (3.75-mm) needles.

---

stitches are cast on for the sleeves than specified. A deep rib at the waist, tiny vintage buttons, and contrasting edges enhances the retro look. The front bands are continuations of the lower body ribbing—at the top of the ribbing the band stitches are placed on a holder, then the fronts are worked to the neck. The band stitches are picked up and worked until they measure the same length as the front. To facilitate seaming the bands to the fronts, extra "seam" stitches are added when the band breaks for the body.

Note: To make ribbing draw in less, work it on larger needles.

Back

With CC and smaller needles, CO 108 sts. Cut off CC. With MC, purl 1 (WS) row, then work k1, p1 rib until piece measures 6" (15 cm) from beg, ending with a WS row. Change to larger needles and St st. Work even until piece measures 11" (28 cm) from beg, ending with a WS row. **Shape armholes**: BO 6 sts at beg of next 2 rows, then BO 4 sts at beg of foll 2 rows, then dec 1 st each end of needle every RS row 4 times—80 sts rem. Cont even until armholes measure 8½" (21.5 cm), ending with a WS row. **Shape shoulders**: BO 7 sts at beg of next 6 rows—38 sts rem. BO all sts.

Left Front

With CC and smaller needles, CO 54 sts for front, place marker (pm), then CO 5 more sts for button band—59 sts total. Cut off CC. With MC, purl 1 (WS) row, then work k1, p1 rib until piece measures 6" (15 cm) from beg, ending with a WS row. *Next row*: (RS) Change to larger needles, k53, k1f&b (to provide an extra st for seaming button band later), remove m, place rem 5 sts on holder to work later for button band—55 sts rem. Cont working St st on rem 55 sts until piece measures same as back to armhole, ending with a WS row. **Shape armhole**: (RS) BO 6 sts at beg of row, work to end. At armhole edge (beg of RS rows), BO 4 sts once, then dec 1 st at beg of needle every RS row 4 times—41 sts rem. Cont even until armhole measures 7" (18 cm), ending with a RS row. **Shape crewneck**: (WS) BO 11 sts (seam st + 10 front sts) at beg of row, work to end—30 sts rem. At neck edge (beg of WS rows), BO 3 sts once, then BO 2 sts 2 times, then dec 1 st every RS row 2 times—21 sts rem. Cont even until armhole measures same as back to shoulder, ending with WS row. **Shape shoulder**: BO 7 sts at beg of next 3 RS rows. **Button band**: Place 5 held button band sts on smaller needles. With RS facing, join yarn at seam edge and work as foll: K1f&b (to provide an extra st for seaming), work in established rib to end—6 sts. Cont in rib as established until piece measures to neck edge when slightly stretched. Place sts on holder. With yarn threaded on a tapestry needle, sew button band to front, working 1 st from each edge into seam. Mark placement of 11 buttons, one about ½" (1.3 cm) up from lower edge, one 1" (2.5 cm) down from neck edge, and the others evenly spaced in between (the 12th button will be in the neckband).

Right Front

With CC and smaller needles, CO 5 sts for buttonhole band, pm, then CO 54 more sts for front—59 sts total. Cut off CC. With MC, purl 1 (WS) row, then work k1, p1 rib as for left front, and *at the same time*, on RS rows, work each buttonhole opposite markers for buttons as foll: K1, p1, k1, yo, k2tog, work in rib to end. Cont in rib until piece measures 6" (15 cm) from beg, ending with a RS row. *Next row*: (WS) Work 53 sts in rib, k1f&b (to provide an extra st for seaming), place rem 5 sts on holder to work later for buttonhole band—55 sts rem. Change to larger needles and work St st until piece measures same as back to armhole, ending with a RS row. **Shape armhole**: (WS) BO 6 sts at beg of row, work to end. At armhole edge (beg of WS rows), BO 4 sts once, then dec 1 st at end of needle every RS row 4 times—41 sts rem. Cont even until armhole measures 7" (18 cm), ending with a WS row. **Shape crewneck**: (RS) BO 11 sts (seam st + 10 front sts) at beg of row, work to end—30 sts rem. At neck edge (beg of RS rows), BO 3 sts once, then BO 2 sts 2 times, then dec 1 st every RS row 2 times—21 sts rem. Cont even until armhole measures same as back to shoulder, ending with RS row. **Shape shoulder**: BO 7 sts at beg of next 3 WS rows. **Buttonhole band**: Place 5 held buttonhole band sts on smaller needles. With WS facing, join yarn at seam edge and work as foll: K1f&b (to provide an extra st for seaming), work in established rib to end—6 sts. Cont in rib as established until piece measures to neck edge when slightly stretched, working buttonholes opposite markers as before. Place sts on holder. With yarn threaded on a tapestry needle, sew buttonhole band to front, working 1 st from each edge into seam.

Sleeves

With CC and smaller needles, CO 62 sts. (Note: sleeve is shortened 3" [7.5 cm] and begins with more sts that specified on chart.) Cut off CC. With MC, purl 1 (WS) row, then work k1, p1 rib until piece measures 1" (2.5 cm) from beg. Change to larger needles and St st, inc 1 st each end of needle every 4 rows 6 times, then every 6 rows 10 times—94 sts. Cont even until piece measures 13" (33 cm) from beg, ending with a WS row. *Shape cap*: BO 6 sts at beg of next 2 rows, then BO 4 sts at beg of foll 2 rows, then dec 1 st each end of needle every RS row 14 times—46 sts rem. BO 2 sts at beg of next 6 rows, then BO 3 sts at beg of next 4 rows—22 sts rem. BO all sts.

Finishing

Block pieces to measurements. With yarn threaded on a tapestry needle, sew shoulder seams. Sew sleeve caps into armholes. Sew sleeve and side seams. *Neckband*: With smaller needles and RS facing, place 6 held buttonhole band sts on needle, join MC and pick up and knit 97 sts around neck opening to button band sts, place 6 held button band sts onto needle—109 sts. Cut off yarn. With WS facing, rejoin MC to center front edge and cont in established rib as foll: Work 5 sts, work the next 2 sts tog (last band st and first right front st), work to last 7 sts, work 2 sts tog (last left front st and first band st), work to end—107 sts rem. Cont in rib until neckband measures ½" (1.3 cm). On next row,

work buttonhole as before. Cont in rib until band measures 1" (2.5 cm), ending with a WS row. With RS facing and CC, BO all sts in rib. Weave in loose ends. Sew buttons to button band, opposite buttonholes. Block again if desired.

Diagonal Eyelet Pullover

This set-in sleeve pull-over features a diagonal lace pattern and crew-neck with a side-split collar. Other than the stitch pattern, which interestingly gets the same gauge as stockinette, this sweater follows

Finished Size: 38" (96.5 cm) bust/chest circumference.
Yarn: Indiecita Alpaca Worsted Weight (100% alpaca; 102 yd [93 m]/50 g): #181 grape, 11 balls. Yarn distributed by Plymouth Yarn.
Needles: Body and sleeves—Size 7 (4.5 mm): straight. Ribbing—Size 6 (4 mm): straight. Collar—Sizes 6 and 7 (4 and 4.5 mm): 16" (40-cm) circular (cir). Adjust needle size if necessary to obtain the correct gauge.
Notions: Tapestry needle.
Gauge: 5 sts and 7 rows = 1" (2.5 cm) in diagonal eyelet pattern on size 7 (4.5-mm) needles; 5 sts and 7 rows = 1" (2.5 cm) in stockinette stitch on size 7 (4.5-mm) needles.

the basic instructions from start to finish. The collar begins with a smaller needle at the neck edge, then changes to a larger one for the last couple of inches to provide additional flair so that it falls against the body gracefully.

Back

With smaller straight needles, CO 94 sts. Work k1, p1 rib until piece measures 2" (2.5 cm) from beg, ending with a WS row. Change to larger straight needles. Work the first and last st in garter st for selvedges and the center 92 sts according to Diagonal Eyelet chart (beg and end chart as indicated) until piece measures 13" (33 cm) from beg, ending with a WS row. *Shape armholes*: BO 5 sts at beg of next 2 rows, then BO 3 sts at beg of foll 2 rows. Dec 1 st each end of needle every RS row 4 times—70 sts rem. Cont even until armholes measure 9" (23 cm), ending with a WS row. *Shape shoulders*: BO 7 sts at beg of next 2 rows, then BO 6 sts at beg of foll 4 rows—32 sts rem. BO all sts.

Front

Work as back until armholes measure 7½" (19 cm), ending with a WS row—70 sts rem. *Shape crewneck*: Keeping in patt, work 27 sts, join new yarn and BO 16 sts, work to end—27 sts each side. Working each side separately, at each neck edge BO 3 sts 1 time, then BO 2 sts 1 time, then dec 1 st every RS row 3 times—19 sts rem each side.

Cont even if necessary until armholes measure same as back to shoulders, ending with a WS row. Shape shoulders as for back.

Sleeves

With smaller straight needles, CO 46 sts. Work k1, p1 rib until piece measures 2" (5 cm) from beg, ending with a WS row. Change to larger straight needles. Work the first st and last st in garter st for selvedges and the center 44 sts according to Diagonal Eyelet chart (beg and end as indicated), inc 1 st inside selvedge st each end of needle every 4 rows 10 times, then every 6 rows 8 times, working new sts into patt—82 sts. Cont even until piece measures 16½" (42 cm) from beg, ending with a WS row. *Shape cap*: BO 5 sts at beg of next 2 rows, then BO 3 sts at beg of foll 2 rows, then dec 1 st each end of needle every RS row 4 times—58 sts rem. Dec 1 st each end of needle every RS row 8 more times, the BO 2 sts at beg of next 6 rows, then BO 3 sts at beg of next 4 rows—18 sts rem. BO all sts.

Finishing

Block pieces to measurements. With yarn threaded on a tapestry needle, sew shoulder seams. Sew sleeve caps into armholes. Sew sleeve and side seams. *Collar*: With smaller 16" (40-cm) cir needle, RS facing, and beg at left shoulder seam, pick up and knit 87 sts around neck opening (about 3 sts for every 4 rows down to center front neck, 1 st for each BO st across front neck, about 3 sts for every 4 rows up to shoulder, and about 1 st for each BO st across back neck). Adjust st count if necessary to achieve an odd number of sts. Do not join. With WS facing, work k1, p1 rib across all sts (beg and end with k1) until collar measures about 4" (10 cm). Change to larger cir needle and cont in rib for 2" (5 cm) more. Loosely BO all sts in patt. With yarn threaded on a tapestry needle, work a bar tack at the neckline to reinforce the base of the split collar. Weave in loose ends. Block again if desired.

Diagonal Eyelet

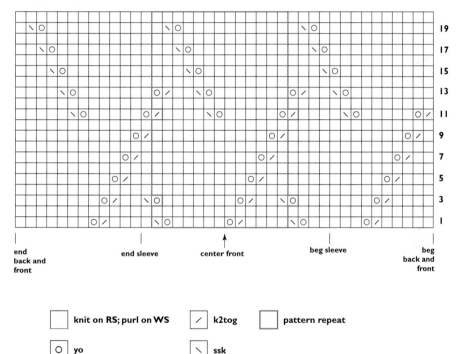

knit on **RS**; purl on **WS**	/ k2tog	pattern repeat
O yo	\ ssk	

personaltouches waist shaping

Sometimes a little shaping at the waist is all that's needed to turn a casual boxy sweater into a sleek and slimming dressy sweater.

For waist shaping to work well, it should coincide with the natural waistline. That is, the narrowest width on the sweater should fall at the narrowest width on the body. Most patterns call for waist shaping to decrease about an inch's worth of stitches in width at each side, front, and back, for a total of four inches reduced in circumference. Waist shaping allows you to custom-fit a sweater to a bottom-heavy or top-heavy figure. If the wearer's hips are broader than her bust (or his chest), you may want to have more stitches at the hips, decrease for the waist, then increase fewer stitches than were decreased to reach the bust circumference. Conversely, if the wearer's bust is larger than her hips, you may want to increase extra stitches above the waist.

Decreases should be equally spaced to make a gentle curve inward followed by a gentle curve outward. Typically, the narrowest circumference is maintained for about an inch between the last decrease and the first increase.

Shaping a Waist with Decreases

The easiest way to draw in the waist is to work a series of decreases at the side seams of the front(s) and back of a sweater. For balance, work one decrease at the beginning of the row and one at the end of the row—there will be a total of 2 stitches decreased. *Work even until the piece measures 1" (2.5 cm) from the decrease, then repeat the decrease row. Repeat from * until the number of stitches decreased at each side represents about an inch (2.5 cm) in width (i.e., total width of back is 2" [5 cm] narrower). *Work even for about an inch, then increase one stitch at the beginning of the row and one at the end of the row; there will be a total of 2 stitches increased. Repeat from * until you have the same number of stitches you began with (before the first decrease).

The Zip-Front Jacket on page 133 has decreased waist shaping.

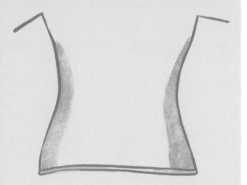

personal**touches** waist shaping

Shaping a Waist with Ribbing

An easy way to shape the waist of a sweater is to add ribbing along the side edges. The natural tendency of ribbing (columns of knit and purl stitches) to contract will cause the garment width to narrow. Because there is play in the amount that ribbing draws in—it can either be blocked in a stretched position for a more open look or left contracted—you can fine-tune how much the garment narrows by how much you block the ribbing. On its own, the ribbing will contract where there is little resistance (at the waist) and expand as needed to accommodate bust and hips.

The Ribbed-Sleeve Pullover on page 166 has ribs along the side edges. The Cropped Cardigan on page 99 takes this concept to the extreme, with the entire lower body worked in rib.

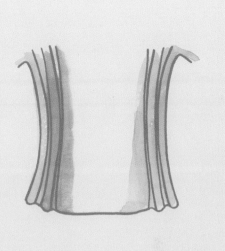

saddle shoulder sweaters

Named for the extensions of the sleeves that lay across the tops of the shoulders to connect the sleeve caps to the neck, saddle shoulder sweaters have a comfortable fit. The shoulder straps (also called saddles, sleeve straps, or sleeve extensions) can be added to most any type of sweater by extending two or three inches at the top edge of the sleeve cap across the shoulders. The construction used here is most closely related to the set-in sleeve style on page 70. The front and back are worked just like their set-in sleeve counterparts but the total armhole depth is shorter than desired by one-half of the saddle width—the shoulder strap adds the last inch or so to the armhole depth. The shoulder stitches are bound off in a series of steps to accommodate the natural slope of the body at the shoulders. The well-fitting sleeve caps are worked as for a set-in sleeve style, but instead of binding off the final two inches or so of stitches, these stitches are continued from shoulder to neck edge across the width of the shoulder. A shoulder strap can range in width from quite narrow—just a few stitches—to the entire width of the sweater yoke. The shoulder straps in these instructions are wide enough to feature a design element, but not so wide as to interfere with the neck shaping.

Like sweaters featuring set-in sleeves, saddle shoulder sweaters have no excess fabric at the armholes. They have a clean, tailored silhouette that is well suited for close-fitting variations. Most importantly, the shoulder strap provides a prominent area to showcase a design element, such as a cable, that can travel up the center of the sleeve and across the shoulder (see the Diamond Cable Pullover on

Three sweater variations following the saddle shoulder chart. Top to bottom: Diamond Cable Pullover at 46" (117 cm) circumference and 4 stitches/inch, Cartridge Rib Pullover at 34" (86.5 cm) circumference and 5 stitches/inch, and Zip-Front Jacket at 38" (96.5 cm) circumference and 6 stitches/inch. Step-by-step instructions for these sweaters begin on page 132.

page 136). Close attention should be paid to measuring the length of the shoulder straps and sewing them to the fronts and back to avoid puckers.

basic anatomy

The following saddle shoulder sweaters are worked in pieces—back, front(s), and sleeves—from the lower edges upward. The back is worked straight to the armhole (with waist shaping if desired, see pages 104–105), a few stitches are bound off at once, followed by a series of decreases to create a smooth curve until the armhole is in line with the shoulder bone, then the piece is worked straight to an inch or so less than the desired armhole depth. The shoulders stitches are bound off in a series of steps. For the pullover version, the front is identical to the back to the point where stitches are bound off and/or decreased to shape the crew- or V-neck. For the cardigan version, the front is worked in two pieces—each with half the number of stitches used for the back. The sleeves are widened for the upper arm by paired increases worked at specific intervals until the desired width is achieved. At the underarm, the sleeve cap is shaped with a series of decreases worked at different rates to create the rounded shape necessary to accommodate the armhole, ending with the number of stitches required for the shoulder strap. The shoulder strap stitches are worked for the width of the shoulder. After the pieces are blocked, they are sewn together (first the shoulder strap is sewn in place between the front and back shoulders, then the rest of the sleeve cap is sewn into the armhole, and finally, the sleeve and side seams are sewn in a continuous line) and the neck is finished off with the desired edging.

To use the following chart to make a saddle shoulder sweater, you need to choose yarn, determine your gauge (see page 6), and pick a size based on the desired finished bust/chest circumference. You'll also need straight needles in the size necessary to obtain the desired gauge (and needles one or two sizes smaller for edgings, if appropriate), a tapestry needle, and buttons for cardigan versions: 5 to 7 for child sizes, 7 to 9 for adult sizes. Gauge runs vertically along the left side of the chart; finished bust/chest circumference is listed horizontally across the top. The chart for children's sizes begins on page 109; schematics are on page 116. The chart for adult sizes begins on page 117; schematics are on page 131.

sizing child

Finished Chest Circumference

	26	28	30	32	34"
	66	71	76	81.5	86.5 cm

GAUGE

Yarn Requirements

GAUGE	26	28	30	32	34"
3	250	310	380	450	510 yd
	229	283	347	411	466 m
4	350	440	530	630	730
	320	402	485	576	668
5	440	560	670	800	920
	402	512	613	732	841
6	620	790	950	1130	1290
	567	722	869	1033	1180
7	690	870	1050	1240	1420
	631	796	960	1134	1298

Pullover Back

CO:

GAUGE	26	28	30	32	34"
3	40	42	46	48	52 sts.
4	52	56	60	64	68
5	64	70	74	80	86
6	78	84	90	96	102
7	90	98	106	112	120

Work edging of choice (see pages 35–37), then cont even until piece measures desired length to armhole, or about:

7¾	8¾	10¼	11¾	13¼"
19.5	22	26	30	33.5 cm

Shape Armholes

At beg of next 2 rows BO:

GAUGE	26	28	30	32	34"
3	2	2	2	2	3 sts.
4	3	3	3	3	3
5	4	4	4	4	4
6	5	5	5	5	5
7	5	5	5	5	6

At beg of foll 2 rows BO:

GAUGE	26	28	30	32	34"
3	2	2	2	2	2 sts.
4	3	3	3	3	3

Finished Chest Circumference

	26	28	30	32	34"
	66	71	76	81.5	86.5 cm

GAUGE	26	28	30	32	34"
5	3	3	3	3	3
6	4	4	4	4	4
7	4	4	4	4	4

Dec 1 st each end of needle every RS row:

GAUGE	26	28	30	32	34"
3	1	1	1	2	2 time(s).
4	1	1	1	2	2
5	1	1	1	3	2
6	1	1	1	2	2
7	2	2	2	3	3

There will remain:

GAUGE	26	28	30	32	34"
3	30	32	36	36	38 sts.
4	38	42	46	48	52
5	48	54	58	60	68
6	58	64	70	74	80
7	68	76	84	88	94

Cont even until armholes measure:

4¾	5¾	6¼	6¾	7¼"
12	14.5	16	17	18.5 cm

Shape Shoulders

At beg of next 2 rows BO:

GAUGE	26	28	30	32	34"
3	4	4	5	5	5 sts.
4	5	5	6	6	7
5	6	7	7	8	9
6	5	6	6	7	8
7	6	7	7	8	9

At beg of foll 2 rows BO:

GAUGE	26	28	30	32	34"
3	4	4	4	4	5 sts.
4	4	5	5	6	7
5	6	7	7	7	9
6	5	5	6	6	7
7	5	6	7	8	8

Finished Chest Circumference

	26	28	30	32	34"
	66	71	76	81.5	86.5 cm

At beg of foll 2 rows BO (if number is zero, omit these rows):

	26	28	30	32	34"
3	0	0	0	0	0 sts.
4	0	0	0	0	0
5	0	0	0	0	0
6	4	5	5	6	7
7	5	6	6	7	8

BO rem sts for back neck:

	26	28	30	32	34"
3	14	16	18	18	18 sts.
4	20	22	24	24	24
5	24	26	30	30	32
6	30	32	36	36	36
7	36	38	44	42	44

Pullover Front with Crewneck

(See page 111 for V-neck option.) Work as for back until armholes measure (ending with a WS row):

4	5	5½	6	6½"
10	12.5	14	15	16.5 cm

There will be:

	26	28	30	32	34"
3	30	32	36	36	38 sts.
4	38	42	46	48	52
5	48	54	58	60	68
6	58	64	70	74	80
7	68	76	84	88	94

Shape Crewneck

With RS facing, work across:

	26	28	30	32	34"
3	12	12	13	13	14 sts,
4	15	16	16	17	19
5	19	20	21	22	26
6	23	24	25	27	30
7	27	28	30	32	35

join new yarn and BO for front neck:

	26	28	30	32	34"
3	6	8	10	10	10 sts,
4	8	10	14	14	14

	26	28	30	32	34"
	66	71	76	81.5	86.5 cm
5	10	14	16	16	16
6	12	16	20	20	20
7	14	20	24	24	24

work to end. There will be the foll number of sts at each side:

	26	28	30	32	34"
3	12	12	13	13	14 sts.
4	15	16	16	17	19
5	19	20	21	22	26
6	23	24	25	27	30
7	27	28	30	32	35

Working each side separately, at each neck edge BO 3 sts (if number is zero, omit these rows):

	26	28	30	32	34"
3	0	0	0	0	0 time(s).
4	0	0	0	0	0
5	1	1	1	1	1
6	1	1	1	1	1
7	2	1	1	1	1

Then BO 2 sts:

	26	28	30	32	34"
3	1	1	1	1	1 time(s).
4	2	2	1	1	1
5	1	1	1	1	2
6	2	1	1	1	1
7	1	2	2	2	2

Then dec 1 st at neck edge every RS row:

	26	28	30	32	34"
3	2	2	2	2	2 time(s).
4	2	2	3	3	3
5	2	1	2	2	1
6	2	3	3	3	3
7	3	2	3	2	3

At the same time, when armholes measure same as back to shoulder,

Finished Chest Circumference

26	28	30	32	34"
66	71	76	81.5	86.5 cm

Shape Shoulders
At each armhole edge, BO:

	26	28	30	32	34"
3	4	4	5	5	5 sts
4	5	5	6	6	7
5	6	7	7	8	9
6	5	6	6	7	8
7	6	7	7	8	9

once, then BO:

	26	28	30	32	34"
3	4	4	4	4	5 sts
4	4	5	5	6	7
5	6	7	7	7	9
6	5	5	6	6	7
7	5	6	7	8	8

once, then BO rem (if number is zero, omit this row):

	26	28	30	32	34"
3	0	0	0	0	0 sts.
4	0	0	0	0	0
5	0	0	0	0	0
6	4	5	5	6	7
7	5	6	6	7	8

Pullover Front with V-Neck
Work as for back until armholes measure:

1¼	1¾	1¾	2¼	2¾"
3.2	4.5	4.5	5.5	7 cm

With RS facing, work to center of row. Turn and work these sts only (place rem sts on a holder to work later). Cont to work armhole shaping as for back, if necessary, and *at the same time* dec 1 st at neck edge every RS row:

	26	28	30	32	34"
3	5	6	7	7	7 times.
4	9	10	11	11	11
5	12	12	14	14	16

	26	28	30	32	34"
66	71	76	81.5	86.5 cm

	26	28	30	32	34"
6	15	16	18	18	18
7	18	19	22	21	22

Then dec 1 st at neck edge every 4 rows (if number is zero, omit these rows):

	26	28	30	32	34"
3	2	2	2	2	2 time(s).
4	1	1	1	1	1
5	0	1	1	1	0
6	0	0	0	0	0
7	0	0	0	0	0

There will remain:

	26	28	30	32	34"
3	8	8	9	9	10 sts.
4	9	10	11	12	14
5	12	14	14	15	18
6	14	16	17	19	22
7	16	19	20	23	25

Work even until armhole measures same as back to shoulder. Shape shoulder as for crewneck version. Rejoin yarn at neck edge of held sts and work as for first half, reversing neck and shoulder shaping.

Sleeves
CO:

	26	28	30	32	34"
3	18	20	22	22	24 sts.
4	24	26	28	30	32
5	30	32	36	38	40
6	36	40	42	46	48
7	42	46	48	52	56

Work edging of choice for desired length or until piece measures about:

1½	1½	1½	2	2"
3.8	3.8	3.8	5	5 cm

saddle shoulder

Finished Chest Circumference

	26	28	30	32	34"
	66	71	76	81.5	86.5 cm

Change to St st and inc 1 st each end of needle every 4 rows (if number is zero, omit these rows):

3	0	0	0	0	0 time(s).
4	0	4	3	3	4
5	0	8	4	6	8
6	1	10	11	10	14
7	0	12	15	13	17

Then inc 1 st each end of needle every 6 rows:

3	5	7	8	9	10 times.
4	7	6	8	9	9
5	9	5	9	9	8
6	10	5	6	8	6
7	12	5	5	8	6

There will be:

3	28	34	38	40	44 sts.
4	38	46	50	54	58
5	48	58	62	68	72
6	58	70	76	82	88
7	66	80	88	94	102

Work even if necessary until piece measures desired length to armhole, or about:

	11	11¾	13	14½	15"
	28	30	33	37	38 cm

Shape Cap

At beg of next 2 rows BO:

3	2	2	2	2	3 sts.
4	3	3	3	3	3
5	4	4	4	4	4
6	5	5	5	5	5
7	5	5	5	5	6

At beg of foll 2 rows BO:

3	2	2	2	2	2 sts.
4	3	3	3	3	3
5	3	3	3	3	3
6	4	4	4	4	4
7	4	4	4	4	4

Dec 1 st each end of needle every RS row:

3	1	1	1	2	2 time(s).
4	1	1	1	2	2
5	1	1	1	3	2
6	1	1	1	2	2
7	2	2	2	3	3

There will remain:

3	18	24	28	28	30 sts.
4	24	32	36	38	42
5	32	42	46	48	54
6	38	50	56	60	66
7	44	58	66	70	76

Dec 1 st each end of needle every 4 rows (if number is zero, omit these rows):

3	0	2	1	2	1 time(s).
4	1	0	0	0	1
5	1	1	0	0	0
6	0	0	0	0	0
7	1	0	0	0	0

Then dec 1 st each end of needle every 2 rows:

3	4	2	5	3	5 times.
4	3	7	9	9	5
5	4	6	10	8	9
6	7	8	10	9	9
7	6	10	11	9	9

Then BO 2 sts at beg of next (if number is zero, omit these rows):

3	0	0	0	0	0 rows.
4	0	0	0	0	4
5	0	2	0	2	4
6	0	4	4	6	8
7	0	2	4	8	10

26	28	30	32	34"
66	71	76	81.5	86.5 cm

26	28	30	32	34"
66	71	76	81.5	86.5 cm

At beg of foll 2 rows, BO:

3	2	5	5	6	6 sts.
4	4	5	5	6	7
5	3	3	4	4	4
6	3	3	4	4	5
7	4	5	6	6	6

At beg of foll 2 rows, BO (if number is zero, omit these rows):

3	0	0	0	0	0 sts.
4	0	0	0	0	0
5	3	4	4	5	5
6	3	4	4	5	5
7	5	6	6	6	7

There will remain:

3	6	6	6	6	6 sts.
4	8	8	8	8	8
5	10	10	10	10	10
6	12	12	12	12	12
7	12	12	12	12	12

Shoulder Strap
Cont even until piece measures:

2½	2¾	2¾	3	3½"
6.5	7	7	7.5	9 cm

from last BO. BO all sts.

Finishing
Block pieces to measurements.

Join saddles: With yarn threaded on a tapestry needle, sew front edges of sleeve caps to front armholes. Sew front edges of saddle shoulder straps to BO edges of front shoulders, easing in any fullness. Sew back edges of sleeve caps to back armholes. Sew back edge of left shoulder strap to BO edge of back shoulder, easing in fullness.

Neckband: Choose a crewneck finish on pages 66–67 or a V-neck finish on pages 68–69. With smaller needles, RS facing, and beg at right shoulder opening, pick up and knit 1 st for each BO st and about 3 sts for every 4 rows along sloped edges around neck opening. Adjust st count if necessary to achieve a full multiple of the edging patt you've chosen, plus 2 extra "seam" sts. Work in chosen patt until neckband measures ¾" (2 cm), or desired length. BO all sts in patt.
Seams: Sew rem shoulder and neckband seam. Sew sleeve and side seams.
Weave in loose ends. Block again, if desired.

Cardigan Back
Work as for pullover version.

Cardigan Left Front with Crewneck
(See page 115 for V-neck option.) CO:

3	20	21	23	24	26 sts.
4	26	28	30	32	34
5	32	35	37	40	43
6	39	42	45	48	51
7	45	49	53	56	60

Work edging of choice (as for back), then cont even until piece measures same as back to armhole, ending with a WS row.

Shape Armhole
At beg of next RS row BO:

3	2	2	2	2	3 sts.
4	3	3	3	3	3
5	4	4	4	4	4
6	5	5	5	5	5
7	5	5	5	5	6

saddle shoulder

Finished Chest Circumference

	26	28	30	32	34"		26	28	30	32	34"
	66	71	76	81.5	86.5 cm		66	71	76	81.5	86.5 cm

At beg of foll RS row BO:

3	2	2	2	2	2 sts.
4	3	3	3	3	3
5	3	3	3	3	3
6	4	4	4	4	4
7	4	4	4	4	4

Dec 1 st at beg of needle every RS row:

3	1	1	1	2	2 time(s).
4	1	1	1	2	2
5	1	1	1	3	2
6	1	1	1	2	2
7	2	2	2	3	3

There will remain:

3	15	16	18	18	19 sts.
4	19	21	23	24	26
5	24	27	29	30	34
6	29	32	35	37	40
7	34	38	42	44	47

Cont even until armhole measures:

4	5	5½	6	6½"
10	12.5	14	15	16.5 cm

Shape Crewneck
At beg of next WS row, BO:

3	3	4	5	5	5 sts,
4	4	5	7	7	7
5	5	7	8	8	8
6	6	8	10	10	10
7	7	10	12	12	12

work to end. At neck edge (beg of WS rows) BO 3 sts (if number is zero, omit these rows):

3	0	0	0	0	0 time(s).
4	0	0	0	0	0
5	1	1	1	1	1
6	1	1	1	1	1
7	2	1	1	1	1

Then BO 2 sts:

3	1	1	1	1	1 time(s).
4	2	2	1	1	1
5	1	1	1	1	2
6	2	1	1	1	1
7	1	2	2	2	2

Then dec 1 st at neck edge every RS row:

3	2	2	2	2	2 time(s).
4	2	2	3	3	3
5	2	1	2	2	1
6	2	3	3	3	3
7	3	2	3	2	3

There will remain:

3	8	8	9	9	10 sts.
4	9	10	11	12	14
5	12	14	14	15	18
6	14	16	17	19	22
7	16	19	20	23	25

Cont even until piece measures same as back to shoulder, ending with a WS row.

Shape Shoulder
At armhole edge (beg of RS row), BO:

3	4	4	5	5	5 sts.
4	5	5	6	6	7
5	6	7	7	8	9
6	5	6	6	7	8
7	6	7	7	8	9

At beg of foll RS row, BO:

3	4	4	4	4	5 sts.
4	4	5	5	6	7
5	6	7	7	7	9
6	5	5	6	6	7
7	5	6	7	8	8

Finished Chest Circumference

	26	28	30	32	34"
	66	71	76	81.5	86.5 cm

At beg of foll RS row, BO (if number is zero, omit this row):

	26	28	30	32	34"
3	0	0	0	0	0 sts.
4	0	0	0	0	0
5	0	0	0	0	0
6	4	5	5	6	7
7	5	6	6	7	8

Cardigan Right Front with Crewneck

Work as for left front with crewneck, but reverse shaping (i.e., BO for armhole and shoulder at beg of WS rows; shape neck at beg of RS rows).

Cardigan Left Front with V-Neck

Work as for crewneck option until armhole measures:

	1¼	1¾	1¾	2¼	2¾"
	3.2	4.5	4.5	5.5	7 cm

Cont to work armhole shaping as for back, if necessary, and *at the same time* dec 1 st at neck edge (end of row) every RS row:

	26	28	30	32	34"
3	5	6	7	7	7 times.
4	9	10	11	11	11
5	12	12	14	14	16
6	15	16	18	18	18
7	18	19	22	21	22

Then dec 1 st at neck edge every 4 rows (if number is zero omit these rows):

	26	28	30	32	34"
3	2	2	2	2	2 times.
4	1	1	1	1	1
5	0	1	1	1	0
6	0	0	0	0	0
7	0	0	0	0	0

There will remain:

	26	28	30	32	34"
3	8	8	9	9	10 sts.
4	9	10	11	12	14

	26	28	30	32	34"
	66	71	76	81.5	86.5 cm
5	12	14	14	15	18
6	14	16	17	19	22
7	16	19	20	23	25

Work even until armhole measures same as back to shoulder. Shape shoulder as for crewneck version.

Cardigan Right Front with V-Neck

Work as for left front with V-neck but reverse shaping (i.e., BO for armhole and shoulder at beg of WS rows; shape neck at beg of RS rows).

Finishing

Block pieces to measurements.

Join saddles: With yarn threaded on a tapestry needle, sew front edges of sleeve caps to front armholes. Sew front edge of each saddle shoulder strap to BO edge of each front shoulder, easing in any fullness. Sew back edges of sleeve caps to back armholes. Sew back edge of each shoulder strap to BO edge of each back shoulder, easing in fullness.

Neckband: Choose a crewneck finish on pages 66–67 or a V-neck finish on pages 68–69. With smaller needles, RS facing, and beg at center front, pick up and knit 1 st for every BO st and about 3 sts for every 4 rows along sloped edges around neck opening for a crewneck. (Combine neckband with button and buttonhole bands for a V-neck version.) Adjust st count if necessary to achieve a full multiple of the edging patt you've chosen. Work in chosen patt until neckband measures ¾" (2 cm), or desired length. BO all sts in patt.

Button band: (on left front for females; right front for males) With smaller needles and RS facing, pick up and knit about 3 sts for every 4 rows along center front edge. Adjust sts if necessary to achieve a full multiple of the edging pattern you've chosen. Work in chosen pattern until band measures ¾" (2 cm). BO all sts in patt. Mark placement of desired number of buttons, one ½" (1.3 cm) up from CO edge, one at beg of neck shaping, and the others evenly spaced in between.

Buttonhole band: (on right front for females; left front for males) Work as for button band, working one-row buttonholes (see Glossary) opposite markers when band measures between ¼" and ½" (.6 and 1.3 cm). BO all sts in patt.

Seams: Sew sleeve and side seams. Weave in loose ends. Sew buttons to button band opposite buttonholes. Block again, if desired.

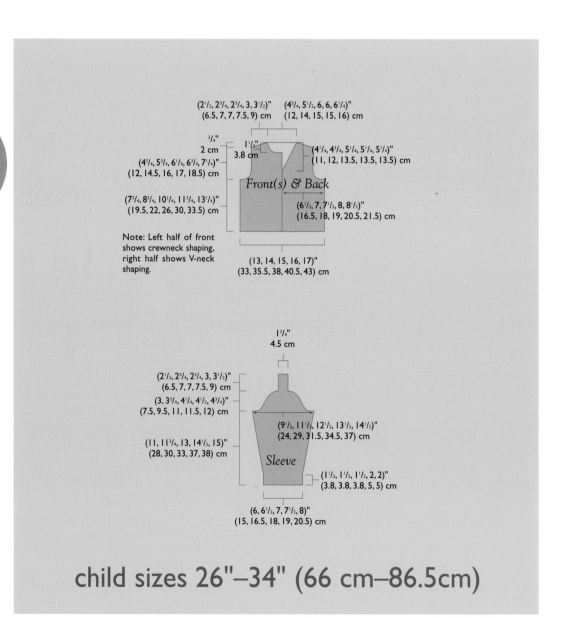

child sizes 26"–34" (66 cm–86.5cm)

sizing adult

Finished Bust/Chest Circumference

36	38	40	42	44	46	48	50	52	54"
91.5	96.5	101.5	106.5	112	117	122	127	132	137 cm

Yarn Requirements

GAUGE										
3	570	620	680	730	780	830	870	900	940	980 yd
	521	567	622	668	713	759	796	823	860	896 m
4	810	870	960	1040	1110	1180	1230	1280	1330	1380
	741	796	878	951	1015	1079	1125	1170	1216	1262
5	1020	1100	1210	1310	1400	1480	1550	1610	1680	1740
	933	1006	1106	1198	1280	1353	1417	1472	1536	1591
6	1440	1560	1710	1850	1970	2100	2190	2280	2380	2470
	1317	1426	1564	1692	1801	1920	2003	2085	2176	2259
7	1590	1710	1880	2030	2170	2310	2420	2510	2620	2710
	1454	1564	1719	1856	1984	2112	2213	2295	2396	2478

saddle shoulder

Pullover Back
CO:

3	54	58	60	64	66	70	72	76	78	82 sts.
4	72	76	80	84	88	92	96	100	104	108
5	90	94	100	106	110	116	120	126	130	136
6	108	114	120	126	132	138	144	150	156	162
7	126	134	140	148	154	162	168	176	182	190

Work edging of choice (see pages 35–37), then cont even until piece measures desired length to armhole, or about:

13	13	13½	14¼	15	15¼	15½	15¾	16	16¼
33	33	34.5	36	38	38.5	39.5	40	40.5	41.5 cm

Shape Armholes
At beg of next 2 rows BO:

3	3	3	3	3	3	3	3	4	4	5 sts.
4	4	4	4	4	4	4	5	5	5	6
5	5	5	5	5	5	5	6	6	6	7
6	6	6	6	6	6	6	7	7	7	8
7	7	7	7	7	7	7	8	9	9	10

Finished Bust/Chest Circumference

	36	38	40	42	44	46	48	50	52	54"
	91.5	96.5	101.5	106.5	112	117	122	127	132	137 cm

At beg of foll 2 rows BO:

3	2	2	2	2	2	2	2	2	2	2 sts.
4	3	3	3	3	3	3	3	3	3	3
5	3	3	3	3	3	3	3	3	3	3
6	4	4	4	4	4	4	4	4	4	4
7	4	4	4	4	4	4	4	4	4	4

Dec 1 st each end of needle every RS row:

3	2	3	3	3	4	4	4	5	5	5 times.
4	3	3	4	4	4	5	5	6	7	7
5	3	4	5	5	5	6	6	8	9	9
6	4	5	6	6	6	7	8	9	11	11
7	5	5	7	7	7	9	9	10	12	12

There will remain:

3	40	42	44	48	48	52	54	54	56	58 sts.
4	52	56	58	62	66	68	70	72	74	76
5	68	70	74	80	84	88	90	92	94	98
6	80	84	88	94	100	104	106	110	112	116
7	94	102	104	112	118	122	126	130	132	138

Cont even until armholes measure:

	7½	8	8½	8¾	9	9	9¼	9½	9¾	10"
	19	20.5	21.5	22	23	23	23.5	24	25	25.5 cm

Shape Shoulders

At beg of next 2 rows BO:

3	5	6	6	7	7	5	5	5	5	6 sts.
4	7	8	8	9	10	7	7	7	7	7
5	6	7	7	8	8	9	9	9	9	9
6	7	8	8	9	10	10	10	11	10	11
7	8	10	10	11	12	12	12	12	12	13

At beg of foll 2 rows BO:

3	5	5	6	7	7	5	5	5	5	5 sts.
4	6	7	8	8	9	6	6	7	7	7
5	6	6	7	8	8	8	8	8	9	9
6	7	7	8	9	10	10	10	10	10	11
7	8	9	10	11	11	11	12	12	12	13

saddle shoulder

Finished Bust/Chest Circumference

	36	38	40	42	44	46	48	50	52	54"
	91.5	96.5	101.5	106.5	112	117	122	127	132	137 cm

At beg of foll 2 rows BO (if number is zero, omit these rows):

3	0	0	0	0	0	5	5	5	5	5 sts.
4	0	0	0	0	0	6	6	6	6	7
5	6	6	7	7	8	8	8	8	8	9
6	7	7	8	9	9	10	9	10	10	10
7	8	9	9	10	11	11	11	12	12	12

BO rem sts for back neck:

3	20	20	20	20	20	22	24	24	26	26 sts.
4	26	26	26	28	28	30	32	32	34	34
5	32	32	32	34	36	38	40	42	42	44
6	38	40	40	40	42	44	48	48	52	52
7	46	46	46	48	50	54	56	58	60	62

Pullover Front with Crewneck

(See page 122 for V-neck option.) Work as for back until armholes measure:

	6¾	7¼	7¾	8	8¼	8¼	8½	8¾	9	9¼"
	17	18.5	19.5	20.5	21	21	21.5	22	23	23.5 cm

There will be:

3	40	42	44	48	48	52	54	54	56	58 sts.
4	52	56	58	62	66	68	70	72	74	76
5	68	70	74	80	84	88	90	92	94	98
6	80	84	88	94	100	104	106	110	112	116
7	94	102	104	112	118	122	126	130	132	138

Shape Crewneck

With RS facing, work across:

3	15	16	17	19	18	20	21	21	21	22 sts,
4	19	21	22	24	25	26	27	28	28	29
5	26	27	29	32	32	34	35	36	36	38
6	30	32	34	37	38	40	41	43	43	45
7	35	39	40	44	45	47	49	51	51	54

join new yarn and BO for front neck:

3	10	10	10	10	12	12	12	12	14	14 sts,
4	14	14	14	14	16	16	16	16	18	18
5	16	16	16	16	20	20	20	20	22	22
6	20	20	20	20	24	24	24	24	26	26
7	24	24	24	24	28	28	28	28	30	30

Finished Bust/Chest Circumference

	36	38	40	42	44	46	48	50	52	54"
	91.5	96.5	101.5	106.5	112	117	122	127	132	137 cm

work to end. There will be the foll number of sts at each side:

3	15	16	17	19	18	20	21	21	21	22 sts.
4	19	21	22	24	25	26	27	28	28	29
5	26	27	29	32	32	34	35	36	36	38
6	30	32	34	37	38	40	41	43	43	45
7	35	39	40	44	45	47	49	51	51	54

Working each side separately, at each neck edge BO 3 sts (if number is zero, omit these rows):

3	0	0	0	0	0	0	0	0	0	0 time(s).
4	0	0	0	1	0	1	1	1	1	1
5	1	1	1	1	1	1	1	2	1	2
6	1	1	1	1	1	1	2	2	2	2
7	2	2	2	2	2	2	2	2	2	2

Then BO 2 sts:

3	1	1	1	1	1	1	2	2	2	2 time(s).
4	2	2	2	1	2	1	1	1	1	1
5	1	1	1	2	1	2	2	1	2	1
6	2	2	2	2	2	2	2	2	2	2
7	1	1	1	2	1	2	3	3	3	4

Then dec 1 st at neck edge every RS row:

3	3	3	3	3	2	3	2	2	2	2 times.
4	2	2	2	2	2	2	3	3	3	3
5	3	3	3	2	3	2	3	3	3	3
6	2	3	3	3	2	3	2	2	3	3
7	3	3	3	2	3	3	2	3	3	2

At the same time, when armholes measure same as back to shoulders,

Shape Shoulders

At each armhole edge, BO:

3	5	6	6	7	7	5	5	5	5	6 sts
4	7	8	8	9	10	7	7	7	7	7
5	6	7	7	8	8	9	9	9	9	9
6	7	8	8	9	10	10	10	11	10	11
7	8	10	10	11	12	12	12	12	12	13

Finished Bust/Chest Circumference									
36	38	40	42	44	46	48	50	52	54"
91.5	96.5	101.5	106.5	112	117	122	127	132	137 cm

once, then BO:

	36	38	40	42	44	46	48	50	52	54"
3	5	5	6	7	7	5	5	5	5	5 sts
4	6	7	8	8	9	6	6	7	7	7
5	6	6	7	8	8	8	8	8	9	9
6	7	7	8	9	10	10	10	10	10	11
7	8	9	10	11	11	11	12	12	12	13

once, then BO rem (if number is zero, omit this row):

	36	38	40	42	44	46	48	50	52	54"
3	0	0	0	0	0	5	5	5	5	5 sts.
4	0	0	0	0	0	6	6	6	6	7
5	6	6	7	7	8	8	8	8	8	9
6	7	7	8	9	9	10	9	10	10	10
7	8	9	9	10	11	11	11	12	12	12

Pullover Front with V-Neck

Work as for back until armholes measure:

36	38	40	42	44	46	48	50	52	54"
3½	3½	4	4	4¼	4¼	4½	4½	4½	4¾"
9	9	10	10	11	11	11.5	11.5	11.5	12 cm

With RS facing, work to center of row. Turn and work these sts only (place rem sts on a holder to work later). Cont to work armhole shaping as for back, if necessary, and *at the same time* dec 1 st at neck edge every RS row:

	36	38	40	42	44	46	48	50	52	54"
3	10	9	9	8	8	10	12	12	13	13 times.
4	13	13	13	14	14	15	16	16	17	17
5	16	16	16	17	18	19	20	21	21	22
6	19	20	20	20	21	22	24	24	26	26
7	23	23	23	24	25	27	28	29	30	31

Then dec 1 st at neck edge every 4 rows (if number is zero, omit these rows):

	36	38	40	42	44	46	48	50	52	54"
3	0	1	1	2	2	1	0	0	0	0 time(s).
4	0	0	0	0	0	0	0	0	0	0
5	0	0	0	0	0	0	0	0	0	0
6	0	0	0	0	0	0	0	0	0	0
7	0	0	0	0	0	0	0	0	0	0

There will remain:

	36	38	40	42	44	46	48	50	52	54"
3	10	11	12	14	14	15	15	15	15	16 sts.
4	13	15	16	17	19	19	19	20	20	21
5	18	19	21	23	24	25	25	25	26	27

Finished Bust/Chest Circumference

	36	38	40	42	44	46	48	50	52	54"
	91.5	96.5	101.5	106.5	112	117	122	127	132	137 cm

6	21	22	24	27	29	30	29	31	30	32
7	24	28	29	32	34	34	35	36	36	38

Work even until armhole measures same as back to shoulder. Shape shoulder as for crew-neck version. Rejoin yarn at neck edge of held sts and work as for first half, reversing neck and shoulder shaping.

Sleeves
CO:

3	28	28	30	30	30	32	32	32	34	34 sts.
4	38	38	40	40	40	44	44	44	46	46
5	46	46	50	50	50	54	54	56	58	58
6	56	56	60	60	60	66	66	66	68	68
7	66	66	70	70	70	76	76	76	80	80

Work edging of choice for desired length or until piece measures about:

	2½	2½	2½	2½	2½	2½	2½	2½	2½	2½"
	6.5	6.5	6.5	6.5	6.5	6.5	6.5	6.5	6.5	6.5 cm

Change to St st and inc 1 st each end of needle every 2 rows (if number is zero, omit these rows):

3	0	0	0	0	0	0	0	0	0	0 time(s).
4	0	0	0	0	0	0	0	0	0	0
5	0	0	0	0	0	0	0	0	0	0
6	0	0	0	0	0	0	0	0	1	1
7	0	0	0	0	0	0	0	2	2	7

Then inc 1 st each end of needle every 4 rows (if number is zero, omit these rows):

3	0	2	1	3	5	5	5	8	8	11 time(s).
4	0	4	7	9	10	7	10	13	13	16
5	6	10	12	14	16	15	18	18	18	24
6	9	16	18	20	24	17	23	26	27	28
7	10	19	21	25	30	25	28	30	30	27

Then inc 1 st each end of needle every 6 rows (if number is zero, omit these rows):

3	9	9	10	9	8	8	8	6	6	4 time(s).
4	12	10	8	7	7	9	7	5	5	3
5	10	8	7	6	5	6	4	4	4	0
6	10	6	5	4	2	7	3	1	0	0
7	11	6	5	3	0	4	2	0	0	0

saddle shoulder

Finished Bust/Chest Circumference

	36	38	40	42	44	46	48	50	52	54"
	91.5	96.5	101.5	106.5	112	117	122	127	132	137 cm

There will be:

3	46	50	52	54	56	58	58	60	62	64 sts.
4	62	66	70	72	74	76	78	80	82	84
5	78	82	88	90	92	96	98	100	102	106
6	94	100	106	108	112	114	118	120	124	126
7	108	116	122	126	130	134	136	140	144	148

Work even if necessary until piece measures desired length to armhole, or about:

16	16½	16¾	17	17½	17¾	18¼	18¾	18¾	18½"
40.5	42	42.5	43	44.5	45	46.5	47.5	47.5	47 cm

Shape Cap
At beg of next 2 rows BO:

3	3	3	3	3	3	3	3	4	4	5 sts.
4	4	4	4	4	4	4	5	5	5	6
5	5	5	5	5	5	5	6	6	6	7
6	6	6	6	6	6	6	7	7	7	8
7	7	7	7	7	7	7	8	9	9	10

At beg of foll 2 rows BO:

3	2	2	2	2	2	2	2	2	2	2 sts.
4	3	3	3	3	3	3	3	3	3	3
5	3	3	3	3	3	3	3	3	3	3
6	4	4	4	4	4	4	4	4	4	4
7	4	4	4	4	4	4	4	4	4	4

Dec 1 st each end of needle every RS row:

3	2	3	3	3	4	4	4	4	5	5 times.
4	3	3	4	4	4	5	5	6	7	7
5	3	4	5	5	5	6	6	8	9	9
6	4	5	6	6	6	7	8	9	11	11
7	5	5	7	7	7	9	9	10	12	12

There will remain:

3	32	34	36	38	38	40	40	40	40	40 sts.
4	42	46	48	50	52	52	52	52	52	52
5	56	58	62	64	66	68	68	66	66	68
6	66	70	74	76	80	80	80	80	80	80
7	76	84	86	90	94	94	94	94	94	96

Finished Bust/Chest Circumference

	36	38	40	42	44	46	48	50	52	54"
	91.5	96.5	101.5	106.5	112	117	122	127	132	137 cm

Dec 1 st each end of needle every 4 rows (if number is zero, omit these rows):

	36	38	40	42	44	46	48	50	52	54	
3	1	1	1	1	1	1	3	3	3	3	time(s).
4	0	0	0	1	0	2	3	4	1	2	
5	0	0	0	0	0	4	4	2	4	3	
6	0	0	0	1	0	4	4	3	3	4	
7	0	0	0	0	0	4	4	4	4	5	

Then dec 1 st each end of needle every 2 rows (if number is zero, omit these rows):

	36	38	40	42	44	46	48	50	52	54	
3	6	6	7	8	7	6	2	2	1	3	time(s).
4	10	11	10	8	11	5	4	0	7	6	
5	9	8	9	9	10	1	3	4	1	3	
6	10	8	9	8	9	1	2	3	2	1	
7	12	11	11	12	11	0	0	0	1	0	

Then BO 2 sts at beg of next (if number is zero, omit these rows):

	36	38	40	42	44	46	48	50	52	54	
3	0	0	0	0	0	2	2	2	4	2	rows.
4	0	0	2	4	2	2	2	4	4	4	
5	4	6	6	6	6	8	6	8	6	6	
6	6	10	10	10	12	12	10	10	12	10	
7	6	10	10	10	12	16	18	18	16	14	

At beg of foll 2 rows, BO:

	36	38	40	42	44	46	48	50	52	54	
3	5	6	6	6	7	6	7	7	7	7	sts.
4	6	7	7	7	8	8	9	9	8	8	
5	4	4	5	5	5	7	7	6	7	8	
6	5	5	5	6	6	7	7	7	7	8	
7	6	6	7	7	8	8	7	7	8	9	

At beg of foll 2 rows, BO (if number is zero, omit these rows):

	36	38	40	42	44	46	48	50	52	54	
3	0	0	0	0	0	0	1	1	0	0	st(s).
4	0	0	0	0	0	3	2	3	0	0	
5	5	5	5	6	6	7	7	6	8	7	
6	5	5	6	6	6	7	8	8	7	8	
7	6	7	7	8	8	9	8	8	8	10	

There will remain:

	36	38	40	42	44	46	48	50	52	54	
3	8	8	8	8	8	10	10	10	10	10	sts.
4	10	10	10	10	10	12	12	12	12	12	
5	12	12	12	12	12	14	14	14	14	14	
6	14	14	14	14	14	18	18	18	18	18	
7	16	16	16	16	16	20	20	20	20	20	

saddle shoulder

Finished Bust/Chest Circumference									
36	38	40	42	44	46	48	50	52	54"
91.5	96.5	101.5	106.5	112	117	122	127	132	137 cm

Shoulder Strap

Cont even until piece measures:

3½	3¾	4	4½	4¾	5	5	5	5	5¼"
9	9.5	10	11.5	12	12.5	12.5	12.5	12.5	13.5 cm

from last BO. BO all sts.

Finishing

Block pieces to measurements.

Join saddles: With yarn threaded on a tapestry needle, sew front edges of sleeve caps to front armholes. Sew front edges of saddle shoulder straps to BO edges of front shoulders, easing in any fullness. Sew back edges of sleeve caps to back armholes. Sew back edge of left shoulder strap to BO edge of back shoulder, easing in fullness.

Neckband: Choose a crewneck finish on pages 66–67 or a V-neck finish on pages 68–69. With smaller needles, RS facing, and beg at right shoulder opening, pick up and knit 1 st for each BO st and about 3 sts for every 4 rows along sloped edges around neck opening. Adjust st count if necessary to achieve a full multiple of the edging patt you've chosen, plus 2 extra "seam" sts. Work in chosen patt until neckband measures 1" (2.5 cm), or desired length. BO all sts in patt.

Seams: Sew rem shoulder and neckband seam. Sew sleeve and side seams. Weave in loose ends. Block again, if desired.

Cardigan Back

Work as for pullover version.

Cardigan Left Front with Crewneck

(See page 129 for V-neck option.) CO:

3	27	29	30	32	33	35	36	38	39	41 sts.
4	36	38	40	42	44	46	48	50	52	54
5	45	47	50	53	55	58	60	63	65	68
6	54	57	60	63	66	69	72	75	78	81
7	63	67	70	74	77	81	84	88	91	95

Work edging of choice (as for back), then cont even until piece measures same as back to armhole, ending with a WS row.

Shape Armhole

At beg of next RS row BO:

3	3	3	3	3	3	3	3	4	4	5 sts.
4	4	4	4	4	4	4	5	5	5	6

Finished Bust/Chest Circumference

	36	38	40	42	44	46	48	50	52	54"
	91.5	96.5	101.5	106.5	112	117	122	127	132	137 cm

5	5	5	5	5	5	5	6	6	6	7
6	6	6	6	6	6	6	7	7	7	8
7	7	7	7	7	7	7	8	9	9	10

At beg of foll RS row BO:

3	2	2	2	2	2	2	2	2	2	2 sts.
4	3	3	3	3	3	3	3	3	3	3
5	3	3	3	3	3	3	3	3	3	3
6	4	4	4	4	4	4	4	4	4	4
7	4	4	4	4	4	4	4	4	4	4

Dec 1 st at beg of needle every RS row:

3	2	3	3	3	4	4	4	5	5	5 times.
4	3	3	4	4	4	5	5	6	7	7
5	3	4	5	5	5	6	6	8	9	9
6	4	5	6	6	6	7	8	9	11	11
7	5	5	7	7	7	9	9	10	12	12

There will remain:

3	20	21	22	24	24	26	27	27	28	29 sts.
4	26	28	29	31	33	34	35	36	37	38
5	34	35	37	40	42	44	45	46	47	49
6	40	42	44	47	50	52	53	55	56	58
7	47	51	52	56	59	61	63	65	66	69

Cont even until armhole measures:

	6¾	7¼	7¾	8	8¼	8¼	8½	8¾	9	9¼"
	17	18.5	19.5	20.5	21	21	21.5	22	23	23.5 cm

Shape Crewneck
At beg of next WS row, BO:

3	5	5	5	5	6	6	6	6	7	7 sts,
4	7	7	7	7	8	8	8	8	9	9
5	8	8	8	8	10	10	10	10	11	11
6	10	10	10	10	12	12	12	12	13	13
7	12	12	12	12	14	14	14	14	15	15

saddle shoulder

Finished Bust/Chest Circumference

	36	38	40	42	44	46	48	50	52	54"
	91.5	96.5	101.5	106.5	112	117	122	127	132	137 cm

work to end. At neck edge (beg of WS rows) BO 3 sts (if number is zero, omit these rows):

3	0	0	0	0	0	0	0	0	0	0 time(s).
4	0	0	0	1	0	1	1	1	1	1
5	1	1	1	1	1	1	1	2	1	2
6	1	1	1	1	1	1	2	2	2	2
7	2	2	2	2	2	2	2	2	2	2

Then BO 2 sts:

3	1	1	1	1	1	1	2	2	2	2 time(s).
4	2	2	2	1	2	1	1	1	1	1
5	1	1	1	2	1	2	2	1	2	1
6	2	2	2	2	2	2	2	2	2	2
7	1	1	1	2	1	2	3	3	3	4

Then dec 1 st at neck edge every RS row:

3	3	3	3	3	2	3	2	2	2	2 times.
4	2	2	2	2	2	2	3	3	3	3
5	3	3	3	2	3	2	3	3	3	3
6	2	3	3	3	2	3	2	2	3	3
7	3	3	3	2	3	3	2	3	3	2

There will remain:

3	10	11	12	14	14	15	15	15	15	16 sts.
4	13	15	16	17	19	19	19	20	20	21
5	18	19	21	23	24	25	25	25	26	27
6	21	22	24	27	29	30	29	31	30	32
7	24	28	29	32	34	34	35	36	36	38

Cont even until piece measures same as back to shoulder, ending with a WS row.

Shape Shoulder
At armhole edge (beg of RS row), BO:

3	5	6	6	7	7	5	5	5	5	6 sts.
4	7	8	8	9	10	7	7	7	7	7
5	6	7	7	8	8	9	9	9	9	9
6	7	8	8	9	10	10	10	11	10	11
7	8	10	10	11	12	12	12	12	12	13

saddle shoulder

Finished Bust/Chest Circumference

36	38	40	42	44	46	48	50	52	54"
91.5	96.5	101.5	106.5	112	117	122	127	132	137 cm

At beg of foll RS row, BO:

3	5	5	6	7	7	5	5	5	5	5 sts.
4	6	7	8	8	9	6	6	7	7	7
5	6	6	7	8	8	8	8	8	9	9
6	7	7	8	9	10	10	10	10	10	11
7	8	9	10	11	11	11	12	12	12	13

At beg of foll RS row, BO (if number is zero, omit this row):

3	0	0	0	0	0	5	5	5	5	5 sts.
4	0	0	0	0	0	6	6	6	6	7
5	6	6	7	7	8	8	8	8	8	9
6	7	7	8	9	9	10	9	10	10	10
7	8	9	9	10	11	11	11	12	12	12

Cardigan Right Front with Crewneck

Work as for left front with crewneck, but reverse shaping (i.e., BO for armhole and shoulder at beg of WS rows; shape neck at beg of RS rows).

Cardigan Left Front with V-Neck

Work as for crewneck option until armhole measures:

3½	3½	4	4	4¼	4¼	4½	4½	4½	4¾"
9	9	10	10	11	11	11.5	11.5	11.5	12 cm

Cont to work armhole shaping as for back, if necessary, and *at the same time* dec 1 st at neck edge (end of row) every RS row:

3	10	9	9	8	8	19	12	12	13	13 times.
4	13	13	13	14	14	15	16	16	17	17
5	16	16	16	17	18	19	20	21	21	22
6	19	20	20	20	21	22	24	24	26	26
7	23	23	23	24	25	27	28	29	30	31

Then dec 1 st at neck edge every 4 rows (if number is zero, omit these rows):

3	0	1	1	2	2	1	0	0	0	0 time(s).
4	0	0	0	0	0	0	0	0	0	0
5	0	0	0	0	0	0	0	0	0	0
6	0	0	0	0	0	0	0	0	0	0
7	0	0	0	0	0	0	0	0	0	0

Finished Bust/Chest Circumference

	36	38	40	42	44	46	48	50	52	54"
	91.5	96.5	101.5	106.5	112	117	122	127	132	137 cm

There will remain:

3	10	11	12	14	14	15	15	15	15	16 sts.
4	13	15	16	17	19	19	19	20	20	21
5	18	19	21	23	24	25	25	25	26	27
6	21	22	24	27	29	30	29	31	30	32
7	24	28	29	32	34	34	35	36	36	38

Work even until armhole measures same as back to shoulder. Shape shoulder as for crew-neck version.

Cardigan Right Front with V-Neck

Work as for left front with V-neck but reverse shaping (i.e., BO for armhole and shoulder at beg of WS rows; shape neck at beg of RS rows).

Finishing

Block pieces to measurements.

Join saddles: With yarn threaded on a tapestry needle, sew front edges of sleeve caps to front armholes. Sew front edge of each saddle shoulder strap to BO edge of front shoulder, easing in any fullness. Sew back edges of sleeve caps to back armholes. Sew back edge of each shoulder strap to BO edge of back shoulder, easing in fullness.

Neckband: Choose a crewneck finish on pages 66–67 or a V-neck finish on pages 68–69. With smaller needles, RS facing, and beg at center front, pick up and knit 1 st for every BO st and about 3 sts for every 4 rows along sloped edges around neck opening for a crewneck. (Combine neckband with button and buttonhole bands for a V-neck version.) Adjust st count if necessary to achieve a full multiple of the edging patt you've chosen. Work in chosen patt until neckband measures 1" (2.5 cm), or desired length. BO all sts in patt.

Button band: (on left front for females; right front for males) With smaller needles and RS facing, pick up and knit about 3 sts for every 4 rows along center front edge. Adjust sts if necessary to achieve a full multiple of the edging pattern you've chosen. Work in chosen pattern until band measures 1" (2.5 cm). BO all sts in patt. Mark placement of desired number of buttons, one ½" (1.3 cm) up from CO edge, one at beg of neck shaping, and the others evenly spaced in between.

Buttonhole band: (on right front for females; left front for males) Work as for button band, working one-row buttonholes (see Glossary) opposite markers when band measures between ¼" and ½" (.6 and 1.3 cm). BO all sts in patt.

Seams: Sew sleeve and side seams.

Weave in loose ends. Sew buttons to button band opposite buttonholes. Block again, if desired.

saddle shoulder

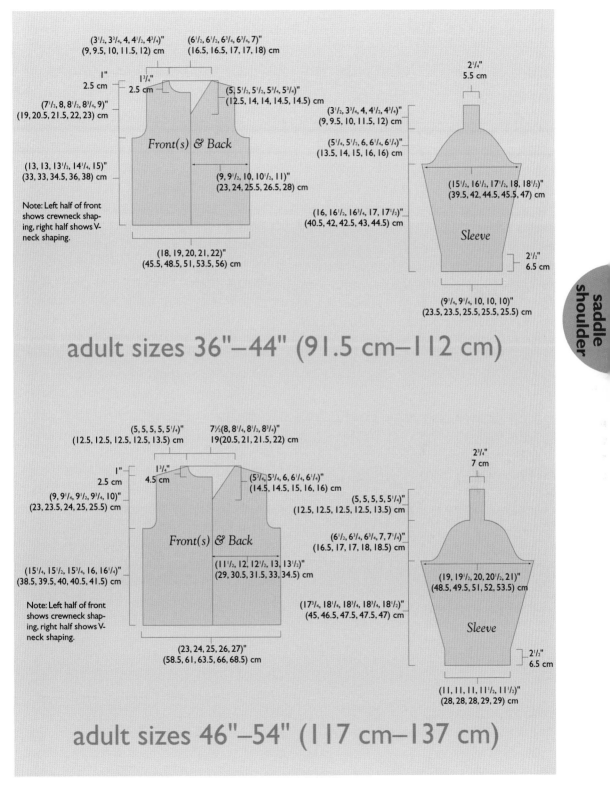

(3½, 3¾, 4, 4½, 4¾)"
(9, 9.5, 10, 11.5, 12) cm

(6½, 6½, 6¾, 6¾, 7)"
(16.5, 16.5, 17, 17, 18) cm

2¼"
5.5 cm

1"
2.5 cm

1¾"
2.5 cm

(5, 5½, 5½, 5¾, 5¾)"
(12.5, 14, 14, 14.5, 14.5) cm

(7½, 8, 8½, 8¾, 9)"
(19, 20.5, 21.5, 22, 23) cm

(3½, 3¾, 4, 4½, 4¾)"
(9, 9.5, 10, 11.5, 12) cm

Front(s) & Back

(5¼, 5½, 6, 6¼, 6¼)"
(13.5, 14, 15, 16, 16) cm

(13, 13, 13½, 14¼, 15)"
(33, 33, 34.5, 36, 38) cm

(9, 9½, 10, 10½, 11)"
(23, 24, 25.5, 26.5, 28) cm

(15½, 16½, 17½, 18, 18½)"
(39.5, 42, 44.5, 45.5, 47) cm

Note: Left half of front shows crewneck shaping, right half shows V-neck shaping.

(16, 16½, 16¾, 17, 17½)"
(40.5, 42, 42.5, 43, 44.5) cm

Sleeve

2½"
6.5 cm

(18, 19, 20, 21, 22)"
(45.5, 48.5, 51, 53.5, 56) cm

(9¼, 9¼, 10, 10, 10)"
(23.5, 23.5, 25.5, 25.5, 25.5) cm

saddle shoulder

adult sizes 36"–44" (91.5 cm–112 cm)

(5, 5, 5, 5, 5¼)"
(12.5, 12.5, 12.5, 12.5, 13.5) cm

7½(8, 8¼, 8½, 8¾)"
19(20.5, 21, 21.5, 22) cm

2¾"
7 cm

1"
2.5 cm

1¾"
4.5 cm

(5¾, 5¾, 6, 6¼, 6¼)"
(14.5, 14.5, 15, 16, 16) cm

(9, 9¼, 9½, 9¾, 10)"
(23, 23.5, 24, 25, 25.5) cm

(5, 5, 5, 5, 5¼)"
(12.5, 12.5, 12.5, 12.5, 13.5) cm

Front(s) & Back

(6½, 6¾, 6¾, 7, 7½)"
(16.5, 17, 17, 18, 18.5) cm

(11½, 12, 12½, 13, 13½)"
(29, 30.5, 31.5, 33, 34.5) cm

(19, 19½, 20, 20½, 21)"
(48.5, 49.5, 51, 52, 53.5) cm

(15¼, 15½, 15¾, 16, 16¼)"
(38.5, 39.5, 40, 40.5, 41.5) cm

Note: Left half of front shows crewneck shaping, right half shows V-neck shaping.

(17¾, 18¼, 18¾, 18¾, 18½)"
(45, 46.5, 47.5, 47.5, 47) cm

Sleeve

2½"
6.5 cm

(23, 24, 25, 26, 27)"
(58.5, 61, 63.5, 66, 68.5) cm

(11, 11, 11, 11½, 11½)"
(28, 28, 28, 29, 29) cm

adult sizes 46"–54" (117 cm–137 cm)

Cartridge Rib Pullover

A simple texture pattern adds interest to this V-neck variation of the basic saddle shoulder pullover. Prominent vertical ribs in the overall pattern extend across, and accentuate, the shoulder straps. The diagonal lines of the overlapping V-neck provide contrast. Each piece is worked on one less stitch than specified in the chart to accommodate the odd number of stitches in the cartridge rib pattern. On the front, the odd, center stitch is placed on a holder at the base of the V-neck shaping.

Finished Size: 34" (86.5 cm) chest circumference.
Yarn: Louet Gems Topaz (100% merino; 168 yd [153 m]/100 g): lavender, 6 skeins.
Needles: Body and sleeves—Size 10 (6 mm). Edging—Size 8 (5 mm). Adjust needle size if necessary to obtain the correct gauge.
Notions: Stitch holders; tapestry needle.
Gauge: 5 sts and 8 rows = 1" (2.5 cm) in cartridge rib on size 10 (6-mm) needles; 5 sts and 7 rows = 1" (2.5 cm) in stockinette stitch on size 7 (4.5-mm) needles.

Cartridge Rib

(multiple of 4 sts + 1)
Row 1: (RS) *K3, sl 1 with yarn in front (wyif); rep from *, end k1.

Row 2: K3, *sl 1 wyif, k3; rep from * to last 2 sts, sl 1 wyif, k1.
Repeat Rows 1 and 2 for pattern.

Back

With smaller needles, CO 86 sts. Work k1, p1 rib until piece measures 2" (5 cm), ending with a WS row. Work Row 1 of cartridge rib to last st, dec 1 st (to allow for patt repeat)—85 sts. Cont even in patt until piece measures 13¼" (33.5 cm) from beg, ending with a WS row. **Shape armholes**: BO 4 sts at beg of next 2 rows, then BO 3 sts at beg of foll 2 rows, then dec 1 st each end of needle every RS row 2 times—67 sts rem. Cont even in patt until armholes measure 7¼" (18.5 cm), ending with a WS row. **Shape shoulders**: BO 9 sts at beg of next 4 rows—31 sts rem. BO all sts in patt.

Front

Work as back until armholes measure 2¾" (7 cm), ending with a WS row—67 sts. **Shape V-neck**: Keeping in patt, work 33 sts, place center st on holder, join new yarn and work to end—33 sts each side. Working each side separately, at each neck edge dec 1 st every RS row 12 times, then every 4 rows 3 times—18 sts rem each side. Cont even in patt until piece measures same as back to shoulders. **Shape shoulders**: At each armhole edge, BO 9 sts 4 times.

Sleeves

With smaller needles, CO 40 sts. Work k1, p1 rib until piece measures 2" (5 cm), ending with a WS row. Work Row 1 of cartridge rib to last st, inc 1 st (to allow for patt repeat)—41 sts.

Cont in patt as established, and *at the same time* inc 1 st each end of needle every 4 rows 8 times, then every 6 rows 8 times, working new sts into patt—73 sts. Cont even in patt until piece measures 15" (38 cm) from beg, ending with a WS row. **Shape cap**: BO 4 sts at beg of next 2 rows, then BO 3 sts at beg of foll 2 rows, then dec 1 st each end of needle every RS row 2 times—55 sts rem. Dec 1 st each end of needle every RS row 9 more times—37 sts rem. BO 2 sts at beg of next 4 rows, then BO 4 sts at beg of foll 2 rows, then BO 5 sts at beg of next 2 rows—11 sts rem. **Shoulder strap**: On next row (WS) inc 1 st at each end of needle for seam sts—13 sts. Cont even in patt until piece measures 3½" (9 cm) from last BO row. Place sts on holder.

Finishing

Block pieces to measurements. With yarn threaded on a tapestry needle, sew sleeve seams. Sew front edges of sleeve caps to front armholes. Sew front edges of shoulder straps to BO edges of front shoulders, easing in any fullness and securing live seam sts at each side. Sew back edges of sleeve caps to back armholes. Sew back edges of shoulder straps to BO edges of back shoulder, working selvedge sts into seams and easing in fullness. Sew side seams. Weave in loose ends. **Neckband**: With smaller cir needle, RS facing, and beg at right side of V at front, pick up and knit about 3 sts for every 4 rows to shoulder strap (about 36 sts), work 11 shoulder strap sts in patt, pick up and knit 1 st for every BO st of back neck (31 sts), work 11 shoulder strap sts in patt, pick up and knit about 3 sts for every row to center front neck (about 36 sts), k1 held st at

base of V—125 sts total. Do not join. Work k1, p1 rib for 1" (2.5 cm), ending with a WS row. BO all sts in patt. Tack edges of neckband down to front V-neck edges. Weave in loose ends. Block again if desired.

Zip-Front Jacket

The basic saddle shoulder cardigan is worked in double seed stitch and edged with contrasting I-cord in this zippered jacket. Waist shaping, worked at the side seams, gives the body a tailored look. Stitches for the

Finished Size: 38" (96.5 cm) bust/chest circumference, zipped.
Yarn: Louet Gems Opal (100% merino; 225 yd [205 m]/100 g): tobacco (MC), 6 skeins; mustard (CC), 1 skein. Contrasting waste yarn.
Needles: Body and sleeves—Size 6 (4 mm): 24" (60-cm) circular (cir) and set of 2 double-pointed (dpn). Neckband—Size 3 (3.25 mm): 24" (60-cm) cir and set of 2 dpn. Adjust needle size if necessary to obtain the correct gauge.
Notions: Tapestry needle; 20" (51-cm) separating zipper; straight pins; contrasting sewing thread; matching sewing thread; sewing needle.
Gauge: 6 sts and 9 rows = 1" (2.5 cm) in double seed stitch on size 6 (4-mm) needles; 6 sts and 8 rows = 1" (2.5 cm) in stockinette stitch on size 5 (3.75-mm) needles.

body and sleeves are provisionally cast on to provide live stitches for the I-cord edging, which is worked as it is attached to the cast-on edge after the knitting is complete. The body and sleeves are worked 1" (2.5 cm) shorter than specified in the chart to allow for the I-cord edging. The zipper, sewn in by hand, is hidden behind the I-cord along the fronts, resulting in a sleek appearance.

Double Seed Stitch:

(multiple of 4 sts)
Rows 1 and 2: *K2, p2; rep from *.
Rows 3 and 4: *P2, k2; rep from *.
Repeat Rows 1–4 for pattern.

Back

With MC, larger cir needle, and using a provisional method (see Glossary), CO 114 sts. Do not join. *Set-up row:* (WS) Knit the first st and last st of every row for selvedge sts, work center 112 sts in double seed st. Work 6 rows as established. ***Shape waist:*** (RS) Dec 1 st inside selvedge st each end of needle—112 sts rem. Work 7 rows even. Rep the last 8 rows 5 more times—102 sts rem. Work even for 1½" (3.8 cm). *Next row:* Inc 1 st inside selvedge st each of needle—104 sts. Work 7 rows even. Rep the last 8 rows 5 more times, working new sts in patt—114 sts. Cont even until piece measures 12" (30.5 cm) from beg (1" [2.5 cm] less than specified on chart to allow for edging that will be added later), ending with a WS row. ***Shape armholes:*** BO 6 sts at beg of next 2 rows, then BO 4 sts at beg of foll 2 rows, then dec 1 st each end of needle inside selvedge sts every RS row 5 times—84 sts rem. Cont even until armholes

measure 8" (20.5 cm), ending with a WS row. ***Shape shoulders:*** BO 8 sts at beg of next 2 rows, then BO 7 sts at beg of foll 4 rows—40 sts rem. BO all sts in patt.

Left Front

With MC, larger cir needle, and using a provisional method, CO 58 sts (57 sts + 1 st to allow for patt rep). Do not join. *Set-up row:* (WS) Knit the first and last st for selvedge sts as for back, and work center 56 sts in double seed st. Work 6 rows as established. ***Shape waist:*** (RS) Dec 1 st inside selvedge st at beg of row, work to end—57 sts rem. Work 7 rows even. Rep the last 8 rows 5 more times—52 sts rem. Work even for 1½" (3.8 cm). *Next row:* Inc 1 st inside selvedge st at beg of row, work to end—53 sts. Work 7 rows even. Rep the last 8 rows 5 more times—58 sts. Cont even until piece measures 12" (30.5 cm) from beg, ending with a WS row. ***Shape armhole:*** (RS) BO 6 sts at beg of row, work to end. At armhole edge (beg of RS rows), BO 4 sts once, then dec 1 st at beg of row every RS row 5 times—43 sts rem. Cont even until armhole measures 7¼" (18.5 cm), ending with a RS row. ***Shape crewneck:*** (WS) BO 10 sts, work to end—33 sts rem. At neck edge (beg of WS rows), BO 3 sts once, then BO 2 sts 2 times, then BO 1 st 4 times—22 sts rem (21 sts + 1 st to balance patt). *At the same time,* when armhole measures 8" (20.5 cm), ending with a WS row. ***Shape shoulder:*** At armhole edge (beg of RS rows), BO 8 sts once, then BO 7 sts 2 times.

Right Front

Work as left front but reverse shaping by working waist shaping at end of RS rows, neck shaping at beg of RS rows, and shoulder shaping at beg of WS rows.

Sleeves

With MC, larger cir needle, and using a provisional method, CO 56 sts. Do not join. Work in double seed st until piece measures 1" (2.5 cm) from beg, ending with a WS row. (Note: sleeve shaping is adjusted from chart to give more tapered angle to sleeve.) Inc 1 st inside selvedge st each end of needle every 4 rows 8 times, then every 6 rows 14 times, working new sts into patt—100 sts. Cont even until piece measures 16½" (42 cm) from beg, ending with a WS row. **Shape cap**: BO 6 sts at beg of next 2 rows, then BO 4 sts at beg of foll 2 rows, then dec 1 st each end of needle every RS row 13 times—54 sts rem. BO 2 sts at beg of next 10 rows, then BO 5 sts at beg of next 4 rows—14 sts rem. **Shoulder strap**: On next row (WS), inc 1 st at each end of needle for edge st—16 sts. Cont in patt (working edge sts in garter st) until piece measures 3¾" (9.5 cm) from last BO row. BO all sts in patt.

Finishing

Block pieces to measurements. **Cuffs**: Carefully remove waste yarn from provisional CO on sleeve and place 56 live sts onto larger cir needle. With larger dpn and CC, CO 4 sts. Work 4-st I-cord (see Glossary), working last st tog with first picked-up st to join cord to sleeve. *At the same time* work 2 picked-up sts tog (k2tog) about every 6 rows to draw in cuff. When all picked-up sts have been worked, BO rem 4 I-cord sts. With yarn threaded on a tapestry needle, sew BO edge

to CO edge. Sew sleeve seam. With yarn threaded on a tapestry needle, sew front edges of sleeve caps to front armholes. Sew front edges of shoulder straps to BO edges of front shoulders, easing in fullness and securing live seam sts at each side. Sew back edges of sleeve caps to back armholes. Sew back edges of shoulder straps to BO edges of back shoulders, easing in fullness and securing live seam sts at each side. Sew side seams. Weave in loose ends. **Lower body band**: Carefully remove waste yarn from provisional CO and place 230 live sts onto larger cir needle. With larger dpn and CC, CO 4 sts. Work 4-st I-cord, working last st tog with first picked-up st to join cord to lower body edge. When all picked-up sts have been worked, BO rem 4 I-cord sts. **Neckband**: With smaller cir needle, CC, and beg at center front, pick up and knit 28 sts along right front neck, 14 sts across shoulder strap, 38 sts across back neck, 14 sts across other shoulder strap, and 28 sts along left front neck—122 sts total. Break yarn. With smaller dpn and CC, CO 4 sts. With RS of neckband facing, work 4-st I-cord, working last st of cord tog with first st of picked-up sts as for lower body band. When all picked-up sts have been worked, BO rem 4 I-cord sts. **Front bands**: With smaller cir needle, CC, and RS facing, pick up and knit 170 sts along front edge (2 sts in each I-cord and about 1 st for every row). Break yarn. With smaller dpn and CC, CO 4 sts. With RS facing, work 4-st I-cord, working last st of cord tog with first st of picked-up st, and *at the same time* work 2 picked-up sts, tog every 4 or 5 rows to prevent band from flaring. When all picked-up sts have been worked, BO rem 4 I-cord sts. Rep for other band. **Zipper**: With RS facing and zipper closed, pin zipper to fronts so that I-cord meets at center. With contrasting sewing thread, baste zipper in place. Turn piece to WS. With matching sewing thread and needle, stitch outer edges of zipper to fronts, being careful to follow a single row of sts in the knitting to keep zipper straight. Turn to RS and stitch MC edge of each front to zipper, close to teeth. Remove basting. Weave in loose ends. Block again if desired.

Diamond Cable Pullover

A combination of stitch patterns give this loose-fitting saddle-shoulder pullover a comfortable, casual look. A narrow version of the center body cable panel is worked on the sleeves and continues across the shoulder strap. The gauge for this sweater is determined by the moss stitch pattern; extra stitches are added on the first row to account for the natural tendency of the cables to draw in the width. The ribbed neckband is finished off with a simple rolled edge.

Moss Stitch
(multiple of 2 sts)
Rows 1 and 2: *K1, p1; rep from *.
Rows 3 and 4: *P1, k1; rep from *.
Repeat Rows 1–4 for pattern.

Finished Size: 46" (117 cm) bust/chest circumference.
Yarn: Louet Gems Sapphire (100% merino; 103 yd [94 m]/100 g): terra cotta, 10 skeins.
Needles: Body and sleeves—size 10½ (6.5 mm). Neckband—size 10 (6 mm): 16" (40-cm) circular (cir). Adjust needle size if necessary to obtain the correct gauge.
Notions: Markers (m); cable needle (cn); tapestry needle.
Gauge: 4 sts and 6 rows = 1" (2.5 cm) in moss stitch on size 10½ (6.5-mm) needles. 4 sts and 6 rows = 1" (2.5 cm) in stockinette stitch on size 9 (5.5-mm) needles.

Back
With larger needles, CO 92 sts. *Set-up row:* (WS) Work 22 sts in moss st, place marker (pm), work set-up row of Diamond Cable chart over 48 sts (working incs as specified in set-up row), pm, work 22 sts in moss st—102 sts (92 sts + 10 sts inc'd for cables). Rep Rows 1–24 of chart until piece measures 15¼" (38.5 cm) from beg, ending with a WS row. **Shape armholes**: BO 4 sts at beg of next 2 rows, then BO 3 sts at beg of foll 2 rows, then dec 1 st each end of needle every RS row 5 times—78 sts rem (68 sts + 10 extra sts for cables). Cont even until armholes measure 9" (23 cm), ending with a WS row. **Shape shoulders**: BO 7 sts at beg of next 2 rows, then BO 6 sts at beg of foll 4 rows, working

Sleeve

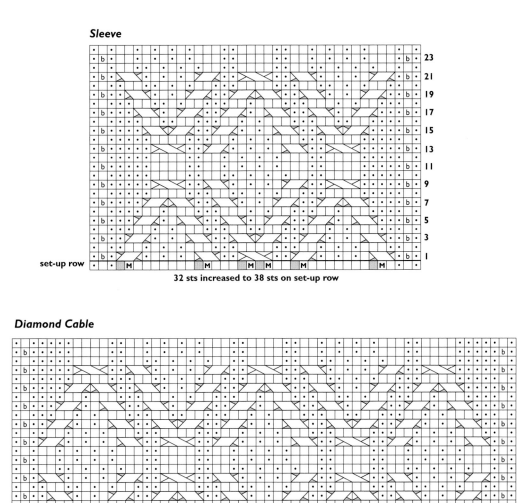

32 sts increased to 38 sts on set-up row

Diamond Cable

48 sts increased to 58 sts on set-up row

knit on RS; purl on WS	no stitch
• purl on RS; knit on WS	⊐⊐ 2/1RPC: sl 1 st onto cn and hold in back, k2, p1 from cn
b k1tbl	⊏⊏ 2/1RPC: sl 2 sts onto cn and hold in front, p1, k2 from cn
M Make 1 (see Glossary), then purl next st	⋈ 2/2LC: sl 2 st onto cn and hold in front, k2, k2 from cn

cables as k2tog (on RS rows) or p2tog (on WS rows) as they are bound off to prevent flaring (10 sts dec'd for cables)—30 sts rem. BO all sts.

Front

Work as back until armholes measure 8¼" (21 cm), ending with a WS row—78 sts. **Shape crewneck:** Work in patt to center 20 sts (16 sts + 4 sts inc'd for cables), join new yarn and BO these center sts, working k2 sts of cables as k2tog, work in patt to end—29 sts rem each side. Working each side separately, at each neck edge, BO 3 sts once, then BO 2 sts once, then dec 1 st every RS row 2 times, and *at the same time* when piece measures same as back to shoulders, **Shape shoulders:** At armhole edge, BO 7 sts once, then BO 6 sts 2 times, working k2 sts of rem cables as k2tog (3 sts dec'd for cables at each side).

Sleeves

With larger needles, CO 44 sts. *Set-up row:* (WS) Work 6 sts in moss st, pm, work set-up row of Sleeve chart over 32 sts (inc 6 sts as specified), pm, work 6 sts moss st—50 sts. Cont as established until piece measures 2½" (6.5 cm) from beg, ending with a WS row. Inc 1 st each end of needle every 4 rows 7 times, then every 6 rows 9 times, working new sts into moss st patt—82 sts. Cont even until piece measures 17¾" (45 cm) from beg, ending with a WS row. **Shape cap:** BO 4 sts at beg of next 2 rows, then BO 3 sts at beg of foll 2 rows, then dec 1 st each end of needle every RS row 5 times—58 sts rem (52 sts + 6 extra sts for cables). Dec 1 st each end of

needle every 4 rows 2 times, then every 2 rows 5 times—44 sts rem. BO 2 sts at beg of next 2 rows, then BO 8 sts at beg of foll 2 rows, working cables as k2tog (on RS rows) or p2tog (on WS rows) as they are bound off to prevent flaring (2 sts dec'd for cables)—22 sts rem. BO 3 sts at beg of next 2 rows, also dec cables as before (2 sts dec'd for cables) as they are bound off—14 sts rem. **Shoulder strap:** On next row (WS), inc 1 st each end of needle for seam sts—16 sts. Cont even as established until piece measures 5" (12.5 cm) from last BO row. Place sts on holder.

Finishing

Block pieces to measurements. With yarn threaded on a tapestry needle, sew sleeve seams. Sew front edges of sleeve caps to front armholes. Sew front edges of shoulder straps to BO edges of front shoulders, easing in fullness and securing live seam sts at each side. Sew back edges of sleeve caps to back armholes. Sew back edges of shoulder straps to BO edges of back shoulders, easing in fullness and securing live seam sts at each side. Sew side seams. Weave in loose ends. **Neckband:** With smaller cir needle, RS facing, and beg at right edge of back neck, pick up and knit 34 sts across back neck, k14 shoulder strap sts, pick up and knit 42 sts across front neck, k14 shoulder strap sts—104 sts total. Work in k2, p2 rib, matching cables from body as much as possible, until neckband measures 1" (2.5 cm). Change to St st and work 5 rnds even. BO all sts kwise. Weave in loose ends. Block again if desired.

raglan sweaters

Sweaters with raglan shaping are distinctive in that the "seams" between the front, back, and sleeves occur in diagonal lines that run from the armholes to the neck edge. Beginning at the armholes, the number of stitches on the front, back, and sleeves decrease at regular intervals so that from the armholes upward, each piece develops a triangular shape. For the raglan seams to lie flat (and the sweater to fit well), the sleeve caps must have the same number of rows as the armholes. It is this characteristic that makes raglan sweaters perfectly suited to circular knitting, and because all of the pieces have the same number of rows from the armhole to the neck, they can be worked at the same time. The raglan lines can be decorative or inconspicuous, depending on the type and sequence of decreases used. See Personal Touches on page 171 for possible variations.

Like sweaters featuring set-in sleeves and saddle shoulders, raglan sweaters fit well and can hang straight from the underarm or be shaped to hug the body (see waist shapings on pages 104–105). However, the diagonal raglan lines running from underarm to neck can interrupt added texture or color patterns. You can, of course, use these "seams" to your advantage and plan breaks in

Three sweater variations following the raglan chart. Top to bottom: Gatsby Cardigan at 40" (101.5 cm) circumference and 3 stitches/inch, Ribbed-Sleeve Pullover at 36" (91.5 cm) circumference and 4 stitches/inch, and Striped Crewneck Pullover at 34" (86.5 cm) circumference and 5 stitches/inch. Step-by-step instructions for these sweaters begin on page 166.

your pattern to coincide with them, as in the Ribbed-Sleeve Pullover on page 166.

basic anatomy

Although raglan sweaters can be worked back and forth in pieces just like the other sweaters in this book, the instructions that follow are for working them in the round from the bottom up (they can also be worked in the round from the top down, but there wasn't space to include this variation here). For the pullover version, the lower body is worked as a tube to the armholes, the sleeves are worked as separate tubes to the armholes, a few stitches are bound off each piece at the underarms, then the pieces are joined together and worked in a tapered tube to the neck. To raise the back neck (and make a better fitting garment) a few short rows (see Glossary) are worked across the back stitches only. The upper body is shaped with paired decreases worked along each of the four "seam" lines denoting the boundaries between the front, back, and sleeves. For the cardigan version, the body stitches are not joined into a round; instead they are worked back and forth in rows with the selvedges forming the center front opening. After the knitting is complete, the only seams to be sewn are the bound-off edges at the underarms.

To use the following chart to make a raglan sweater, you need to choose yarn, determine your gauge (see page 6), and pick a size based on the desired finished bust/chest circumference. You'll also need circular (cir) needles in 16" (40-cm) and 24" or 32" (60- or 80-cm) lengths and a set of 4 or 5 double-pointed (dpn) needles in size to obtain gauge (and needles one or two sizes smaller for edgings, if desired), stitch markers (m), a tapestry needle, and buttons for cardigan versions: 5 to 7 for child sizes, 7 to 9 for adult sizes. Gauge runs vertically along the left side of the chart; finished bust/chest circumference is listed horizontally across the top. The chart for children's sizes begins on page 143; schematics are on page 150. The chart for adult sizes begins on page 151; schematics are on page 165.

sizing child

Finished Chest Circumference

26	28	30	32	34"		26	28	30	32	34"
66	71	76	81.5	86.5 cm		66	71	76	81.5	86.5 cm

GAUGE

Yarn Requirements

3	250	310	380	450	510 yd
	229	283	347	411	466 m
4	350	440	530	630	730
	320	402	485	576	668
5	440	560	670	800	920
	402	512	613	732	841
6	620	790	950	1130	1290
	567	722	869	1033	1180
7	690	870	1050	1240	1420
	631	796	960	1134	1298

Pullover Body

With cir needle, CO:

3	80	84	92	96	104 sts.
4	104	112	120	128	136
5	128	140	148	160	172
6	156	168	180	192	204
7	180	196	212	224	240

Place marker (pm) and join, being careful not to twist sts. Work edging of choice (see pages 35–37), then cont even until piece measures desired length to armhole, or about:

8½	9½	11	12½	14"
21.5	24	28	31.5	35.5 cm

ending last rnd the foll number of sts before marker:

3	2	2	2	2	2 sts.
4	3	3	3	3	3
5	4	4	4	4	4
6	4	4	4	4	4
7	5	5	5	5	5

Divide for Front and Back

*BO:

3	4	4	4	4	4 sts,
4	6	6	6	6	6
5	8	8	8	8	8
6	8	8	8	8	8
7	10	10	10	10	10

work until there are the foll number of sts after BO:

3	36	38	42	44	48 sts.
4	46	50	54	58	62
5	56	62	66	72	78
6	70	76	82	88	94
7	80	88	96	102	110

Rep from * once. The foll number of sts will rem each for front and back:

3	36	38	42	44	48 sts.
4	46	50	54	58	62
5	56	62	66	72	78
6	70	76	82	88	94
7	80	88	96	102	110

Set aside.

Sleeves

With dpn, CO:

3	18	20	22	22	24 sts.
4	24	26	28	30	32
5	30	32	36	38	40
6	36	40	42	46	48
7	42	46	48	52	56

raglan

Finished Chest Circumference

26	28	30	32	34"		26	28	30	32	34"
66	71	76	81.5	86.5 cm		66	71	76	81.5	86.5 cm

Place m and join, being careful not to twist sts. Work edging of choice until piece measures desired length, or about:

1½	1½	1½	2	2"
3.8	3.8	3.8	5	5 cm

Change to St st and inc 1 st each side of marker every 4 rnds (if number is zero, omit these rnds):

3	0	0	0	0	0 time(s).
4	0	0	0	0	0
5	0	0	0	0	0
6	1	0	0	0	0
7	3	1	0	0	0

Then inc 1 st each side of marker every 6 rnds:

3	6	6	6	7	7 times.
4	7	8	8	8	9
5	9	10	9	10	11
6	10	11	12	12	13
7	10	12	15	15	16

There will be:

3	30	32	34	36	38 sts.
4	38	42	44	46	50
5	48	52	54	58	62
6	58	62	66	70	74
7	68	72	78	82	88

Work even if necessary until piece measures:

11½	12	13½	14¾	15½"
29	30.5	34.5	37.5	39.5 cm

from beg, or desired length to underarm, ending the foll number of sts before end-of-rnd marker:

3	2	2	2	2	2 sts.
4	3	3	3	3	3
5	4	4	4	4	4

6	4	4	4	4	4
7	5	5	5	5	5

BO:

3	4	4	4	4	4 sts,
4	6	6	6	6	6
5	8	8	8	8	8
6	8	8	8	8	8
7	10	10	10	10	10

work to end. There will remain:

3	26	28	30	32	34 sts.
4	32	36	38	40	44
5	40	44	46	50	54
6	50	54	58	62	66
7	58	62	68	72	78

Set aside. Make another sleeve to match.

Pullover Yoke with Crew Neck

(See page 146 for V-neck option.) With RS facing, join all pieces as foll:

Knit across:

3	26	28	30	32	34 sts
4	32	36	38	40	44
5	40	44	46	50	54
6	50	54	58	62	66
7	58	62	68	72	78

of left sleeve, pm, knit across:

3	36	38	42	44	48 sts
4	46	50	54	58	62
5	56	62	66	72	78
6	70	76	82	88	94
7	80	88	96	102	110

of front, pm, knit across:

3	26	28	30	32	34 sts
4	32	36	38	40	44

Finished Chest Circumference

	26	28	30	32	34"
	66	71	76	81.5	86.5 cm

5	40	44	46	50	54
6	50	54	58	62	66
7	58	62	68	72	78

of right sleeve, pm, knit across:

3	36	38	42	44	48 sts
4	46	50	54	58	62
5	56	62	66	72	78
6	70	76	82	88	94
7	80	88	96	102	110

of back, pm for end of rnd.
There will be:

3	124	132	144	152	164 sts.
4	156	172	184	196	212
5	192	212	224	244	264
6	240	260	280	300	320
7	276	300	328	348	376

Shape Raglan

Next rnd: Dec as foll: *K2tog, knit to 2 sts before next m, ssk, slip m; rep from * 3 more times—8 sts dec'd. Work 3 rnds even.

Dec 8 sts in this manner every 4 rnds (if number is zero, omit these rnds):

3	0	2	2	2	2 time(s)
4	0	1	1	2	1
5	0	1	2	1	1
6	0	0	0	0	0
7	0	0	0	0	0

more. Then rep dec rnd every 2 rnds:

3	11	10	11	12	13 times.
4	14	15	16	16	19
5	17	18	18	21	23
6	18	24	26	28	30
7	20	27	28	32	33

	26	28	30	32	34"
	66	71	76	81.5	86.5 cm

Then rep dec rnd every rnd , working decs on WS rows as *purl to 2 sts before m, p2tog, slip m, ssp; rep from * 3 more times, purl to end (if number is zero, omit these rnds):

3	0	0	0	0	0 times.
4	0	0	0	0	0
5	0	0	0	0	0
6	4	0	0	0	0
7	5	0	2	0	2

At the same time, when piece measures:

	3¼	4¼	4¾	5¼	5¾"
	8.5	11	12	13.5	14.5 cm

from joining rnd, **Shape crewneck**: Cont working raglan decs as established, BO at center front:

3	4	6	8	8	8 sts,
4	4	6	10	10	10
5	6	8	12	12	12
6	8	12	16	16	16
7	10	16	20	20	20

work to end. Working back and forth in rows and cont working raglan decs as established, at each neck edge BO 3 sts (if number is zero, omit these rows):

3	0	0	0	0	0 time(s).
4	1	0	0	0	0
5	1	1	1	1	1
6	1	1	1	1	1
7	1	1	1	1	1

Then BO 2 sts:

3	1	1	1	1	1 time(s).
4	1	2	1	2	2
5	1	1	1	1	1
6	2	1	1	1	1
7	2	2	1	2	2

Finished Chest Circumference

	26	28	30	32	34"
	66	71	76	81.5	86.5 cm

Then dec 1 st at each neck edge every RS row:

	26	28	30	32	34"
3	2	1	1	1	2 time(s).
4	1	1	2	1	1
5	2	2	1	2	3
6	1	2	1	2	3
7	2	1	2	1	2

After all neck and raglan decs have been completed, there will remain:

	26	28	30	32	34"
3	16	16	18	18	20 sts.
4	20	20	22	24	24
5	28	30	32	34	36
6	32	34	36	38	40
7	40	44	46	48	50

BO all sts.

Pullover Yoke with V-Neck

Work as for crewneck version until yoke measures:

	26	28	30	32	34"
	½	1	1	1½	2"
	1.3	2.5	2.5	3.8	5 cm

Work to center of front sts. Turn and work back and forth in rows, and *at the same time* cont to work raglan shaping as for crewneck version, and *also at the same time* dec 1 st at each neck edge every RS row (if number is zero, omit these rows):

	26	28	30	32	34"
3	1	0	0	0	2 time(s).
4	1	0	1	3	3
5	4	4	4	6	8
6	5	5	5	7	9
7	7	9	8	10	12

Then dec 1 st at neck edge every 4 rows:

	26	28	30	32	34"
3	5	6	7	7	6 times.
4	7	8	8	7	7
5	6	7	8	7	6

Finished Chest Circumference

	26	28	30	32	34"
	66	71	76	81.5	86.5 cm

	26	28	30	32	34"
6	7	8	9	8	7
7	7	7	9	8	7

After all neck and raglan decs have been completed, there will remain:

	26	28	30	32	34"
3	16	16	18	18	20 sts.
4	20	20	22	24	24
5	28	30	32	34	36
6	32	34	36	38	40
7	40	44	46	48	50

BO all sts.

Finishing

Block to measurements. With yarn threaded on a tapestry needle, sew underarm seams.

Neckband: Choose a crewneck finish on pages 66–67 or a V-neck finish on pages 68–69. With smaller dpn, RS facing, and beg at back right raglan line, pick up and knit 1 st for each BO st and about 3 sts for every 4 rows along sloped edges around neck opening. Adjust st count if necessary to achieve a full multiple of the edging patt you've chosen. Place m and join. Work in chosen pattern until neckband measures ¾" (2 cm), or desired length. BO all sts in patt. Weave in loose ends. Block again, if desired.

Cardigan Body

Work as for pullover body, but do not join into a rnd (i.e., work the body sts back and forth in rows, with opening at center front) until piece measures desired length to armhole, or about:

	26	28	30	32	34"
	8½	9½	11	12½	14"
	21.5	24	28	31.5	35.5 cm

ending with a RS row.

raglan

Finished Chest Circumference

26	28	30	32	34"
66	71	76	81.5	86.5 cm

26	28	30	32	34"
66	71	76	81.5	86.5 cm

Divide for Fronts and Back

With WS facing, purl across:

3	18	19	21	22	24 sts
4	23	25	27	29	31
5	28	31	33	36	39
6	35	38	41	44	47
7	40	44	48	51	55

for left front, BO:

3	4	4	4	4	4 sts
4	6	6	6	6	6
5	8	8	8	8	8
6	8	8	8	8	8
7	10	10	10	10	10

for left underarm, purl across:

3	36	38	42	44	48 sts
4	46	50	54	58	62
5	56	62	66	72	78
6	70	76	82	88	94
7	80	88	96	102	110

for back, BO:

3	4	4	4	4	4 sts
4	6	6	6	6	6
5	8	8	8	8	8
6	8	8	8	8	8
7	10	10	10	10	10

for right underarm, purl across:

3	18	19	21	22	24 sts
4	23	25	27	29	31
5	28	31	33	36	39
6	35	38	41	44	47
7	40	44	48	51	55

for right front. Set aside.

Sleeves

Work sleeves as for pullover version.

Cardigan Yoke with Crewneck

(See page 149 for V-neck option.) Join all pieces as foll:

With RS facing, knit across:

3	18	19	21	22	24 sts
4	23	25	27	29	31
5	28	31	33	36	39
6	35	38	41	44	47
7	40	44	48	51	55

of right front, pm, knit across:

3	26	28	30	32	34 sts
4	32	36	38	40	44
5	40	44	46	50	54
6	50	54	58	62	66
7	58	62	68	72	78

of right sleeve, pm, knit across:

3	36	38	42	44	48 sts
4	46	50	54	58	62
5	56	62	66	72	78
6	70	76	82	88	94
7	80	88	96	102	110

of back, pm, knit across:

3	26	28	30	32	34 sts
4	32	36	38	40	44
5	40	44	46	50	54
6	50	54	58	62	66
7	58	62	68	72	78

of left sleeve, pm, knit across:

3	18	19	21	22	24 sts
4	23	25	27	29	31
5	28	31	33	36	39
6	35	38	41	44	47
7	40	44	48	51	55

Finished Chest Circumference

26	28	30	32	34"		26	28	30	32	34"
66	71	76	81.5	86.5 cm		66	71	76	81.5	86.5 cm

of left front. There will be:

3	124	132	144	152	164 sts.
4	156	172	184	196	212
5	192	212	224	244	264
6	240	260	280	300	320
7	276	300	328	348	376

Work 1 WS row even.

Shape Raglan

Next row: Dec as foll: *Knit to 2 sts before m, ssk, slip m, k2tog; rep from * 3 more times, knit to end of row—8 sts dec'd. Work 3 rows even.

Dec 8 sts every 4 rows in this manner (if number is zero, omit these rows):

3	0	2	2	2	2 time(s).
4	0	1	1	2	1
5	0	1	2	1	1
6	0	0	0	0	0
7	0	0	0	0	0

Then rep dec row every 2 rows:

3	11	10	11	12	13 times.
4	14	15	16	16	19
5	17	18	18	21	23
6	18	24	26	28	30
7	20	27	28	32	33

Then rep dec row every row (see page 145 for working decs on WS rows; if number is zero, omit these rows):

3	0	0	0	0	0 times.
4	0	0	0	0	0
5	0	0	0	0	0
6	4	0	0	0	0
7	5	0	2	0	2

At the same time, when piece measures

3¼	4¼	4¾	5¼	5¾"
8.5	11	12	13.5	14.5 cm

from joining row,

Shape Crewneck

Cont working raglan decs as established, BO at beg of next 2 rows:

3	2	3	4	4	4 sts.
4	2	3	5	5	5
5	3	4	6	6	6
6	4	6	8	8	8
7	5	8	10	10	10

Cont working raglan decs as established, at each neck edge BO 3 sts (if number is zero, omit these rows):

3	0	0	0	0	0 time(s).
4	1	0	0	0	0
5	1	1	1	1	1
6	1	1	1	1	1
7	1	1	1	1	1

Then BO 2 sts:

3	1	1	1	1	1 time(s).
4	1	2	1	2	2
5	1	1	1	1	1
6	2	1	1	1	1
7	2	2	1	2	2

Then dec 1 st at each neck edge every RS row:

3	2	1	1	1	2 time(s).
4	1	1	2	1	1
5	2	2	1	2	3
6	1	2	1	2	3
7	2	1	2	1	2

raglan

Finished Chest Circumference

26	28	30	32	34"
66	71	76	81.5	86.5 cm

After all neck and raglan decs have been completed, there will remain:

3	16	16	18	18	20 sts.
4	20	20	22	24	24
5	28	30	32	34	36
6	32	34	36	38	40
7	40	44	46	48	50

BO all sts.

Cardigan Yoke with V-Neck

Work as for crewneck version until yoke measures:

½	1	1	1 ½	2"
1.3	2.5	2.5	3.8	5 cm

Shape V-Neck

Cont to work raglan shaping as for crewneck version, and *at the same time* dec 1 st at each neck edge every RS row (if number is zero, omit these rows):

3	1	0	0	0	2 time(s).
4	1	0	1	3	3
5	4	4	4	6	8
6	5	5	5	7	9
7	7	9	8	10	12

Then dec 1 st at neck edge every 4 rows:

3	5	6	7	7	6 times.
4	7	8	8	7	7
5	6	7	8	7	6
6	7	8	9	8	7
7	7	7	9	8	7

After all neck and raglan decs have been completed, there will remain:

3	16	16	18	18	20 sts.
4	20	20	22	24	24
5	28	30	32	34	36

Finished Chest Circumference

26	28	30	32	34"
66	71	76	81.5	86.5 cm

6	32	34	36	38	40
7	40	44	46	48	50

BO all sts.

Finishing

Block to measurements. With yarn threaded on a tapestry needle, sew underarm seams.

Neckband: Choose a crewneck finish on pages 66–67 or a V-neck finish on pages 68–69. With smaller needles, RS facing, and beg at center front, pick up and knit 1 st for every BO st and about 3 sts for every 4 rows along sloped edges around neck opening for a crewneck. (Combine neckband with button and buttonhole bands for a V-neck version.) Adjust st count if necessary to achieve a full multiple of the edging pattern you've chosen. Work edging pattern of choice for ¾" (2 cm) or desired length. BO all sts.

Button band: (on left front for females; right front for males) With smaller needles and RS facing, pick up and knit about 3 sts for every 4 rows along center front edge. Adjust st count if necessary to achieve a full multiple of the edging pattern you've chosen. Work in chosen pattern until band measures ¾" (2 cm). BO all sts in patt. Mark placement of desired number of buttons, one ½" (1.3 cm) up from CO edge, one at beg of neck shaping, and the others evenly spaced in between.

Buttonhole band: (on right front for females; left front for males) Work as for button band, working one-row buttonholes (see Glossary) opposite markers when band measures between ¼" and ½" (.6 and 1.3 cm). BO all sts in patt.

Weave in loose ends. Sew buttons to button band opposite buttonholes. Block again, if desired.

raglan

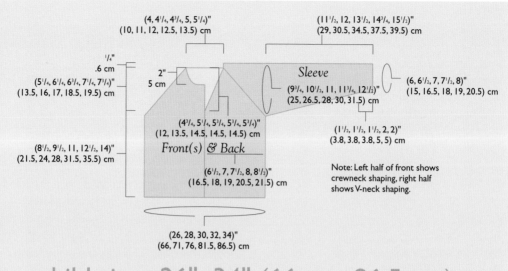

(4, 4¼, 4¾, 5, 5¼)"
(10, 11, 12, 12.5, 13.5) cm

(11½, 12, 13½, 14¾, 15½)"
(29, 30.5, 34.5, 37.5, 39.5) cm

¼"
.6 cm

(5¼, 6¼, 6¾, 7¼, 7¾)"
(13.5, 16, 17, 18.5, 19.5) cm

2"
5 cm

Sleeve

(9¾, 10½, 11, 11¾, 12½)"
(25, 26.5, 28, 30, 31.5) cm

(6, 6½, 7, 7½, 8)"
(15, 16.5, 18, 19, 20.5) cm

(4¾, 5¼, 5¾, 5¾, 5¾)"
(12, 13.5, 14.5, 14.5, 14.5) cm

Front(s) & Back

(8½, 9½, 11, 12½, 14)"
(21.5, 24, 28, 31.5, 35.5) cm

(1½, 1½, 1½, 2, 2)"
(3.8, 3.8, 3.8, 5, 5) cm

(6½, 7, 7½, 8, 8½)"
(16.5, 18, 19, 20.5, 21.5) cm

Note: Left half of front shows crewneck shaping, right half shows V-neck shaping.

(26, 28, 30, 32, 34)"
(66, 71, 76, 81.5, 86.5) cm

child sizes 26"–34" (66 cm–86.5 cm)

quicktips for circular knitting

- Sometimes a vertical line of loose stitches develops at the boundaries between double-pointed needles. To avoid such unsightly stitches, when you reach the end of a double-pointed needle, work two or three stitches from the next needle onto the working needle. Doing so will move the boundary between the needles and will help prevent a column of loose stitches from forming. If you move the boundary, remember to use a marker to designate the beginning of the round.

- When you're working the yoke on raglan or yoke sweaters, push the sleeves to the inside of the sweater to keep them from getting tangled with the yarn and to make the knitting more manageable.

- Place a safety pin or open-coil marker at the center front when you're working the joining round on the yoke of circular-yoke sweaters. Then it will be easy to lay the sweater flat and measure the correct distance to the first decrease round. Likewise, mark the first decrease round to make it easy to measure the distance to the next decrease round, and so on.

raglan

sizing adult

Finished Bust/Chest Circumference

36	38	40	42	44	46	48	50	52	54"
91.5	96.5	101.5	106.5	112	117	122	127	132	137 cm

Yarn Requirements

GAUGE											
3	570	620	680	730	780	830	870	900	940	980 yd
	521	567	622	668	713	759	796	823	860	896 m
4	810	870	960	1040	1110	1180	1230	1280	1330	1380
	741	796	878	951	1015	1079	1125	1170	1216	1262
5	1020	1100	1210	1310	1400	1480	1550	1610	1680	1740
	933	1006	1106	1198	1280	1353	1417	1472	1536	1591
6	1440	1560	1710	1850	1970	2100	2190	2280	2380	2470
	1317	1426	1564	1692	1801	1920	2003	2085	2176	2259
7	1590	1710	1880	2030	2170	2310	2420	2510	2620	2710
	1454	1564	1719	1856	1984	2112	2213	2295	2396	2478

Pullover Body

With cir needle, CO:

3	108	116	120	128	132	140	144	152	156	164 sts.
4	144	152	160	168	176	184	192	200	208	216
5	180	188	200	212	220	232	240	252	260	272
6	216	228	240	252	264	276	288	300	312	324
7	252	268	280	296	308	324	336	352	364	380

Place marker (pm) and join, being careful not to twist sts. Work edging of choice (see pages 35–37), then cont even until piece measures desired length to armhole, or about:

14	14	14½	15¼	16	16¼	16½	16¾	17	17¼"
35.5	35.5	37	38.5	40.5	41.5	42	42.5	43	44 cm

ending last rnd the foll number of sts before marker:

3	3	3	3	3	3	4	4	4	4	4 sts.
4	4	4	4	4	4	6	6	6	6	6
5	5	5	5	5	5	7	7	7	7	7
6	6	6	6	6	6	9	9	9	9	9
7	7	7	7	7	7	10	10	10	10	10

raglan

Finished Bust/Chest Circumference

36	38	40	42	44	46	48	50	52	54"
91.5	96.5	101.5	106.5	112	117	122	127	132	137 cm

Divide for Front and Back
*BO:

	36	38	40	42	44	46	48	50	52	54"
3	6	6	6	6	6	8	8	8	8	8 sts,
4	8	8	8	8	8	12	12	12	12	12
5	10	10	10	10	10	14	14	14	14	14
6	12	12	12	12	12	18	18	18	18	18
7	14	14	14	14	14	20	20	20	20	20

work until there are the foll number of sts after BO:

	36	38	40	42	44	46	48	50	52	54"
3	48	52	54	58	60	62	64	68	70	74 sts,
4	64	68	72	76	80	80	84	88	92	96
5	80	84	90	96	100	102	106	112	116	122
6	96	102	108	114	120	120	126	132	138	144
7	112	120	126	134	140	142	148	156	162	170

rep from * once. There will rem the foll number of sts each for front and back:

	36	38	40	42	44	46	48	50	52	54"
3	48	52	54	58	60	62	64	68	70	74 sts.
4	64	68	72	76	80	80	84	88	92	96
5	80	84	90	96	100	102	106	112	116	122
6	96	102	108	114	120	120	126	132	138	144
7	112	120	126	134	140	142	148	156	162	170

Set aside.

Sleeves
With dpn, CO:

	36	38	40	42	44	46	48	50	52	54"
3	28	28	30	30	30	32	32	32	34	34 sts.
4	38	38	40	40	40	44	44	44	46	46
5	46	46	50	50	50	54	54	54	58	58
6	56	56	60	60	60	66	66	66	68	68
7	66	66	70	70	70	76	76	76	80	80

Place m and join, being careful not to twist sts. Work edging of choice until piece measures desired length from beg, or about 2½" (6.5 cm).

Finished Bust/Chest Circumference

36	38	40	42	44	46	48	50	52	54"
91.5	96.5	101.5	106.5	112	117	122	127	132	137 cm

Change to St st and inc 1 st each side of marker every 4 rnds (if number is zero, omit these rnds):

	36	38	40	42	44	46	48	50	52	54"
3	0	0	0	0	0	0	0	0	0	0 times.
4	0	0	0	0	0	0	0	0	0	0
5	0	0	0	0	0	0	0	0	0	0
6	0	0	0	0	0	0	0	0	0	2
7	0	0	0	0	0	0	0	0	0	6

Then inc 1 st each side of marker every 6 rnds (if number is zero, omit these rnds):

	36	38	40	42	44	46	48	50	52	54"
3	0	0	0	0	0	0	2	4	3	6 times.
4	0	0	0	0	0	0	2	4	7	10
5	0	0	0	2	3	5	11	16	11	17
6	0	0	0	2	8	5	11	16	19	21
7	0	0	0	7	12	14	19	24	23	21

Then inc 1 st each side of marker every 8 rnds (if number is zero, omit these rnds):

	36	38	40	42	44	46	48	50	52	54"
3	6	7	7	8	9	9	8	7	8	6 time(s).
4	7	8	9	10	11	11	10	9	7	5
5	10	11	11	11	11	9	5	2	6	2
6	11	13	13	13	9	11	7	4	2	0
7	13	15	15	11	8	6	3	0	1	0

There will be:

	36	38	40	42	44	46	48	50	52	54"
3	40	42	44	46	48	50	52	54	56	58 sts.
4	52	54	58	60	62	66	68	70	74	76
5	66	68	72	76	78	82	86	90	92	96
6	78	82	86	90	94	98	102	106	110	114
7	92	96	100	106	110	116	120	124	128	134

Work even if necessary until piece measures:

16¾	17¼	17¾	18½	19	19¾	20¼	20½	20½	20¾"
42.5	44	45	47	48.5	50	51.5	52	52	52.5 cm

from beg, or desired length to underarm, ending the foll number of sts before end-of-rnd marker:

	36	38	40	42	44	46	48	50	52	54"
3	3	3	3	3	3	4	4	4	4	4 sts.
4	4	4	4	4	4	6	6	6	6	6
5	5	5	5	5	5	7	7	7	7	7

Finished Bust/Chest Circumference

	36	38	40	42	44	46	48	50	52	54"
	91.5	96.5	101.5	106.5	112	117	122	127	132	137 cm
6	6	6	6	6	6	9	9	9	9	9
7	7	7	7	7	7	10	10	10	10	10

BO:

	36	38	40	42	44	46	48	50	52	54"
3	6	6	6	6	6	8	8	8	8	8 sts,
4	8	8	8	8	8	12	12	12	12	12
5	10	10	10	10	10	14	14	14	14	14
6	12	12	12	12	12	18	18	18	18	18
7	14	14	14	14	14	20	20	20	20	20

work to end. There will remain:

	36	38	40	42	44	46	48	50	52	54"
3	34	36	38	40	42	42	44	46	48	50 sts.
4	44	46	50	52	54	54	56	58	62	64
5	56	58	62	66	68	68	72	76	78	82
6	66	70	74	78	82	80	84	88	92	96
7	78	82	86	92	96	96	100	104	108	114

Set aside. Make another sleeve to match.

Pullover Yoke with Crewneck

(See page 158 for V-neck option.) With RS facing, join pieces as foll:
Knit across:

	36	38	40	42	44	46	48	50	52	54"
3	34	36	38	40	42	42	44	46	48	50 sts
4	44	46	50	52	54	54	56	58	62	64
5	56	58	62	66	68	68	72	76	78	82
6	66	70	74	78	82	80	84	88	92	96
7	78	82	86	92	96	96	100	104	108	114

of left sleeve, pm, knit across:

	36	38	40	42	44	46	48	50	52	54"
3	48	52	54	58	60	62	64	68	70	74 sts
4	64	68	72	76	80	80	84	88	92	96
5	80	84	90	96	100	102	106	112	116	122
6	96	102	108	114	120	120	126	132	138	144
7	112	120	126	134	140	142	148	156	162	170

raglan

Finished Bust/Chest Circumference

36	38	40	42	44	46	48	50	52	54"
91.5	96.5	101.5	106.5	112	117	122	127	132	137 cm

of front, pm, knit across:

3	34	36	38	40	42	42	44	46	48	50 sts
4	44	46	50	52	54	54	56	58	62	64
5	56	58	62	66	68	68	72	76	78	82
6	66	70	74	78	82	80	84	88	92	96
7	78	82	86	92	96	96	100	104	108	114

of right sleeve, pm, knit across:

3	48	52	54	58	60	62	64	68	70	74 sts
4	64	68	72	76	80	80	84	88	92	96
5	80	84	90	96	100	102	106	112	116	122
6	96	102	108	114	120	120	126	132	138	144
7	112	120	126	134	140	142	148	156	162	170

of back, pm for end of rnd. There will be:

3	164	176	184	196	204	208	216	228	236	248 sts.
4	216	228	244	256	268	268	280	292	308	320
5	272	284	304	324	336	340	356	376	388	408
6	324	344	364	384	404	400	420	440	460	480
7	380	404	424	452	472	476	496	520	540	568

Shape Raglan

Next rnd: Dec as foll: *K2tog, knit to 2 sts before next m, ssk, slip m; rep from * 3 more times—8 sts dec'd. Work 3 rnds even.

Dec 8 sts in this manner every 4 rnds (if number is zero, omit these rnds):

3	4	4	4	4	4	4	3	3	3	2 time(s).
4	3	3	3	3	3	4	3	3	2	2
5	2	3	3	1	1	2	1	0	0	0
6	1	1	1	0	0	2	1	0	0	0
7	0	0	1	0	0	0	0	0	0	0

Then rep dec rnd every 2 rnds:

3	10	11	12	13	14	14	16	17	18	20 times.
4	16	17	19	20	21	19	21	22	25	26
5	22	22	24	28	29	27	30	33	34	36
6	28	30	32	35	37	32	35	38	40	40
7	34	36	37	41	41	42	42	42	42	41

raglan

Finished Bust/Chest Circumference

36	38	40	42	44	46	48	50	52	54"
91.5	96.5	101.5	106.5	112	117	122	127	132	137 cm

Then rep dec rnd every rnd, working decs on WS rows as *purl to 2 sts before m, p2tog, slip m, ssp; rep from * 3 more times, purl to end (if number is zero, omit these rnds):

3	0	0	0	0	0	0	0	0	0	0 times.
4	0	0	0	0	0	0	0	0	0	0
5	0	0	0	0	0	0	0	0	0	0
6	0	0	0	0	0	0	0	0	0	2
7	0	0	0	0	2	0	2	4	6	10

At the same time, when piece measures

6	6½	7	7¼	7½	7¼	7½	7¾	8	8¼"
15	16.5	18	18.5	19	18.5	19	19.5	20.5	21 cm

from joining rnd,

Shape Crewneck

Cont working raglan decs as established, BO at center front:

3	6	6	6	6	8	8	8	8	10	10 sts,
4	10	10	10	10	12	12	12	12	14	14
5	12	12	12	12	16	16	16	16	18	18
6	16	16	16	16	20	20	20	20	22	22
7	20	20	18	20	24	24	24	24	26	26

work to end. Working back and forth in rows and cont working raglan decs as established, at each neck edge BO 3 sts (if number is zero, omit these rows):

3	0	1	1	1	1	1	1	1	1	1 time(s).
4	1	1	1	1	1	1	1	2	1	2
5	1	1	1	2	1	2	2	2	2	3
6	1	1	2	2	2	3	3	3	3	3
7	1	2	3	3	2	3	3	3	3	3

Then BO 2 sts:

3	2	1	1	2	1	2	2	2	2	2 time(s).
4	1	2	2	2	2	3	3	2	3	2
5	2	3	3	2	3	2	2	3	3	2
6	3	3	2	2	2	2	2	3	3	3
7	3	2	2	2	3	2	3	4	4	4

raglan

Finished Bust/Chest Circumference

36	38	40	42	44	46	48	50	52	54"
91.5	96.5	101.5	106.5	112	117	122	127	132	137 cm

Then dec 1 st at each neck edge every RS row:

3	2	2	2	1	2	1	1	2	1	2 time(s).
4	2	1	1	2	2	1	2	2	2	2
5	2	1	2	2	2	3	3	2	2	2
6	1	2	2	3	2	2	3	2	2	3
7	2	3	2	2	2	3	2	2	2	3

After all neck and raglan decs have been completed, there will remain:

3	26	28	28	30	30	32	32	34	34	36 sts.
4	32	34	34	36	38	44	46	48	48	50
5	42	44	46	48	50	58	58	60	62	64
6	48	50	52	54	56	70	72	74	76	78
7	58	62	64	66	68	76	78	82	84	86

BO all sts.

Pullover Yoke with V-Neck

Work as for crewneck version until yoke measures:

2½	2½	3	3	3¼	3¼	3½	3½	3½	3¾"
6.5	6.5	7.5	7.5	8.5	8.5	9	9	9	9.5 cm

Work to center of front sts. Turn and work back and forth in rows, and *at the same time* cont to work raglan shaping as for crewneck version, and *also at the same time* dec 1 st at each neck edge every RS row:

3	5	5	5	7	7	9	9	10	9	11 times.
4	8	8	8	10	12	14	16	17	16	18
5	11	11	13	15	16	20	20	21	23	24
6	14	14	16	17	19	25	26	27	28	29
7	17	19	21	22	24	28	29	31	32	33

Then dec 1 st at neck edge every 4 rows (if number is zero, omit these rows):

3	4	5	5	4	4	3	3	3	4	3 time(s).
4	4	5	5	4	3	2	1	1	2	1
5	4	5	4	3	3	1	1	1	0	0
6	4	5	4	4	3	0	0	0	0	0
7	4	4	3	3	2	0	0	0	0	0

Finished Bust/Chest Circumference

36	38	40	42	44	46	48	50	52	54"
91.5	96.5	101.5	106.5	112	117	122	127	132	137 cm

After all neck and raglan decs have been completed, there will remain:

3	26	28	28	30	30	32	32	34	34	36 sts.
4	32	34	34	36	38	44	46	48	48	50
5	42	44	46	48	50	58	58	60	62	64
6	48	50	52	54	56	70	72	74	76	78
7	58	62	64	66	68	76	78	82	84	86

BO all sts.

Finishing

Block to measurements. With yarn threaded on a tapestry needle, sew underarm seams.
Neckband: Choose a crewneck finish on pages 66–67 or a V-neck finish on pages 68–69. With smaller dpn, RS facing, and beg at back right raglan line, pick up and knit 1 st for each BO st and about 3 sts for every 4 rows along sloped edges around neck opening. Adjust st count if necessary to achieve a full multiple of the edging patt you've chosen. Place m and join. Work in chosen pattern until neckband measures 1" (2.5 cm), or desired length. BO all sts in patt. Weave in loose ends. Block again, if desired.

Cardigan Body

Work as for pullover body, but do not join into a rnd (i.e., work the body sts back and forth in rows, with opening at center front) until piece measures desired length to armholes, or about:

14	14	14½	15¼	16	16¼	16½	16¾	17	17¼"
35.5	35.5	37	38.5	40.5	41.5	42	42.5	43	44 cm

ending with a WS row.

Divide for Fronts and Back

With WS facing, purl across:

3	24	26	27	29	30	31	32	34	35	37 sts
4	32	34	36	38	40	40	42	44	46	48
5	40	42	45	48	50	51	53	56	58	61
6	48	51	54	57	60	60	63	66	69	72
7	56	60	63	67	70	71	74	78	81	85

for left front, BO:

3	6	6	6	6	6	8	8	8	8	8 sts
4	8	8	8	8	8	12	12	12	12	12
5	10	10	10	10	10	14	14	14	14	14
6	12	12	12	12	12	18	18	18	18	18
7	14	14	14	14	14	20	20	20	20	20

Finished Bust/Chest Circumference

	36	38	40	42	44	46	48	50	52	54"
	91.5	96.5	101.5	106.5	112	117	122	127	132	137 cm

for left underarm, purl across:

3	48	52	54	58	60	62	64	68	70	74 sts
4	64	68	72	76	80	80	84	88	92	96
5	80	84	90	96	100	102	106	112	116	122
6	96	102	108	114	120	120	126	132	138	144
7	112	120	126	134	140	142	148	156	162	170

for back, BO:

3	6	6	6	6	6	8	8	8	8	8 sts
4	8	8	8	8	8	12	12	12	12	12
5	10	10	10	10	10	14	14	14	14	14
6	12	12	12	12	12	18	18	18	18	18
7	14	14	14	14	14	20	20	20	20	20

for right underarm, purl across:

3	24	26	27	29	30	31	32	34	35	37 sts
4	32	34	36	38	40	40	42	44	46	48
5	40	42	45	48	50	51	53	56	58	61
6	48	51	54	57	60	60	63	66	69	72
7	56	60	63	67	70	71	74	78	81	85

for right front. Set aside.

Sleeves
Work sleeves as for pullover version.

Cardigan Yoke with Crewneck
(See page 163 for V-neck option.) Join all pieces as foll:
With RS facing, knit across:

3	24	26	27	29	30	31	32	34	35	37 sts
4	32	34	36	38	40	40	42	44	46	48
5	40	42	45	48	50	51	53	56	58	61
6	48	51	54	57	60	60	63	66	69	72
7	56	60	63	67	70	71	74	78	81	85

of right front, pm, knit across:

3	34	36	38	40	42	42	44	46	48	50 sts
4	44	46	50	52	54	54	56	58	62	64
5	56	58	62	66	68	68	72	76	78	82
6	66	70	74	78	82	80	84	88	92	96
7	78	82	86	92	96	96	100	104	108	114

raglan

Finished Bust/Chest Circumference

	36	38	40	42	44	46	48	50	52	54"
	91.5	96.5	101.5	106.5	112	117	122	127	132	137 cm

of right sleeve, pm, knit across:

	36	38	40	42	44	46	48	50	52	54"
3	48	52	54	58	60	62	64	68	70	74 sts
4	64	68	72	76	80	80	84	88	92	96
5	80	84	90	96	100	102	106	112	116	122
6	96	102	108	114	120	120	126	132	138	144
7	112	120	126	134	140	142	148	156	162	170

of back, pm, knit across:

	36	38	40	42	44	46	48	50	52	54"
3	34	36	38	40	42	42	44	46	48	50 sts
4	44	46	50	52	54	54	56	58	62	64
5	56	58	62	66	68	68	72	76	78	82
6	66	70	74	78	82	80	84	88	92	96
7	78	82	86	92	96	96	100	104	108	114

of left sleeve, pm, knit across:

	36	38	40	42	44	46	48	50	52	54"
3	24	26	27	29	30	31	32	34	35	37 sts
4	32	34	36	38	40	40	42	44	46	48
5	40	42	45	48	50	51	53	56	58	61
6	48	51	54	57	60	60	63	66	69	72
7	56	60	63	67	70	71	74	78	81	85

of left front. There will be:

	36	38	40	42	44	46	48	50	52	54"
3	164	176	184	196	204	208	216	228	236	248 sts.
4	216	228	244	256	268	268	280	292	308	320
5	272	284	304	324	336	340	356	376	388	408
6	324	344	364	384	404	400	420	440	460	480
7	380	404	424	452	472	476	496	520	540	568

Work 1 row even on WS.

Shape Raglan
Next row: Dec as foll: Knit to 2 sts before m, *ssk, sl m, k2tog; rep from * 3 more times, knit to end of row—8 sts dec'd. Work 3 rows even.

Dec 8 sts every 4 rows in this manner (if number is zero, omit these rows):

	36	38	40	42	44	46	48	50	52	54"
3	4	4	4	4	4	4	3	3	3	2 time(s).
4	3	3	3	3	3	4	3	3	2	2
5	2	3	3	1	1	2	1	0	0	0
6	1	1	1	0	0	2	1	0	0	0
7	0	0	1	0	0	0	0	0	0	0

raglan

Finished Bust/Chest Circumference

	36	38	40	42	44	46	48	50	52	54"
	91.5	96.5	101.5	106.5	112	117	122	127	132	137 cm

Then rep dec row every 2 rows:

3	10	11	12	13	14	14	16	17	18	20 times.
4	16	17	19	20	21	19	21	22	25	26
5	22	22	24	28	29	27	30	33	34	36
6	28	30	32	35	37	32	35	38	40	40
7	34	36	37	41	41	42	42	42	42	41

Then rep dec row every row (see page 157 for working decs on WS rows. If number is zero, omit these rows):

3	0	0	0	0	0	0	0	0	0	0 times.
4	0	0	0	0	0	0	0	0	0	0
5	0	0	0	0	0	0	0	0	0	0
6	0	0	0	0	0	0	0	0	0	2
7	0	0	0	0	2	0	2	4	6	10

At the same time, when piece measures

	6	6½	7	7¼	7½	7¼	7½	7¾	8	8¼"
	15	16.5	18	18.5	19	18.5	19	19.5	20.5	21 cm

from joining rnd,

Shape Crewneck
Cont working raglan decs as established, BO at beg of next 2 rows:

3	3	3	3	3	4	4	4	4	5	5 sts.
4	5	5	5	5	6	6	6	6	7	7
5	6	6	6	6	8	8	8	8	9	9
6	8	8	8	8	10	10	10	10	11	11
7	10	10	9	10	12	12	12	12	13	13

Cont working raglan decs as established, at each neck edge BO 3 sts (if number is zero, omit these rows):

3	0	1	1	1	1	1	1	1	1	1 time(s).
4	1	1	1	1	1	1	1	2	1	2
5	1	1	1	2	1	2	2	2	2	3
6	1	1	2	2	2	3	3	3	3	3
7	1	2	3	3	2	3	3	3	3	3

Finished Bust/Chest Circumference

	36	38	40	42	44	46	48	50	52	54"
	91.5	96.5	101.5	106.5	112	117	122	127	132	137 cm

Then BO 2 sts:

3	2	1	1	2	1	2	2	2	2	2 time(s).
4	1	2	2	2	2	3	3	2	3	2
5	2	3	3	2	3	2	2	3	3	2
6	3	3	2	2	2	2	2	3	3	3
7	3	2	2	2	3	2	3	4	4	4

Then dec 1 st at each neck edge every RS row:

3	2	2	2	1	2	1	1	2	1	2 time(s).
4	2	1	1	2	2	1	2	2	2	2
5	2	1	2	2	2	3	3	2	2	2
6	1	2	2	3	2	2	3	2	2	3
7	2	3	2	2	2	3	2	2	2	3

After all neck and raglan decs have been completed, there will remain:

3	26	28	28	30	30	32	32	34	34	36 sts.
4	32	34	34	36	38	44	46	48	48	50
5	42	44	46	48	50	58	58	60	62	64
6	48	50	52	54	56	70	72	74	76	78
7	58	62	64	66	68	76	78	82	84	86

BO all sts.

Cardigan Yoke with V-Neck

Work yoke as for crewneck version until yoke measures:

	2½	2½	3	3	3¼	3¼	3½	3½	3½	3¾"
	6.5	6.5	7.5	7.5	8.5	8.5	9	9	9	9.5 cm

Shape V-Neck

Cont to work raglan shaping as for crewneck version, and *at the same time* dec 1 st at each neck edge every RS row:

3	5	5	5	7	7	9	9	10	9	11 times.
4	8	8	8	10	12	14	16	17	16	18
5	11	11	13	15	16	20	20	21	23	24
6	14	14	16	17	19	25	26	27	28	29
7	17	19	21	22	24	28	29	31	32	33

raglan

Finished Bust/Chest Circumference									
36	38	40	42	44	46	48	50	52	54"
91.5	96.5	101.5	106.5	112	117	122	127	132	137 cm

Then dec 1 st at each neck edge every 4 rows (if number is zero, omit these rows):

3	4	5	5	4	4	3	3	3	4	3 time(s).
4	4	5	5	4	3	2	1	1	2	1
5	4	5	4	3	3	1	1	1	0	0
6	4	5	4	4	3	0	0	0	0	0
7	4	4	3	3	2	0	0	0	0	0

After all neck and raglan decs have been completed, there will remain:

3	26	28	28	30	30	32	32	34	34	36 sts.
4	32	34	34	36	38	44	46	48	48	50
5	42	44	46	48	50	58	58	60	62	64
6	48	50	52	54	56	70	72	74	76	78
7	58	62	64	66	68	76	78	82	84	86

BO all sts.

Finishing

Block to measurements. With yarn threaded on a tapestry needle, sew underarm seams.
Neckband: Choose a crewneck finish on pages 66–67 or a V-neck finish on pages 68–69. With smaller needles, RS facing, and beg at center front, pick up and knit 1 st for every BO st and about 3 sts for every 4 rows along sloped edges around neck opening for a crewneck. (Combine neckband with button and buttonhole bands for a V-neck version.) Adjust st count if necessary to achieve a full multiple of the edging pattern you've chosen. Work edging pattern of choice for 1" (2.5 cm).
Button band: (on left front for females; right front for males) With smaller needles and RS facing, pick up and knit about 3 sts for every 4 rows along center front edge. Adjust st count if necessary to achieve a full multiple of the edging pattern you've chosen. Work in chosen pattern until band measures 1" (2.5 cm). BO all sts in patt. Mark placement of desired number of buttons, one ½" (1.3 cm) up from CO edge, one at beg of neck shaping, and the others evenly spaced in between.
Buttonhole band: (on right front for females; left front for males) Work as for button band, working one-row buttonholes (see Glossary) opposite markers when band measures about ½" (1.3 cm). BO all sts in patt.
Weave in loose ends. Sew buttons to button band opposite buttonholes. Block again, if desired.

raglan

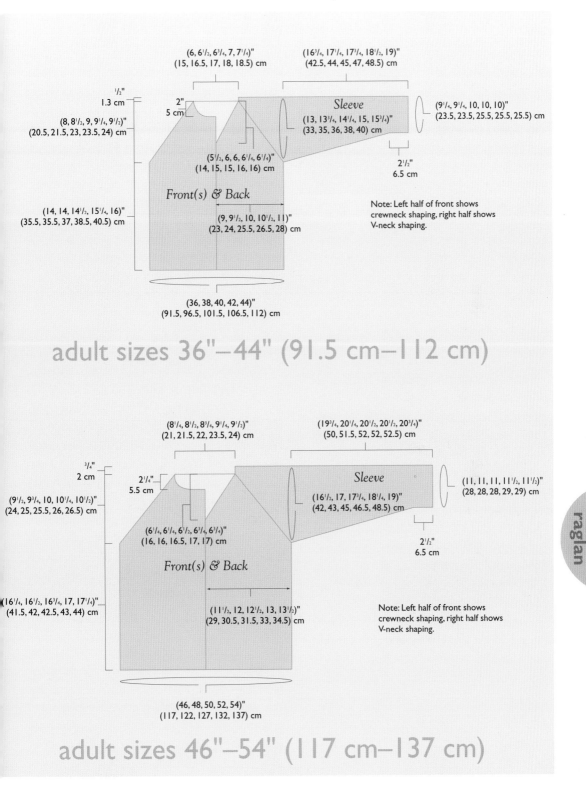

(6, 6¹/₂, 6³/₄, 7, 7¹/₄)"
(15, 16.5, 17, 18, 18.5) cm

(16³/₄, 17¹/₄, 17³/₄, 18¹/₂, 19)"
(42.5, 44, 45, 47, 48.5) cm

¹/₂"
1.3 cm

2"
5 cm

Sleeve
(13, 13³/₄, 14¹/₄, 15, 15¹/₄)"
(33, 35, 36, 38, 40) cm

(9¹/₄, 9¹/₄, 10, 10, 10)"
(23.5, 23.5, 25.5, 25.5, 25.5) cm

(8, 8¹/₂, 9, 9¹/₄, 9¹/₂)"
(20.5, 21.5, 23, 23.5, 24) cm

(5¹/₂, 6, 6, 6¹/₄, 6¹/₄)"
(14, 15, 15, 16, 16) cm

Front(s) & Back

2¹/₂"
6.5 cm

(14, 14, 14¹/₂, 15¹/₄, 16)"
(35.5, 35.5, 37, 38.5, 40.5) cm

(9, 9¹/₂, 10, 10¹/₂, 11)"
(23, 24, 25.5, 26.5, 28) cm

Note: Left half of front shows
crewneck shaping, right half shows
V-neck shaping.

(36, 38, 40, 42, 44)"
(91.5, 96.5, 101.5, 106.5, 112) cm

adult sizes 36"–44" (91.5 cm–112 cm)

(8¹/₄, 8¹/₂, 8³/₄, 9¹/₄, 9¹/₂)"
(21, 21.5, 22, 23.5, 24) cm

(19³/₄, 20¹/₄, 20¹/₂, 20¹/₂, 20³/₄)"
(50, 51.5, 52, 52, 52.5) cm

³/₄"
2 cm

2¹/₄"
5.5 cm

Sleeve
(16¹/₂, 17, 17³/₄, 18¹/₄, 19)"
(42, 43, 45, 46.5, 48.5) cm

(11, 11, 11, 11¹/₂, 11¹/₂)"
(28, 28, 28, 29, 29) cm

(9¹/₂, 9³/₄, 10, 10¹/₄, 10¹/₂)"
(24, 25, 25.5, 26, 26.5) cm

(6¹/₄, 6¹/₄, 6¹/₂, 6³/₄, 6³/₄)"
(16, 16, 16.5, 17, 17) cm

Front(s) & Back

2¹/₂"
6.5 cm

(16¹/₄, 16¹/₂, 16³/₄, 17, 17¹/₄)"
(41.5, 42, 42.5, 43, 44) cm

(11¹/₂, 12, 12¹/₂, 13, 13¹/₂)"
(29, 30.5, 31.5, 33, 34.5) cm

Note: Left half of front shows
crewneck shaping, right half shows
V-neck shaping.

(46, 48, 50, 52, 54)"
(117, 122, 127, 132, 137) cm

adult sizes 46"–54" (117 cm–137 cm)

raglan

Ribbed-Sleeve Pullover

This raglan pullover features wide ribs on the sleeves and along the sides of the body, and a crewneck shape finished off with a front-split collar. The raglan decreases are positioned several stitches away from the seam line on the front and back to accommodate a decorative rib that echoes the one on the sleeves and sides of the body. The ribs give a snug fit to the sleeves and waist, and give the sweater a slimming silhouette.

Finished Size: 36" (91.5 cm) bust/chest circumference.
Yarn: Classic Elite Montera (50% llama, 50% wool; 127 yd [116 m]/100 g): #3829 aqua ice, 6 skeins.
Needles: Body and sleeves—Size 10½ (6.5 mm): 24" (60-cm) circular (cir) and set of 4 double-pointed (dpn). Ribbing—Size 10 (6 mm): 24" (60-cm) cir and set of 4 dpn. Adjust needle size if necessary to obtain the correct gauge.
Notions: Markers (m); stitch holders; tapestry needle.
Gauge: 4 sts and 5½ rnds = 1" (2.5 cm) in stockinette stitch worked in the round on size 10½ (6.5-mm) needles.

Body

With smaller cir needle, CO 144 sts. Place marker (pm) and join, being careful not to twist sts. *Set-up row*: *[K6, p1] 2 times, [k1, p1] 22 times, [k6, p1] 2 times; rep from *. Work rib as established until piece measures 1½" (3.8 cm) from beg. Change to larger cir needle and work wide ribs at each side as established, but work center 43 back and 43 front sts in St st as foll: *[k6, p1] 2 times, k43, p1, [k6, p1] 2 times; rep from *. Cont in this manner until piece measures 14" (35.5 cm) from beg, ending 4 sts before m on last rnd. ***Divide for front and back***: BO 8 sts for underarm, work as established until there are 64 sts on needle for front after BO for front, BO 8 sts for other underarm, work to end for back—64 sts each for front and back. Set aside.

Sleeves

With smaller dpn, CO 38 sts. Place m and join, being careful not to twist sts. Work k1, p1 rib until piece measures 2½" (6.5 cm) from beg, inc 1 st on last rnd (to allow for balance of 3/1 rib)—39 sts. Change to larger dpn and work 3/1 rib as foll: *K3, p1; rep from * to last 3 sts, k3. Cont in rib as established, inc 1 st each side of marker every 8 rnds 7 times, working new sts into rib patt—53 sts. Cont even in patt until piece measures 16¾" (42.5 cm) from beg, ending 4 sts before m on last rnd. *Next rnd*: BO 8 sts, knit to end—45 sts rem. Set aside. Make another sleeve to match.

Yoke

With larger cir needle holding body sts, beg bet back and front sts, and cont in rib as established, work 45 sleeve sts, pm, k64 front sts, pm, work 45 sleeve sts, pm, work 64 back sts, pm, and join—218 sts total; rnd begins at back left armhole. *Next rnd*: Work 45 sleeve sts as established, sl m, k3, p1, pm, knit to last 4 sts of front, pm, p1, k3, sl m, work 45 sleeve sts as established, sl m, k3, p1, pm, work to last 4 sts of back, pm, p1, k3. *Next rnd*: (Dec rnd) *Ssk, work in rib patt as established to last 2 sleeve sts, k2tog, sl m, ssk, knit to last 2 sts of front, k2tog; rep from * for rem sleeve and back—8 sts dec'd. Work 3 rnds even. Rep last 4 rnds 3 more times—186 sts rem. Work dec rnd every other rnd 16 times—58 sts rem. *At the same time*, when piece measures 6" (15 cm) from joining rnd, **Shape crewneck**: Cont working raglan decs, BO 10 sts at center front, work to end. Working back and forth in rows and cont working rib patt on sleeve and raglan decs as established, at each front neck edge BO 3 sts once, then BO 2 sts once, then dec 1 st every other row 2 times, maintaining k3, p1 rib on sleeves as much as possible—34 sts rem after all neck and raglan decs have been completed; 24 sts for back, 5 sts for each sleeve. BO all sts.

Finishing

Block to measurements. With yarn threaded on a tapestry needle, sew underarm seams. **Collar**: With smaller cir needle, RS facing, and beg at center front neck, pick up and knit 7 sts along front neck BO, 11 sts along side neck, 5 sts across sleeve top, 24 sts across back neck BO, 5 sts across sleeve top, 11 sts along side neck, and 7 sts along other front neck—70 sts total. Do not join. Work k1, p1 rib, adjusting st count to maintain established purl sts along raglan line by working k2tog 3 times on first row—67 sts rem. Cont in rib until collar measures 2" (5 cm). Change to larger needle and work even in rib for 2" (5 cm) more. BO all sts in patt. Weave in loose ends. Block again if desired.

Gatsby Cardigan

This casual cardigan features centered double decreases along the raglan lines—three stitches are reduced to one, forming a prominent single-stitch ridge. The body stitches (left front, back, right front) are worked back and forth in rows with the selvedges forming the center front opening. Stitches are picked up along the front edges and worked in single rib for the button and buttonhole bands. The fold-over collar is picked up from the crewneck opening and edged with single rib to prevent the edges from curling.

Finished Size: 40" (101.5 cm) bust/chest circumference, buttoned.
Yarn: Classic Elite Gatsby (70% wool, 15% viscose, 15% nylon; 84 yd [77 m]/100 g): #2132 raspberry, 8 skeins.
Needles: Size 11 (8 mm): 24" (60-cm) circular (cir) and set of 4 double-pointed (dpn). Adjust needle size if necessary to obtain the correct gauge.
Notions: Markers (m); stitch holders; tapestry needle; six ⅞" (2.2-cm) buttons.
Gauge: 3 sts and 4½ rows = 1" (2.5 cm) in stockinette stitch on size 11 (8-mm) needles.

Body

With cir needle, CO 121 sts (120 sts + 1 st to balance rib). Do not join. *K1, p1; rep from *, end k1. Cont in rib as established until piece measures 2" (5 cm) from beg, ending with a WS row. Change to St st and dec 1 st on next row—120 sts. Cont in St st until piece measures 14½" (37 cm) from beg, ending with a RS row. **Divide for fronts and back**: (WS) P27 left front sts, BO 6 sts for underarm, purl until there are 54 sts for back after BO for back, BO 6 sts for other underarm, purl to end for right front—27 sts for each front; 54 sts for back. Do not cut yarn. Set aside.

Sleeves

With dpn, CO 30 sts. Place marker (pm) and join, being careful not to twist sts. Work k1, p1 rib until piece measures 2" (5 cm) from beg. Change to St st and inc 1 st each side of marker every 8 rnds 7 times—44 sts. Cont even if necessary until piece measures 17¾" (45 cm) from beg, ending 3 sts before m on last rnd. *Next rnd*: BO 6 sts, work to end—38 sts rem. Set aside. Make another sleeve to match.

Yoke

With cir needle and RS facing, k27 right front sts, pm, k38 sleeve sts, pm, k54 back sts, pm, k38 sleeve sts, pm, k27 left front sts—184 sts total. Purl 1 row. *Dec row*: (RS) *Knit to 1 st before marker, work centered double dec (sl 2 sts tog kwise, k1, p2sso; remove marker to do so, then replace marker to right of dec); rep from * 3 more times, knit to end—8 sts dec'd. Work 3 rows even. Rep the last 4 rows 4 more times, then work dec row every other row 12 times, and *at the same time* when piece measures 7" (18 cm) from joining row, ending with a WS row, **Shape crewneck**: Cont working raglan decs, BO 3 sts at beg of next

4 rows, then BO 2 sts at beg of next 2 rows, then dec 1 st at each neck edge every RS row 2 times—28 sts rem after all neck and raglan decs have been completed; 20 back sts and 4 sts for each sleeve. BO all sts.

Finishing

Block to measurements. With yarn threaded on a tapestry needle, sew underarm seams. **Button band**: With cir needle, RS facing, and beg at neck edge, pick up and knit 85 sts along center left front edge (about 4 sts for every 5 rows). Do not join. Work k1, p1 rib for 5 rows. BO all sts in patt. Mark placement of 6 buttons, one ¾" (2 cm) up from lower edge, one ½" (1.3 cm) down from neck edge, and the others evenly spaced in between. **Buttonhole band**: With cir needle, RS facing, and beg at lower body edge, pick up and knit 85 sts along center right front edge. Do not join. Work k1, p1 rib for 2 rows. On next row, cont in rib and work buttonholes (k2tog, yo) opposite markers for buttons. Cont in established rib for 2 more rows. BO all sts in patt. **Collar**: With WS facing and beg at left front neck, pick up and knit 13 sts along left front neck BO, 1 st in raglan line, 6 sts across sleeve top, 1 st in raglan line, 25 sts across back neck BO, 1 st in raglan line, 6 sts across sleeve top, 1 st in raglan line, and 13 sts along right front neck BO—67 sts total. *Next row*: (WS of collar; RS of sweater) [P1, k1] 2 times, purl to last 4 sts, [k1, p1] 2 times. Work sts as they appear for 15 rows. Maintaining rib as established on both ends, work all sts in k1, p1 rib for 4 rows. Loosely BO all sts. Weave in loose ends. Sew buttons to button band opposite buttonholes. Block again if desired.

Striped Crewneck Pullover

With the exception of a few stripes across the yoke, this crewneck pull-over follows the basic raglan chart without deviation. It is worked in the round from the bottom up with stripes beginning about an inch before the armhole on the body and sleeves, then extending into the yoke. The raglan "seams" are worked by pairing right- and left-leaning decreases adjacent to each other, forming prominent diagonal lines from the armholes to the neck, and causing the stripes to bend.

Finished Size: 34" (86.5 cm) bust/chest circumference.
Yarn: Classic Elite Lush (50% angora, 50% wool; 124 yd [113 m]/50 g): #4407 this-tle (light blue; MC), 7 skeins; #4457 blue-berry (navy), #4422 glass green (sage), and #4434 berrisimo (burgundy), 1 skein each.
Needles: Body and sleeves—Size 8 (5 mm): 24" (60-cm) circular (cir) and set of 4 double-pointed (dpn). Ribbing—Size 7 (4.5 mm): 16" and 24" (40- and 60-cm) cir and set of 4 dpn. Adjust needle size if necessary to obtain the correct gauge.
Notions: Markers (m); stitch holders; tap-estry needle.
Gauge: 5 sts and 7 rnds = 1" (2.5 cm) in stockinette stitch worked in the round on size 8 (5-mm) needles.

Stripe Pattern:

Work the number of rnds indicated for each color: 2 navy, 2 light blue, 1 navy, 2 light blue, 6 navy, 3 sage, 2 light blue, 2 sage, 2 light blue, 5 sage, 2 burgundy, 2 sage, 1 burgundy, 2 sage, 5 burgundy, 2 light blue, 1 burgundy—42 rnds total.

Body

With MC and smaller cir needle, CO 172 sts. Place marker (pm) and join, being careful not to twist sts. Work k2, p2 rib until piece meas-ures 2" (5 cm) from beg. Change to larger cir needle and cont in St st until piece meas-ures 13" (33 cm), or 1" (2.5 cm) less than desired length to armhole. Work 7 rnds of stripe patt, ending 4 sts before m on last rnd. ***Divide for front and back***: (8th rnd of stripe patt) BO 8 sts for underarm, knit until there are 78 sts for front after BO, BO 8 sts for underarm, knit to end for back—78 sts each for front and back. Set aside.

Sleeves

With MC and smaller dpn, CO 40 sts. Place m and join, being careful not to twist sts. Work k2, p2 rib until piece measures 2" (5 cm) from beg. Change to larger dpn and cont in St st, and *at the same time* inc 1 st each side of marker every 6 rnds 11 times—62 sts. Cont even until piece measures 14½" (37 cm) from beg, or 1" (2.5 cm) less than desired length to armhole. Work 7 rnds of stripe patt, end-ing 4 sts before m on last rnd. *Next rnd*: (8th rnd of stripe patt) BO 8 sts, knit to end—54 sts rem. Set aside. Make another sleeve to match.

Yoke

With larger cir needle holding body sts, beg between back and front, and cont with 9th rnd of stripe patt, k54 sleeve sts, pm, k78 front sts, pm, k54 sleeve sts, pm, k78 back sts, pm and join into a rnd—264 sts total; rnd begins at back left armhole. *Next rnd*: (Dec rnd) *K2tog, knit to 2 sts before next m, ssk, slip m; rep from * 3 more times—8 sts dec'd. Work 3 rnds even. Rep dec rnd. Work 1 rnd even. Cont in stripe patt, work dec rnd every other rnd 23 times. (*Note:* To maintain color sequence along raglan dec lines, make color changes 2 sts before end-of-rnd marker.) When stripe patt has been completed, cont in MC. *At the same time*, when piece measures 5¾" (14.5 cm) from joining rnd, **Shape crewneck**: Cont working raglan decs, BO 12 sts at center front, work to end. Working back and forth in rows and cont working raglan decs as established, at each neck edge BO 3 sts once, then BO 2 sts once, then dec 1 st every other row 3 times, omitting dec at front raglan when just 1 front st rem—36 sts rem after all neck and raglan decs have been completed; 28 sts for back and 4 sts for each sleeve. BO all sts.

Finishing

Block to measurements. With yarn threaded on a tapestry needle, sew underarm seams. **Neckband**: With shorter, smaller cir needle, MC, RS facing, and beg at back right raglan line, pick up and knit 72 sts evenly spaced around neck opening. Place m and join. Work k2, p2 rib until neckband measures 1" (2.5 cm). BO all sts in patt. Weave in loose ends. Block again if desired.

quick**tips** for perfect buttonholes

- Cardigans knitted at a large gauge of 3 stitches/inch may not need buttonholes. Most buttons will fit through the individual stitches without straining them.

- Unless you're designing a sweater around specific buttons, wait to purchase buttons until your sweater is completed. It's easier to choose the correct size and color when you can lay the buttons on the finished sweater.

personal**touches** raglan decreases

The distinctive diagonal lines typical of raglan sweaters are achieved by working decreases in pairs, left-leaning and right-leaning, along the raglan lines. Depending on the type and sequence of decreases used, the effect can be prominent or subtle. For a wide, gored effect, work a right-leaning decrease (k2tog) followed by a left-leaning decrease (ssk) at each seam line, as in the Striped Crewneck Pullover on page 169. Add a few plain knit stitches—half from the sleeve and half from the body—between the seam-line decreases to accentuate the gore. For a subtle seam, work the decreases in the opposite order—ssk followed by k2tog. For a narrow, prominent ridge, work a centered double decrease at each seam line, as in the Gatsby Cardigan on page 167. For a slightly directional ridge line (and a less refined look), work a simple double decrease by knitting three stitches together (k3tog) at each seam line.

Gored Seam

One Center Stitch

Gored Seam with Several Center Stitches

Subtle Seam

Directional Ridge

Prominent Ridge

seamless yoke sweaters

Sweaters with seamless yokes are constructed without seams. This type of sweater is worked in the round, and decreases used to shape the yoke are evenly distributed around the circumference of the upper sweater, instead of confined to specific regions such as along the diagonal lines of a raglan sweater or along the armhole edge of a set-in sleeve sweater. Because the shoulders and armholes are not well defined, seamless yoke sweaters have a less tailored fit than raglan or set-in sleeve sweaters.

Seamless yoke sweaters are ideal for showcasing texture or color patterns that take advantage of the uninterrupted rounds of straight knitting between decrease rounds. This type of sweater is extremely easy to knit given that it's worked completely in the round from the bottom up (as given in the instructions here) or from the top down. Because there are no seams, this is a good choice for bulky yarns. Except for the few rounds in the yoke that require shaping (decreases), every round is simply knitted. However, there are no stabilizing shoulder seams to prevent sagging, and the neck drops as much in the back as it does in the front (unless extra rows are added to the back neck to prevent this from happening).

Three sweater variations following the seamless yoke chart. Top to bottom: Cabled Yoke Pullover at 40" (101.5 cm) circumference and 4 stitches/inch, Chenille Yoke Cardigan at 40" (101.5 cm) circumference and 4½ stitches/inch, and Child's Fair Isle Pullover at 32" (81.5 cm) circumference and 3 stitches/inch. Step-by-step instructions for these sweaters begin on page 192.

basic anatomy

The instructions that follow are for working round yoke sweaters from the bottom up in a modification of the formula Elizabeth Zimmermann developed along with her EPS system published in issue #26 of *Wool Gathering* in 1982, and which her daughter, Meg Swansen, later updated in issue #65 of *Wool Gathering* in 2001. For the pullover version, the lower body is worked as a tube to the armholes, the sleeves are worked as separate tubes to the armholes, a few stitches are bound off each piece at the underarms (or placed on holders, then grafted, for a truly seamless design), then the pieces are joined together (left sleeve, front yoke, right sleeve, back yoke; the round begins at the left back), and the yoke is worked in a single piece to the neck. The yoke is shaped with four decrease rounds, worked at equal intervals during the yoke depth. In the first decrease round twenty percent of the stitches are decreased, in the second decrease round, twenty-five percent of the stitches are decreases, and thirty-three percent of the stitches are decreased in each of the final two decrease rounds. If a continuous texture or color pattern is being worked on the yoke, as in the Cabled Yoke Pullover on page 196, the placement of the decreases may need to be adjusted slightly to accommodate the pattern. After all of the decreases have been worked, a few short rows can be worked across the back neck stitches to raise the height of the sweater back and produce a better-fitting sweater. For the cardigan version, the body stitches are not joined into a round; instead they are worked back and forth in rows, with the selvedges forming the center front opening. After the knitting is complete, the short bound-off edges at the armholes are the only seams to be sewn.

To use the following chart to make a round yoke sweater, you need to choose yarn, determine your gauge (see page 6), and pick a size based on the desired finished bust/chest circumference. You'll also need circular (cir) needles in 16" (40-cm) and 24" or 32" (60- or 80-cm) lengths and a set of 4 or 5 double-pointed (dpn) needles in size to obtain gauge (and needles one or two sizes smaller for edgings, if desired), stitch markers (m), a tapestry needle, and buttons for cardigan versions: 5 to 7 for child sizes, 7 to 9 for adult sizes. Gauge runs vertically along the left side of the chart; finished bust/chest circumference is listed horizontally across the top. The chart for children's sizes begins on page 175; schematics are on page 180. The chart for adult sizes begins on page 181; schematics are on page 191.

Finished Chest Circumference

26	28	30	32	34"		26	28	30	32	34"
66	71	76	81.5	86.5 cm		66	71	76	81.5	86.5 cm

GAUGE

Yarn Requirements

3	250	310	380	450	510 yd
	229	283	347	411	466 m
4	350	440	530	630	730
	320	402	485	576	668
5	440	560	670	800	920
	402	512	613	732	841
6	620	790	950	1130	1290
	567	722	869	1033	1180
7	690	870	1050	1240	1420
	631	796	960	1134	1298

Pullover Body

With cir needle, CO:

3	80	84	92	96	104 sts.
4	104	112	120	128	136
5	128	140	148	160	172
6	156	168	180	192	204
7	180	196	212	224	240

Place marker (pm) and join, being careful not to twist sts. Work edging of choice (see pages 35–37), then cont even until piece measures desired length to armhole, or about:

8½	9½	11	12½	14"
21.5	24	28	31.5	35.5 cm

ending last rnd the foll number of sts before marker:

3	2	2	2	2	2 sts.
4	3	3	3	3	3
5	4	4	4	4	4
6	4	4	4	4	4
7	5	5	5	5	5

Divide for Front and Back

*BO:

3	4	4	4	4	4 sts,
4	6	6	6	6	6
5	8	8	8	8	8
6	8	8	8	8	8
7	10	10	10	10	10

work until there are the foll number of sts after BO:

3	36	38	42	44	48 sts.
4	46	50	54	58	62
5	56	62	66	72	78
6	70	76	82	88	94
7	80	88	96	102	110

Rep from * once. There will rem the foll number of sts each for front and back:

3	36	38	42	44	48 sts.
4	46	50	54	58	62
5	56	62	66	72	78
6	70	76	82	88	94
7	80	88	96	102	110

Set aside.

Sleeves

With dpn, CO:

3	18	20	22	22	24 sts.
4	24	26	28	30	32
5	30	32	36	38	40
6	36	40	42	46	48
7	42	46	48	52	56

seamless yoke

Place m and join, being careful not to twist sts. Work edging of choice until piece measures desired length, or about:

1½	1½	1½	2	2"
3.8	3.8	3.8	5	5 cm

Change to St st and inc 1 st each side of marker every 4 rnds (if number is zero, omit these rnds):

3	0	0	0	0	0 time(s).
4	0	0	0	0	0
5	0	0	0	0	0
6	1	0	0	0	0
7	3	1	0	0	0

Then inc 1 st each side of marker every 6 rnds:

3	6	6	6	7	7 times.
4	7	8	8	8	9
5	9	10	9	10	11
6	10	11	12	12	13
7	10	12	15	15	16

There will be:

3	30	32	34	36	38 sts.
4	38	42	44	46	50
5	48	52	54	58	62
6	58	62	66	70	74
7	68	72	78	82	88

Work even if necessary until piece measures:

11½	12	13½	14¾	15½"
29	30.5	34.5	37.5	39.5 cm

from beg, or desired length to underarm, ending the foll number of sts before end-of-rnd marker:

3	2	2	2	2	2 sts.
4	3	3	3	3	3
5	4	4	4	4	4

6	4	4	4	4	4
7	5	5	5	5	5

BO:

3	4	4	4	4	4 sts,
4	6	6	6	6	6
5	8	8	8	8	8
6	8	8	8	8	8
7	10	10	10	10	10

work to end. There will remain:

3	26	28	30	32	34 sts.
4	32	36	38	40	44
5	40	44	46	50	54
6	50	54	58	62	66
7	58	62	68	72	78

Set aside. Make another sleeve to match.

Pullover Yoke

With RS facing, join all pieces as foll: Knit across:

3	26	28	30	32	34 sts
4	32	36	38	40	44
5	40	44	46	50	54
6	50	54	58	62	66
7	58	62	68	72	78

of left sleeve, pm, knit across:

3	36	38	42	44	48 sts
4	46	50	54	58	62
5	56	62	66	72	78
6	70	76	82	88	94
7	80	88	96	102	110

of front, pm, knit across:

3	26	28	30	32	34 sts
4	32	36	38	40	44
5	40	44	46	50	54

seamless yoke

Finished Chest Circumference

	26	28	30	32	34"
	66	71	76	81.5	86.5 cm

6	50	54	58	62	66
7	58	62	68	72	78

of right sleeve, pm, knit across:

3	36	38	42	44	48 sts
4	46	50	54	58	62
5	56	62	66	72	78
6	70	76	82	88	94
7	80	88	96	102	110

of back, pm for end of rnd.
There will be:

3	124	132	144	152	164 sts.
4	156	172	184	196	212
5	192	212	224	244	264
6	240	260	280	300	320
7	276	300	328	348	376

Shape Yoke

On the next rnd, dec the foll number of sts as evenly as possible, placing decs close to armholes where they will be less noticeable:

3	4	2	4	2	4 st(s).
4	1	2	4	1	2
5	2	2	4	4	4
6	0	0	0	0	0
7	1	0	3	3	1

There will remain:

3	120	130	140	150	160 sts.
4	155	170	180	195	210
5	190	210	220	240	260
6	240	260	280	300	320
7	275	300	325	345	375

Work even until yoke measures:

1½	1¾	2	2	2"
3.8	4.5	5	5	5 cm

Dec Rnd 1: *K3, k2tog; rep from *. There will remain:

3	96	104	112	120	128 sts.
4	124	136	144	156	168
5	152	168	176	192	208
6	192	208	224	240	256
7	220	240	260	276	300

Work even until yoke measures:

2¾	3¼	3¾	4	4"
7	8.5	9.5	10	10 cm

Dec Rnd 2: *K2, k2tog; rep from *. There will remain:

3	72	78	84	90	96 sts.
4	93	102	108	117	126
5	114	126	132	144	156
6	144	156	168	180	192
7	165	180	195	207	225

Work even until yoke measures:

4	4¾	5¼	5¾	6"
10	12	13.5	14.5	15 cm

Dec Rnd 3: *K1, k2tog; rep from *. There will remain:

3	48	52	56	60	64 sts.
4	62	68	72	78	84
5	76	84	88	96	104
6	96	104	112	120	128
7	110	120	130	138	150

Work even until yoke measures:

5¼	6¼	6¾	7¼	7¾"
13.5	16	17	18.5	19.5 cm

Shape Neck

To raise the back neck (and make a better-fitting sweater), work 2 short rows (see Glossary) as foll: Knit to the left shoulder line,

seamless yoke

wrap the next st, turn work around and purl to the right shoulder line, wrap the next st, turn work around and knit to about 1" (2.5 cm) before previous wrapped st, wrap the next st, turn and purl to about 1" (2.5 cm) from previous wrapped st, wrap the next st, turn, knit to end of rnd. Knit 1 rnd, working wraps tog with wrapped sts to hide the wraps.

Dec Rnd 4: *K1, k2tog; rep from * (if 1 st rem at end of rnd, work it as k1; if 2 sts rem at end of rnd, work them as k2tog). There will remain:

3	32	35	37	40	43 sts.
4	41	45	48	52	56
5	51	56	59	64	69
6	64	69	75	80	85
7	73	80	87	92	100

Neckband

Inc or dec sts if necessary to obtain a full multiple of the edging patt you've chosen. Work in chosen patt until neckband measures ¾" (2 cm), or desired length. BO all sts loosely in patt.

Finishing

Block to measurements. With yarn threaded on a tapestry needle, sew underarm seams. Weave in loose ends.

Cardigan Body

Work as for pullover, but do not join into a rnd (i.e., work the body sts back and forth in rows, with opening at center front) until piece measures desired length to armhole, or about:

8½	9½	11	12½	14"
21.5	24	28	31.5	35.5 cm

ending with a RS row.

Divide for Fronts and Back

With WS facing, purl across:

3	18	19	21	22	24 sts
4	23	25	27	29	31
5	28	31	33	36	39
6	35	38	41	44	47
7	40	44	48	51	55

for left front, BO:

3	4	4	4	4	4 sts
4	6	6	6	6	6
5	8	8	8	8	8
6	8	8	8	8	8
7	10	10	10	10	10

for left underarm, purl across:

3	36	38	42	44	48 sts
4	46	50	54	58	62
5	56	62	66	72	78
6	70	76	82	88	94
7	80	88	96	102	110

for back, BO:

3	4	4	4	4	4 sts
4	6	6	6	6	6
5	8	8	8	8	8
6	8	8	8	8	8
7	10	10	10	10	10

for right underarm, purl across:

3	18	19	21	22	24 sts
4	23	25	27	29	31
5	28	31	33	36	39
6	35	38	41	44	47
7	40	44	48	51	55

for right front. Set aside.

Sleeves

Work sleeves as for pullover version.

Cardigan Yoke

Join all pieces as foll:

With RS facing, knit across:

3	18	19	21	22	24 sts
4	23	25	27	29	31
5	28	31	33	36	39
6	35	38	41	44	47
7	40	44	48	51	55

of right front, pm, knit across:

3	26	28	30	32	34 sts
4	32	36	38	40	44
5	40	44	46	50	54
6	50	54	58	62	66
7	58	62	68	72	78

of right sleeve, pm, knit across:

3	36	38	42	44	48 sts
4	46	50	54	58	62
5	56	62	66	72	78
6	70	76	82	88	94
7	80	88	96	102	110

of back, pm, knit across:

3	26	28	30	32	34 sts
4	32	36	38	40	44
5	40	44	46	50	54
6	50	54	58	62	66
7	58	62	68	72	78

of left sleeve, pm, knit across:

3	18	19	21	22	24 sts
4	23	25	27	29	31
5	28	31	33	36	39
6	35	38	41	44	47
7	40	44	48	51	55

of left front. There will be:

3	124	132	144	152	164 sts.
4	156	172	184	196	212
5	192	212	224	244	264
6	240	260	280	300	320
7	276	300	328	348	376

Shape Yoke

Work as for pullover version (page 177), working back and forth in rows and working dec rows on RS.

Finishing

Block to measurements. With yarn threaded on a tapestry needle, sew underarm seams.

Button band: (on left front for females; right front for males) With smaller needles and RS facing, pick up and knit about 3 sts for every 4 rows along center front edge. Adjust st count if necessary to achieve a full multiple of the edging pattern you've chosen. Work in chosen pattern until band measures ¾" (2 cm). BO all sts in patt. Mark placement of desired number of buttons, one ½" (1.3 cm) up from CO edge, one ½" (1.3 cm) down from BO edge, and the others evenly spaced in between.

Buttonhole band: (on right front for females; left front for males) Work as for button band, working one-row buttonholes (see Glossary) opposite markers when band measures between ¼" and ½" (.6 and 1.3 cm). BO all sts in patt.

Weave in loose ends. Sew buttons to button band opposite buttonholes. Block again, if desired.

seamless yoke

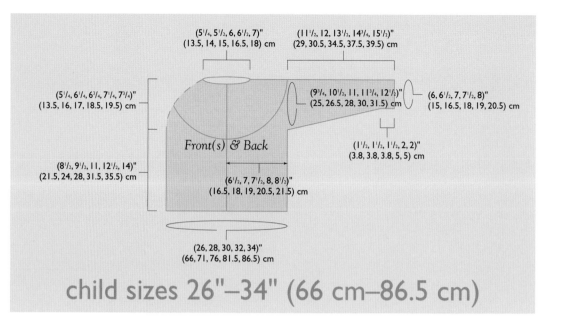

(5¼, 5½, 6, 6½, 7)"
(13.5, 14, 15, 16.5, 18) cm

(11½, 12, 13½, 14¾, 15½)"
(29, 30.5, 34.5, 37.5, 39.5) cm

(5¼, 6¼, 6¾, 7¼, 7¾)"
(13.5, 16, 17, 18.5, 19.5) cm

(9¾, 10½, 11, 11¾, 12½)"
(25, 26.5, 28, 30, 31.5) cm

(6, 6½, 7, 7½, 8)"
(15, 16.5, 18, 19, 20.5) cm

Front(s) & Back

(1½, 1½, 1½, 2, 2)"
(3.8, 3.8, 3.8, 5, 5) cm

(8½, 9½, 11, 12½, 14)"
(21.5, 24, 28, 31.5, 35.5) cm

(6½, 7, 7½, 8, 8½)"
(16.5, 18, 19, 20.5, 21.5) cm

(26, 28, 30, 32, 34)"
(66, 71, 76, 81.5, 86.5) cm

child sizes 26"–34" (66 cm–86.5 cm)

quicktips for flawless color and texture patterns

- Check out the many reference books on stitch patterns to find an interesting allover pattern or edging to plug into the general instructions.

- Consider purchasing one more ball/skein of yarn than suggested for your size and gauge just to be sure you'll have enough, especially if you plan to add a texture pattern or make adjustments to the general instructions.

- If you want to add a stitch pattern that requires an odd number of stitches, add or subtract one stitch from the general instruction chart. Correct for the extra or missing stitch when it's time to bind off for the neck or sleeve cap.

- In a yoke sweater, plan the decrease rounds to cause as little interruption to the pattern as possible. For example, place a decrease round on a solid-color round of a color-work pattern.

- To compensate for the width lost from cable patterns drawing in, increase a stitch or two at the base of each cable column (see Cable Panel Pullover on page 59).

- When you're weaving in ends in a color-work pattern, weave the ends behind the matching color to keep them invisible on the public side of the work.

- When you're working a texture or color pattern, note the row of the pattern you're on when it's time to shape the armholes on the back. Then you can be sure to make the front match by starting the armhole shaping on the same row of the pattern.

seamless yoke

sizing adult

Finished Bust/Chest Circumference									
36	38	40	42	44	46	48	50	52	54"
91.5	96.5	101.5	106.5	112	117	122	127	132	137 cm

Yarn Requirements

GAUGE										
3	570	620	680	730	780	830	870	900	940	980 yd
	521	567	622	668	713	759	796	823	860	896 m
4	810	870	960	1040	1110	1180	1230	1280	1330	1380
	741	796	878	951	1015	1079	1125	1170	1216	1262
5	1020	1100	1210	1310	1400	1480	1550	1610	1680	1740
	933	1006	1106	1198	1280	1353	1417	1472	1536	1591
6	1440	1560	1710	1850	1970	2100	2190	2280	2380	2470
	1317	1426	1564	1692	1801	1920	2003	2085	2176	2259
7	1590	1710	1880	2030	2170	2310	2420	2510	2620	2710
	1454	1564	1719	1856	1984	2112	2213	2295	2396	2478

Pullover Body

With cir needle, CO:

3	108	116	120	128	132	140	144	152	156	164 sts.
4	144	152	160	168	176	184	192	200	208	216
5	180	188	200	212	220	232	240	252	260	272
6	216	228	240	252	264	276	288	300	312	324
7	252	268	280	296	308	324	336	352	364	380

Place marker (pm) and join, being careful not to twist sts. Work edging of choice (see pages 35–37), then cont even until piece measures desired length to armhole, or about:

14	14	14½	15¼	16	16¼	16½	16¾	17	17¼"
35.5	35.5	37	38.5	40.5	41.5	42	42.5	43	44 cm

ending last rnd the foll number of sts before marker:

3	3	3	3	3	3	4	4	4	4	4 sts.
4	4	4	4	4	4	6	6	6	6	6
5	5	5	5	5	5	7	7	7	7	7
6	6	6	6	6	6	9	9	9	9	9
7	7	7	7	7	7	10	10	10	10	10

Divide for Front and Back

*BO:

3	6	6	6	6	6	8	8	8	8	8 sts,
4	8	8	8	8	8	12	12	12	12	12
5	10	10	10	10	10	14	14	14	14	14
6	12	12	12	12	12	18	18	18	18	18
7	14	14	14	14	14	20	20	20	20	20

seamless yoke

	36	38	40	42	44	46	48	50	52	54"
	91.5	96.5	101.5	106.5	112	117	122	127	132	137 cm

work until there are the foll number of sts after BO:

3	48	52	54	58	60	62	64	68	70	74 sts,
4	64	68	72	76	80	80	84	88	92	96
5	80	84	90	96	100	102	106	112	116	122
6	96	102	108	114	120	120	126	132	138	144
7	112	120	126	134	140	142	148	156	162	170

rep from * once. There will rem the foll number of sts each for front and back:

3	48	52	54	58	60	62	64	68	70	74 sts.
4	64	68	72	76	80	80	84	88	92	96
5	80	84	90	96	100	102	106	112	116	122
6	96	102	108	114	120	120	126	132	138	144
7	112	120	126	134	140	142	148	156	162	170

Set aside.

Sleeves
With dpn, CO:

3	28	28	30	30	30	32	32	32	34	34 sts.
4	38	38	40	40	40	44	44	44	46	46
5	46	46	50	50	50	54	54	54	58	58
6	56	56	60	60	60	66	66	66	68	68
7	66	66	70	70	70	76	76	76	80	80

Place m and join, being careful not to twist sts. Work edging of choice until piece measures desired length from beg, or about 2½" (6.5 cm).

Change to St st and inc 1 st each side of marker every 4 rnds (if number is zero, omit these rnds):

3	0	0	0	0	0	0	0	0	0	0 times.
4	0	0	0	0	0	0	0	0	0	0
5	0	0	0	0	0	0	0	0	0	0
6	0	0	0	0	0	0	0	0	0	2
7	0	0	0	0	0	0	0	0	0	6

Then inc 1 st each side of marker every 6 rnds (if number is zero, omit these rnds):

3	0	0	0	0	0	0	2	4	3	6 times.
4	0	0	0	0	0	0	2	4	7	10
5	0	0	0	2	3	5	11	16	11	17
6	0	0	0	2	8	5	11	16	19	21
7	0	0	0	7	12	14	19	24	23	21

seamless yoke

Finished Bust/Chest Circumference

	36	38	40	42	44	46	48	50	52	54"
	91.5	96.5	101.5	106.5	112	117	122	127	132	137 cm

Then inc 1 st each side of marker every 8 rnds (if number is zero, omit these rnds):

	36	38	40	42	44	46	48	50	52	54"
3	6	7	7	8	9	9	8	7	8	6 time(s).
4	7	8	9	10	11	11	10	9	7	5
5	10	11	11	11	11	9	5	2	6	2
6	11	13	13	13	9	11	7	4	2	0
7	13	15	15	11	8	6	3	0	1	0

There will be:

	36	38	40	42	44	46	48	50	52	54"
3	40	42	44	46	48	50	52	54	56	58 sts.
4	52	54	58	60	62	66	68	70	74	76
5	66	68	72	76	78	82	86	90	92	96
6	78	82	86	90	94	98	102	106	110	114
7	92	96	100	106	110	116	120	124	128	134

Work even, if necessary, until piece measures:

	36	38	40	42	44	46	48	50	52	54"
	16¾	17¼	17¾	18½	19	19¾	20¼	20½	20½	20¾"
	42.5	44	45	47	48.5	50	51.5	52	52	52.5 cm

from beg, or desired length to underarm, ending the foll number of sts before end-of-rnd marker:

	36	38	40	42	44	46	48	50	52	54"
3	3	3	3	3	3	4	4	4	4	4 sts.
4	4	4	4	4	4	6	6	6	6	6
5	5	5	5	5	5	7	7	7	7	7
6	6	6	6	6	6	9	9	9	9	9
7	7	7	7	7	7	10	10	10	10	10

BO:

	36	38	40	42	44	46	48	50	52	54"
3	6	6	6	6	6	8	8	8	8	8 sts,
4	8	8	8	8	8	12	12	12	12	12
5	10	10	10	10	10	14	14	14	14	14
6	12	12	12	12	12	18	18	18	18	18
7	14	14	14	14	14	20	20	20	20	20

work to end. There will remain:

	36	38	40	42	44	46	48	50	52	54"
3	34	36	38	40	42	42	44	46	48	50 sts.
4	44	46	50	52	54	54	56	58	62	64
5	56	58	62	66	68	68	72	76	78	82
6	66	70	74	78	82	80	84	88	92	96
7	78	82	86	92	96	96	100	104	108	114

Set aside. Make another sleeve to match.

seamless yoke

Finished Bust/Chest Circumference

36	38	40	42	44	46	48	50	52	54"
91.5	96.5	101.5	106.5	112	117	122	127	132	137 cm

Pullover Yoke

With RS facing, join pieces as foll:

Knit across:

3	34	36	38	40	42	42	44	46	48	50 sts
4	44	46	50	52	54	54	56	58	62	64
5	56	58	62	66	68	68	72	76	78	82
6	66	70	74	78	82	80	84	88	92	96
7	78	82	86	92	96	96	100	104	108	114

of one sleeve, pm, knit across:

3	48	52	54	58	60	62	64	68	70	74 sts
4	64	68	72	76	80	80	84	88	92	96
5	80	84	90	96	100	102	106	112	116	122
6	96	102	108	114	120	120	126	132	138	144
7	112	120	126	134	140	142	148	156	162	170

of front, pm, knit across:

3	34	36	38	40	42	42	44	46	48	50 sts
4	44	46	50	52	54	54	56	58	62	64
5	56	58	62	66	68	68	72	76	78	82
6	66	70	74	78	82	80	84	88	92	96
7	78	82	86	92	96	96	100	104	108	114

of other sleeve, pm, knit across:

3	48	52	54	58	60	62	64	68	70	74 sts
4	64	68	72	76	80	80	84	88	92	96
5	80	84	90	96	100	102	106	112	116	122
6	96	102	108	114	120	120	126	132	138	144
7	112	120	126	134	140	142	148	156	162	170

of back, pm for end of rnd. There will be:

3	164	176	184	196	204	208	216	228	236	248 sts.
4	216	228	244	256	268	268	280	292	308	320
5	272	284	304	324	336	340	356	376	388	408
6	324	344	364	384	404	400	420	440	460	480
7	380	404	424	452	472	476	496	520	540	568

seamless yoke

Finished Bust/Chest Circumference

36	38	40	42	44	46	48	50	52	54"
91.5	96.5	101.5	106.5	112	117	122	127	132	137 cm

Shape Yoke

On the next rnd, dec the foll number of sts as evenly as possible, placing decs close to armholes where they will be less noticeable:

3	4	1	4	1	4	3	1	3	1	3 st(s).
4	1	3	4	1	3	3	0	2	3	0
5	2	4	4	4	1	0	1	1	3	3
6	4	4	4	4	4	0	0	0	0	0
7	0	4	4	2	2	1	1	0	0	3

There will rem:

3	160	175	180	195	200	205	215	225	235	245 sts.
4	215	225	240	255	265	265	280	290	305	320
5	270	280	300	320	335	340	355	375	385	405
6	320	340	360	380	400	400	420	440	460	480
7	380	400	420	450	470	475	495	520	540	565

Work even until yoke measures:

2	2¼	2¼	2½	2½	2½	2½	2½	2¾	2¾"
5	5.5	5.5	6.5	6.5	6.5	6.5	6.5	7	7 cm

Dec Rnd 1: *K3, k2tog; rep from *. There will remain:

3	128	140	144	156	160	164	172	180	188	196 sts.
4	172	180	192	204	212	212	224	232	244	256
5	216	224	240	256	268	272	284	300	308	324
6	256	272	288	304	320	320	336	352	368	384
7	304	320	336	360	376	380	396	416	432	452

Work even until yoke measures:

4	4½	4½	4¾	5	5	5	5	5¼	5½"
10	11.5	11.5	12	12.5	12.5	12.5	12.5	13.5	14 cm

Dec Rnd 2: *K2, k2tog; rep from *. There will remain:

3	96	105	108	117	120	123	129	135	141	147 sts.
4	129	135	144	153	159	159	168	174	183	192
5	162	168	180	192	201	204	213	225	231	243
6	192	204	216	228	240	240	252	264	276	288
7	228	240	252	270	282	285	297	312	324	339

Finished Bust/Chest Circumference

36	38	40	42	44	46	48	50	52	54"
91.5	96.5	101.5	106.5	112	117	122	127	132	137 cm

Work even until yoke measures:

6	6½	6¾	7	7¼	7¼	7½	7½	7¾	8"
15	16.5	17	18	18.5	18.5	19	19	19.5	20.5 cm

Dec Rnd 3: *K1, k2tog; rep from *. There will remain:

3	64	70	72	78	80	82	86	90	94	98 sts.
4	86	90	96	102	106	106	112	116	122	128
5	108	112	120	128	134	136	142	150	154	162
6	128	136	144	152	160	160	168	176	184	192
7	152	160	168	180	188	190	198	208	216	226

Work even until yoke measures:

8	8½	9	9¼	9½	9½	9¾	10	10¼	10½"
20.5	21.5	23	23.5	24	24	25	25.5	26	26.5 cm

Shape Neck

To raise the back neck (and make a better-fitting sweater), work 2 or 3 short rows (see Glossary) as foll: Knit to the left shoulder line, wrap the next st, turn work around and purl to the right shoulder, wrap the next st, *turn work around and knit to about 1" (2.5 cm) before previous wrapped st, wrap the next st, turn and purl to about 1" (2.5 cm) before previous wrapped st, wrap the next st; rep from * if desired, turn, knit to end of rnd. Knit 1 rnd, working wraps tog with wrapped sts to hide the wraps.

Dec Rnd 4: *K1, k2tog; rep from * (if 1 st rem at end of rnd, work it as k1; if 2 sts rem, work them as k2tog). There will remain:

3	43	47	48	52	53	55	57	60	63	65 sts.
4	57	60	64	68	71	71	75	77	81	85
5	72	75	80	85	89	91	95	100	103	108
6	85	91	96	101	107	107	112	117	123	128
7	101	107	112	120	125	127	132	139	144	151

Neckband

Dec sts if necessary to obtain a full multiple of the edging patt you've chosen. Work in chosen patt until neckband measures 1" (2.5 cm), or desired length. BO all sts loosely in patt.

Finishing

Block to measurements. With yarn threaded on a tapestry needle, sew underarm seams. Weave in loose ends.

seamless yoke

Finished Bust/Chest Circumference									
36	38	40	42	44	46	48	50	52	54"
91.5	96.5	101.5	106.5	112	117	122	127	132	137 cm

Cardigan Body

Work as for pullover body, but do not join into a rnd (i.e., work the body sts back and forth in rows, with opening at center front) until piece measures desired length to armholes, or about:

14	14	14½	15¼	16	16¼	16½	16¾	17	17¼"
35.5	35.5	37	38.5	40.5	41.5	42	42.5	43	44 cm

ending with a RS row.

Divide for Fronts and Back

With WS facing, purl across:

3	24	26	27	29	30	31	32	34	35	37 sts
4	32	34	36	38	40	40	42	44	46	48
5	40	42	45	48	50	51	53	56	58	61
6	48	51	54	57	60	60	63	66	69	72
7	56	60	63	67	70	71	74	78	81	85

for left front, BO:

3	6	6	6	6	6	8	8	8	8	8 sts
4	8	8	8	8	8	12	12	12	12	12
5	10	10	10	10	10	14	14	14	14	14
6	12	12	12	12	12	18	18	18	18	18
7	14	14	14	14	14	20	20	20	20	20

for left underarm, purl across:

3	48	52	54	58	60	62	64	68	70	74 sts
4	64	68	72	76	80	80	84	88	92	96
5	80	84	90	96	100	102	106	112	116	122
6	96	102	108	114	120	120	126	132	138	144
7	112	120	126	134	140	142	148	156	162	170

for back, BO:

3	6	6	6	6	6	8	8	8	8	8 sts
4	8	8	8	8	8	12	12	12	12	12
5	10	10	10	10	10	14	14	14	14	14
6	12	12	12	12	12	18	18	18	18	18
7	14	14	14	14	14	20	20	20	20	20

for right underarm, purl across:

3	24	26	27	29	30	31	32	34	35	37 sts
4	32	34	36	38	40	40	42	44	46	48

seamless yoke

Finished Bust/Chest Circumference

| | 36 | 38 | 40 | 42 | 44 | 46 | 48 | 50 | 52 | 54" |
	91.5	96.5	101.5	106.5	112	117	122	127	132	137 cm
5	40	42	45	48	50	51	53	56	58	61
6	48	51	54	57	60	60	63	66	69	72
7	56	60	63	67	70	71	74	78	81	85

for right front. Set aside.

Sleeves
Work sleeves as for pullover version.

Cardigan Yoke
Join all pieces as foll:
With RS facing, knit across:

3	24	26	27	29	30	31	32	34	35	37 sts
4	32	34	36	38	40	40	42	44	46	48
5	40	42	45	48	50	51	53	56	58	61
6	48	51	54	57	60	60	63	66	69	72
7	56	60	63	67	70	71	74	78	81	85

of right front, pm, knit across:

3	34	36	38	40	42	42	44	46	48	50 sts
4	44	46	50	52	54	54	56	58	62	64
5	56	58	62	66	68	68	72	76	78	82
6	66	70	74	78	82	80	84	88	92	96
7	78	82	86	92	96	96	100	104	108	114

of right sleeve, pm, knit across:

3	48	52	54	58	60	62	64	68	70	74 sts
4	64	68	72	76	80	80	84	88	92	96
5	80	84	90	96	100	102	106	112	116	122
6	96	102	108	114	120	120	126	132	138	144
7	112	120	126	134	140	142	148	156	162	170

of back, pm, knit across:

3	34	36	38	40	42	42	44	46	48	50 sts
4	44	46	50	52	54	54	56	58	62	64
5	56	58	62	66	68	68	72	76	78	82
6	66	70	74	78	82	80	84	88	92	96
7	78	82	86	92	96	96	100	104	108	114

seamless
yoke

Finished Bust/Chest Circumference

	36	38	40	42	44	46	48	50	52	54"
	91.5	96.5	101.5	106.5	112	117	122	127	132	137 cm

of left sleeve, pm, knit across:

3	24	26	27	29	30	31	32	34	35	37 sts
4	32	34	36	38	40	40	42	44	46	48
5	40	42	45	48	50	51	53	56	58	61
6	48	51	54	57	60	60	63	66	69	72
7	56	60	63	67	70	71	74	78	81	85

of left front. There will be:

3	164	176	184	196	204	208	216	228	236	248 sts.
4	216	228	244	256	268	268	280	292	308	320
5	272	284	304	324	336	340	356	376	388	408
6	324	344	364	384	404	400	420	440	460	480
7	380	404	424	452	472	476	496	520	540	568

Shape Yoke

Work as for pullover version (page 186), working back and forth in rows, and working dec rows on RS.

Finishing

Block to measurements. With yarn threaded on a tapestry needle, sew underarm seams.
Button band: (on left front for females; right front for males) With smaller needles and RS facing, pick up and knit about 3 sts for every 4 rows along center front edge. Adjust sts if necessary to achieve a full multiple of the edging pattern you've chosen. Work in chosen pattern until band measures 1" (2.5 cm). BO all sts in patt. Mark placement of desired number of buttons, one ½" (1.3 cm) up from CO edge, one ½" (1.3 cm) below BO edge, and the others evenly spaced in between.
Buttonhole band: (on right front for females; left front for males) Work as for button band, working one-row buttonholes (see Glossary) opposite markers when band measures about ½" (1.3 cm). BO all sts in patt.
Weave in loose ends. Sew buttons to button band opposite buttonholes. Block again, if desired.

seamless yoke

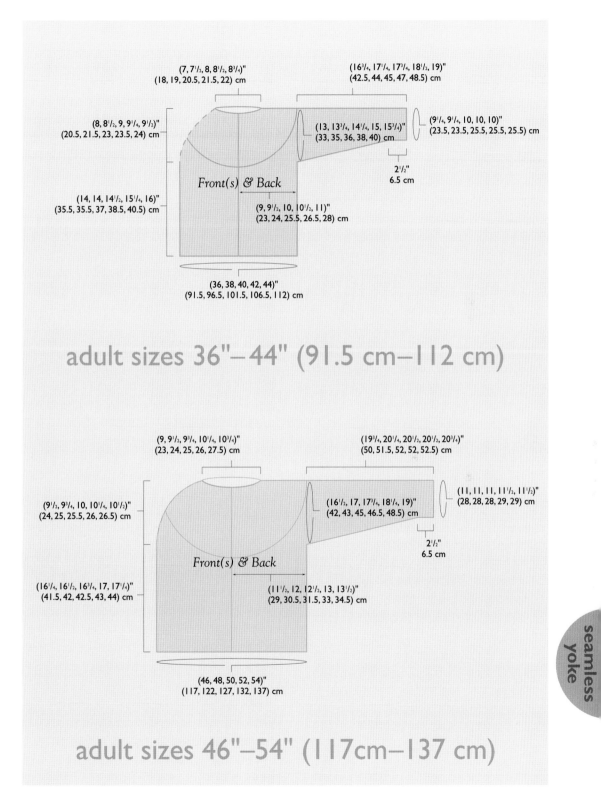

(7, 7½, 8, 8½, 8¾)"
(18, 19, 20.5, 21.5, 22) cm

(16¾, 17¼, 17¾, 18½, 19)"
(42.5, 44, 45, 47, 48.5) cm

(8, 8½, 9, 9¼, 9½)"
(20.5, 21.5, 23, 23.5, 24) cm

(13, 13¾, 14¼, 15, 15¾)"
(33, 35, 36, 38, 40) cm

(9¼, 9¼, 10, 10, 10)"
(23.5, 23.5, 25.5, 25.5, 25.5) cm

2½"
6.5 cm

Front(s) & Back

(14, 14, 14½, 15¼, 16)"
(35.5, 35.5, 37, 38.5, 40.5) cm

(9, 9½, 10, 10½, 11)"
(23, 24, 25.5, 26.5, 28) cm

(36, 38, 40, 42, 44)"
(91.5, 96.5, 101.5, 106.5, 112) cm

adult sizes 36"– 44" (91.5 cm–112 cm)

(9, 9½, 9¾, 10¼, 10¾)"
(23, 24, 25, 26, 27.5) cm

(19¾, 20¼, 20½, 20½, 20¾)"
(50, 51.5, 52, 52, 52.5) cm

(9½, 9¾, 10, 10¼, 10½)"
(24, 25, 25.5, 26, 26.5) cm

(16½, 17, 17¾, 18¼, 19)"
(42, 43, 45, 46.5, 48.5) cm

(11, 11, 11, 11½, 11½)"
(28, 28, 28, 29, 29) cm

2½"
6.5 cm

Front(s) & Back

(16¼, 16½, 16¾, 17, 17¼)"
(41.5, 42, 42.5, 43, 44) cm

(11½, 12, 12½, 13, 13½)"
(29, 30.5, 31.5, 33, 34.5) cm

(46, 48, 50, 52, 54)"
(117, 122, 127, 132, 137) cm

adult sizes 46"–54" (117cm–137 cm)

seamless
yoke

copycats

Child's Fair Isle Pullover

This pullover demonstrates how a color pattern can be worked without interruption on a yoke sweater knitted in the round. The colorwork pattern on the lower body and sleeves repeats over six stitches; the one on the yoke repeats over fifteen stitches, which fits evenly into the 150 yoke stitches of the 32" (81.5 cm) sweater at a gauge of 3 stitches/inch (see page 177). When planning a color-work pattern for a yoke sweater, check the instructions to see how many stitches there will be when the color-work pattern will begin, then choose a pattern that fits evenly

Finished Size: 32" (81.5 cm) chest circumference.
Yarn: Rowan Yorkshire Tweed Chunky (100% wool; 109 yd [100 m]/100 g): #553 pecan (dark orange; MC), 5 balls; #557 olive oil (olive), #556 flaming (burgundy), #554 stout (brown), 1 ball each. Yarn distributed by Westminster Fibers.
Needles: Size 11 (8 mm): 24" (60-cm) circular (cir) and set of 4 double-pointed (dpn). Adjust needle size if necessary to obtain the correct gauge.
Notions: Markers (m); tapestry needle.
Gauge: 3 sts and 5 rnds = 1" (2.5 cm) in stockinette stitch worked in the round on size 11 (8-mm) needles.

into that number. The play of colors against one another obscures the decreases—they are somewhat more noticeable in the decrease round that's worked halfway between the top of the color work and the neck.

Body

With MC and cir needle, CO 96 sts. Place marker (pm) and join, being careful not to twist sts. Work k1, p1 rib for 2 rnds. Change to St st and work 3 rnds even. Work Rnds 1–3 of Lower Body and Cuff chart. Cont in MC until piece measures 12½" (31.5 cm) from beg, ending last rnd 2 sts before marker. *Divide for front and back*: BO 4 sts for left underarm, knit until there are 44 sts after BO for front, BO 4 sts for other underarm, work to end for back—44 sts each for front and back. Set aside.

Sleeves

With MC and dpn, CO 22 sts. Place m and join, being careful not to twist sts. Work k1, p1 rib for 2 rnds. Change to St st and work 3 rnds even, inc 2 sts in last rnd—24 sts. Work Rnd 1–3 of Lower Body and Cuff chart. Cont in MC, and at the same time inc 1 st each side of marker ever 6 rnds 6 times—36 sts. Cont even until piece measures 14¾" (37.5 cm) from beg, ending last rnd 2 sts before marker. BO 4 sts, work to end—32 sts rem. Set aside. Make another sleeve to match.

Yoke

With MC and cir needle holding body sts, beg between back and front, k32 sleeve sts, pm, k44 front sts, pm, k32 sleeve sts, pm, k44 back sts, pm, and join—152 sts. Rnd begins at back left armhole. *Next rnd:* Dec 2 sts (place 1 dec close to each armhole)—150 sts rem. Work 6 rnds even. Work Rnds 1–37 of Yoke chart, working decs as indicated as foll: Work in patt until piece measures 2" (5 cm) from joining rnd. *Dec Rnd 1:* (Rnd 11 of chart) *K3, k2tog; rep from *—120 sts rem. Cont in patt until piece measures 4" (10 cm) from joining rnd. *Dec Rnd 2:* (Rnd 21 of chart) *K2, k2tog; rep from *—90 sts rem. Cont through Rnd 24 of chart, then cont in MC only until yoke measures 5¾" (14.5 cm) from joining rnd. *Dec Rnd 3:* (Rnd 30 of chart) *K1, k2tog; rep from *—60 sts rem. Cont even until yoke measures 7¼" (18.5 cm) from joining rnd (Rnd 35 of chart). **Shape back neck:** To raise the back neck (and make a better-fitting sweater), work 2 short rows (see Glossary) as foll: *Short-row 1:* With RS facing, knit to shoulder line, wrap the next st, turn work around and purl to opposite shoulder line, wrap the next st, and turn work around. *Short-row 2:* With RS facing, knit to about 1" (2.5 cm) before previous wrapped st, wrap the next st, turn, purl to about 1" (2.5 cm) from previous wrapped st, wrap the next st, turn, knit to end of rnd. Knit 1 rnd (Rnd 36 of chart), working wraps tog with wrapped sts to hide the wraps. *Dec Rnd 4:* (Rnd 37 of chart) *K1, k2tog; rep from *—40 sts rem. **Neckband:** Work k1, p1 rib for 3 rnds. BO all sts in rib.

Finishing

Block to measurements. With yarn threaded on a tapestry needle, sew underarm seams. Weave in loose ends. Block again if desired.

Yoke

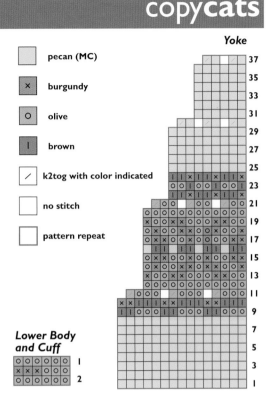

- ☐ pecan (MC)
- ☒ burgundy
- ○ olive
- Ⅰ brown
- ╱ k2tog with color indicated
- ☐ no stitch
- ☐ pattern repeat

Lower Body and Cuff

Chenille Yoke Cardigan

To demonstrate how the charts in this book can be used for additional gauges, this sweater was worked at a gauge of 4½ stitches to the inch, for which there is no listing. However, it's a simple matter of multiplying the gauge (4.5) by the desired chest circumference (40" [101.5 cm]) to determine the number of stitches needed: 4.5 stitches/inch × 40 inches = 180 stitches. A quick perusal of the chart on page 181 shows that a sweater with a 36" (91.5 cm) circumference worked at a gauge of 5 stitches to the inch requires 180 stitches for the body.

copy**cats**

Therefore, it is possible to follow the stitch instructions for the 36" sweater at 5 stitches per inch (first column; third row) and end up with a 40" sweater (third column) at a gauge of 4½ stitches per inch. However, to keep the length measurements consistent with the 40" sweater, follow the third column for the lengths; follow the first column for numbers of stitches.

To maintain a consistent direction of nap on the chenille yarn, lifted increases (working into the stitch below the stitch on the needle) are used to shape the sleeves. The yoke patterning of uneven bands of stockinette and reverse stockinette stitch camouflages the decreases. A simple single-crochet edging is worked around the edges, keeping the sweater from pulling in at the hips, neck, and cuffs.

Finished Size: 40" (101.5 cm) bust/chest circumference, buttoned.
Yarn: Rowan Chunky Cotton Chenille (100% cotton; 153 yd [140 m]/100 g): #390 spook (olive), 6 balls. Yarn distributed by Westminster Fibers.
Needles: Size 4 (3.5 mm): 24" (60-cm) circular (cir) and set of 4 double-pointed (dpn). Adjust needle size if necessary to obtain the correct gauge.
Notions: Marker (m); tapestry needle; size F/5 (3.75-mm) crochet hook; seven ⅝" (1.5-cm) buttons.
Gauge: 4½ stitches and 6½ rows = 1" (2.5 cm) in stockinette stitch on size 4 (3.5-mm) needles.

Yoke Pattern:
Rows 1 and 2: Rev St st (purl on RS; knit on WS).
Rows 3 and 4: St st (knit on RS; purl on WS).
Rows 5–9: Rev St st.
Rows 10–12: St st.
Rows 13 and 14: Rev St st.
Rows 15–17: Garter st (knit every row).
Rows 18–20: St st.
Rows 21–24: Rev St st.
Rows 25–27: Garter st.
Row 28: Purl.
Rows 29–31: Rev St st.
Rows 32 and 33: Purl.
Rows 34 and 35: Knit.
Rows 36–38: Purl.
Rows 39–41: St st.
Row 42: Knit.
Rows 43–46: Purl.
Row 47: Knit.
Rows 48–51: Rev St st.
Rows 52–54: St st.
Row 55: Purl.
Row 56–58: Knit.
Rows 59 and 60: Rev St st.

Body
With cir needle, *loosely* CO 180 sts. Do not join. Work St st until piece measures 14½" (37 cm) from beg, ending with a WS row. **Divide for front and back**: (RS) K40 for right front, BO 10 sts for right underarm, knit until there are 80 sts for back after BO, BO 10 sts for left underarm, knit to end for left front—40 sts for each front; 80 sts for back. Set aside.

Sleeves

With dpn, *loosely* CO 46 sts. Place marker (pm) and join, being careful not to twist sts. Work St st, and *at the same time* use the lifted method (see Glossary) to inc 1 st each side of marker every 8 rnds 10 times—66 sts. Cont even until piece measures 17¾" (45 cm) from beg, ending last rnd 5 sts before marker. BO 10 sts, knit to end—56 sts rem. Set aside. Rep for other sleeve.

Yoke

With cir needle holding body sts and RS facing, k40 front sts, pm, k56 sleeve sts, pm, k80 back sts, pm, k56 sleeve sts, pm, k40 front sts—272 sts. On the next row, dec 2 sts (place 1 dec close to each armhole where they won't be noticeable)—270 sts rem. Beg with Row 1, work through Row 60 of yoke patt, and *at the same time* work 4 dec rows as foll: When yoke measures 2¼" (5.5 cm) from joining row, work *Dec Row 1:* *Work 3 sts, work 2 sts tog; rep from *—216 sts rem. When yoke measures 4½" (11.5 cm) from joining row, work *Dec Row 2:* *Work 2 sts, work 2 sts tog; rep from *—162 sts rem. When yoke measures 6¾" (17 cm) from joining row, work *Dec Row 3:* *Work 1 st, work 2 sts tog; rep from *—108 sts rem. Cont to end of yoke patt, then work St st even, if necessary, until yoke measures 9" (23 cm) from joining row, ending with a WS row. *Shape back neck:* To raise the back neck (and make a better-fitting sweater) work 2 short rows as foll (see Glossary): *Short-row 1:* Knit to left shoulder line, wrap the next st, turn work around and purl to right shoulder line, wrap the next st, turn. *Short-row 2:* Knit to 5 sts before previous wrapped st, wrap the next st, turn, purl to 5 sts before previous wrapped st, wrap the next st, turn, knit to end of row. Knit 1 (WS) row, hiding wraps by working them tog with wrapped sts. *Dec Row 4:* *K1, k2tog; rep from *—72 sts rem. *Loosely* BO all sts.

Finishing

Block pieces to measurements. With yarn threaded on a tapestry needle, sew underarm seams. **Lower edging**: With crochet hook, RS facing, and beg at lower left front, work 1 row single crochet (see Glossary) around entire lower edge, keeping an eye on tension so that edging lays flat. Fasten off. **Neck edging**: With crochet hook, RS facing, and beg at right front neck edge, work 1 row single crochet around neck opening. Fasten off. **Button band**: With crochet hook, RS facing, and beg at left front neck edge, work 1 row single crochet along left front, ch 2, turn, work 1 sc into each sc of previous row, ch 2, turn, work 1 sc into each sc of previous row—3 rows of sc total. Fasten off. Mark placement of 7 buttons on button band, one ½" (1.3 cm) down from neck edge, one ½" (1.3 cm) up from lower edge, and the others evenly spaced in between. **Buttonhole band:** Work as button band, but on second row of sc, work buttonholes opposite markers as foll: ch 2, skip 2 sc. Weave in loose ends. Sew buttons to button band opposite buttonholes. Block again if desired.

Cabled Yoke Pullover

The cable pattern is uninterrupted in the yoke of this seamless pullover. To prevent excessive draw-in of the cables, an extra stitch is added at the base of each cable pair. The sequence of decreases on each decrease round is adjusted slightly to maintain the continuity of the cables. Garter ribs at the lower body and sleeves prevent rolling without pulling in. The back neck is raised with short rows, a somewhat tricky endeavor because to maintain pattern continuity, some of the cable twists need to be made on wrong-side rows.

Finished Size: 40" (101.5 cm) bust/chest circumference.
Yarn: Rowan Yorkshire Tweed Aran (100% wool; 175 yd [160 m]/100 g): #415 maze (dark teal), 6 balls. Yarn distributed by Westminster Fibers.
Needles: Size 10 (6 mm): 24" (60-cm) circular (cir) and set of 4 double-pointed (dpn). Adjust needle size if necessary to obtain the correct gauge.
Notions: Marker (m); tapestry needle.
Gauge: 4 sts and 7 rnds = 1" (2.5 cm) in stockinette stitch worked in the round on size 10 (6-mm) needles.

Body

With cir needle, CO 160 sts. Place marker (pm) and join, being careful not to twist sts. Work garter st (purl 1 rnd, knit 1 rnd) until piece measures 1" (2.5 cm) from beg. Change to St st and work even until piece measures 14½" (37 cm) from beg, ending 4 sts before marker. **Divide for front and back**: BO 8 sts for left underarm, knit until there are 72 sts on needle for front after BO, BO 8 sts for right underarm, knit to end for back—72 sts each for front and back. Set aside.

Sleeves

With dpn, CO 40 sts. Place m and join, being careful not to twist sts. Work garter st until piece measures 1" (2.5 cm) from beg. Change to St st and work even until piece measures 2½" (6.5 cm) from beg. Inc 1 st each side of marker on next rnd, then every 8 rnds 8 more times—58 sts. Cont even until piece measures 17¾" (45 cm) from beg, ending 4 sts before marker. BO 8 sts, work to end—50 sts rem. Set aside. Make another sleeve to match.

Yoke

With cir needle holding body sts, beg between back and front, k50 left sleeve sts, k72 front sts, k50 right sleeve sts, k72 back sts, pm, and join—244 sts total. Rnd begins at back left armhole. *Next rnd*: Knit, dec 1 st at each side of each armhole—4 sts dec'd; 240 sts rem. Work even in St st until piece measures 1" (2.5 cm) from joining rnd. *Set-up rnd*: K5, M1 (see Glossary), *k10, M1; rep from *, end last rep k5—264 sts (240 sts + 24 sts inc'd for cables). Beg with Rnd 1, work 11-st repeat of Yoke chart 24 times around. Cont as charted until piece measures 2¼" (5.5 cm) from joining rnd, ending with a cable rnd (Rnd 9 of chart). *Dec Rnd 1*: (Rnd 10 of chart) *K2, ssk, k4, k2tog, k1; rep from *—216 sts rem; 5 garter sts between cables. Cont in patt until piece measures 4½" (11.5 cm) from joining rnd, ending with a cable rnd (Rnd 25 of chart). *Dec Rnd 2:* (Rnd 26 of chart) *K1, ssk, k4, k2tog; rep from *—168 sts rem; 3 garter sts between cables. Cont in patt until piece measures 6¾" (17 cm) from joining rnd, ending with a cable rnd (Rnd 41 of chart). *Dec Rnd 3:* (Rnd 42 of chart) *K1, ssk, k2, k2tog; rep from *—120 sts rem; 1 garter st between cables. Cont in patt until piece measures 9" (23 cm) from joining rnd, ending with Rnd 57 of chart. **Shape back neck:** Keeping in patt as much as possible, work 3 short rows (see Glossary) as foll: *Short-row 1:* Work 15 sts to shoulder line, wrap next st and turn; with WS facing work 15 sts to beg-of-rnd m, sl m, work 44 sts to opposite shoulder line, wrap next st and turn. *Short-row 2:* With RS facing work 44 sts to marker, sl m, work 10 sts, wrap next st and turn; with WS facing work 10 sts to m, sl m, work 39 sts, wrap next st and turn. *Short-row 3:* With RS facing, work 39 sts to m, sl m, work 5 sts, wrap next st and turn; with WS facing, work 5 sts to m, sl m, work 34 sts, wrap next st and turn. Work to beg-of-rnd m. *Dec Rnd 4:* (Rnd 58 of chart) *K1, ssk, k2tog; rep from *, hiding any wraps—72 sts rem. Cont as charted until piece measures 1½" (3.8 cm) from last dec rnd, ending with a non-cable rnd (Rnd 68 of chart). BO all sts, and *at the same time* dec 1 st in each cable by working each pair of cable sts as ssk.

Finishing

Block to measurements. With yarn threaded on a tapestry needle, sew underarm seams. Weave in loose ends. Block again if desired.

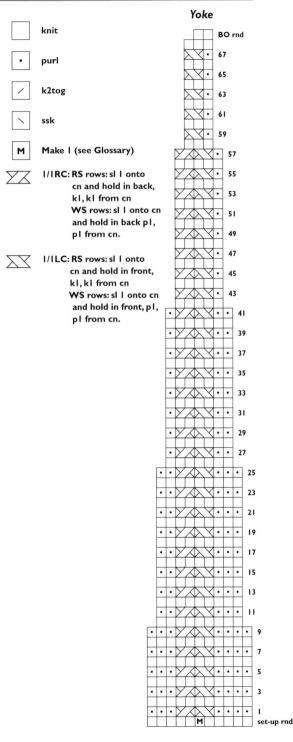

Yoke

□ knit

• purl

╱ k2tog

╲ ssk

M Make 1 (see Glossary)

1/1RC: **RS rows:** sl 1 onto cn and hold in back, k1, k1 from cn
WS rows: sl 1 onto cn and hold in back pl, p1 from cn.

1/1LC: **RS rows:** sl 1 onto cn and hold in front, k1, k1 from cn
WS rows: sl 1 onto cn and hold in front, p1, p1 from cn.

expanding your options

With fifteen sizes and five gauges provided for each of the six sweater styles in this book, you have 450 sets of instructions. Still, that may not be enough. You may want to adjust one of the sweaters to give it a cropped or tunic length. You may want to accommodate a favorite stitch or color pattern. You may fall in love with a yarn that knits up at a gauge that isn't provided here, or you may want to work one of the sweaters (other than the raglan or seamless yoke styles given here) in the round. The following guidelines will help you make these changes with confidence.

Adjusting Body or Sleeve Length

One of the simplest ways to change the look of a sweater is to adjust the body or sleeve length. You can change the overall length of a sweater body by adding or subtracting rows between the lower edge and armholes; the length of the armhole, and consequently the armhole shaping, is unaffected. If you want to lengthen a sweater, work more rows (i.e., inches) before you shape the armholes. To shorten a sweater, work fewer rows. Keep in mind, however, that such changes will affect the amount of yarn you'll need.

Adjustments to sleeve length can be less straightforward. Sleeves taper from the underarms to the cuffs and reflect the natural shape of the arm, which is wider at the bicep than the wrist. This shaping is achieved through regularly spaced increases, for sleeves worked from the bottom up (as in this book). The spacing of the increases is based on the sleeve length from cuff to underarm. If you wish to lengthen a sleeve, you can follow the instructions as written, but add rows in the upper part of the sleeve (at the maximum width) for the desired additional length. If you want to shorten sleeves, you'll need to recalculate the rate of increase based on your desired sleeve length. Doing so is not as difficult as it may seem. Simply use your row gauge to figure out how many rows there will be in your revised length, then divide that number by the number of increase rows you'll have to work to end up with the appropriate new spacing for increase rows.

For example, let's say you want to make a 36" set-in-sleeve sweater at a gauge of 6 stitches/inch, but you want to shorten the sleeve to just 14", instead of the 16" length specified by the chart that begins on page 81 (see the schematic on page 96). Let's also say you're knitting at a gauge of 8 rows per inch. It follows that in 14", you would have $8 \times 14 = 112$ rows in which to work all the

increases for the shaping (assuming you don't plan on working a cuff for part of this distance). Most designers like to end the shaping at least 1" before the underarm, so you'll want to subtract 8 rows from the 112 total, for an adjusted length of 104 rows. (Likewise, if you want to add a cuff, you'll want to subtract the number of rows in the cuff from this number as well.) According to the sleeve instructions on pages 87–88, in 104 rows you'll need to go from 56 stitches to 94 stitches, or a difference of 38 stitches. Sleeve shaping is worked in pairs, one stitch increased at each end of the needle on every shaping, or increase, row. Therefore, we know that there will be 38 ÷ 2 = 19 increase rows. This means that in 112 rows, 19 of them—will involve increases. To space the increase rows evenly, divide the total number of rows in the sleeve by the number of increase rows. In our case, 104 ÷ 19 = 5.47 rows. In other words, you'll want to work the increases about every 5½ rows. Half rows are difficult to work with in knitting, so to simplify things, work half the increase rows at 5-row increments and the other half at 6-row increments. If you prefer to work increases on right-side rows only, work half every 4 rows, and the other half every 6 rows.

You can use the same principle to make a short or three-quarter-length sleeve, as in the Cropped Cardigan on page 99. Measure the circumference of the arm where you want the sleeve to end, then multiply this circumference (allowing the desired amount of ease) by your stitch gauge. Doing so will give you the number of stitches to begin with. The sleeves on the Cropped Cardigan are 3" shorter than specified on the

schematic on page 96. Instead of casting on 56 stitches for a 9¼" circumference, you'll begin the sleeve with 62 stitches for a 10¼" circumference; instead of 19 increase rows worked over 16", you'll work only 16 increase rows over 13".

Adding Stitch or Color Patterns

The charted instructions in this book are intentionally simple; there is little interruption in the way of shaping. The purpose for this approach is twofold: First, the patterns are easy to follow; second, each pattern can be looked at as a blank canvas on which to add your own design.

As long as your gauge matches one of the five gauges specified for the projects in this book, you can work any project in any stitch or color pattern you choose—lace, Aran, or Fair Isle, to name a few. Just work out your gauge by knitting a swatch in the pattern you plan to use in the project; chances are that it will be significantly different from one worked in stockinette stitch. Be aware that textured patterns generally take up more yarn than stockinette stitch, so purchase extra yarn accordingly.

When you're planning a stitch or color pattern, take into account the number of stitches in a pattern repeat and the position of the pattern in relation to the overall dimensions of the knitted piece. If possible, choose a stitch or color pattern that fits into the body of the piece a whole number of times. Your sweater will have a more polished and professional look if there are no partial repeats at the side seams. For example, if the back of your sweater has 96 stitches, you'll want to use a pattern that repeats over a number of stitches that fits evenly into this number, such as 4, 8, or 12 stitches. To prevent the pattern from being interrupted at the side seam, cast on an extra stitch (called a seam stitch or selvedge stitch) at each end of the needle. When you sew the seams, these extra stitches will form the seam allowance. Seam stitches are not necessary for projects worked in the round, which have no seams.

Most stitch or color patterns, except very small ones that repeat over just a few stitches, look best centered on the front, back, and sleeves. Align the focal point of the pattern, such as a cable, with the center stitch on the needles. In general, an odd number of repeats appears more interesting to the eye—for example, group cables in sets of three, five, or seven (see the Cable Panel Pullover on page 59 and the Diamond Cable Pullover on page 136).

Be aware that stitch and color patterns will be interrupted by the shaping of a piece in such places as armholes, necks, and shoulders. Ideally, you'll want to plan ahead so that these interruptions fall at convenient points in the pattern repeat, both vertically and horizontally. For example, a mismatched pattern at the shoulder will make the shoulder seams more conspicuous. To make a "seamless" transition, plan the pattern so that the last row of the repeat is worked just before the shoulder bind-off, or so that half a repeat falls on the back of the shoulder seam and half falls on the front. The best way to tell that a pattern will be centered both horizontally and vertically is to chart it out on graph paper, along with the outline of the garment.

Sometimes you may want to adjust the number of stitches you work with in order to center a stitch or color pattern. For example, all the sweaters in this book are designed to have an even number of stitches across both the front and back. If you choose a stitch or color pattern with an odd-number of stitches in the repeat, you'll either be left with an extra stitch on one side, or the last pattern repeat will be one stitch short of completion. You can work the pattern according to the chart and have a slight distortion of the pattern at one side seam. Or you can simply add or subtract a stitch from the total to give the odd number of stitches that fits your chosen pattern-multiple. If you do so, keep the same number of stitches at the shoulders and adjust the number of stitches (plus or minus one stitch) in the width of the neck opening.

Adjusting for a Different Gauge
All the instructions in this book are written for gauges in whole numbers—3, 4, 5, etc. But if you use the schematics provided, it's a simple matter to adjust these instructions for gauges that fall between.

Let's say you want to knit a sweater with a 40" circumference at a gauge of $4\frac{1}{2}$ stitches to the inch. The gauge tells us that each inch of knitting will require $4\frac{1}{2}$ stitches. It follows that 40" of knitting will require 40 times that number: $40 \times 4\frac{1}{2} = 180$ stitches. If you use the schematics provided to determine the finished width of the upper body, neck, shoulders, etc., and multiply these numbers by the gauge you want, you can calculate the number of stitches to use, then adjust any shaping increases or decreases to correspond.

Another simpler option is to look at the other sizes on the chart. The calculation above tells us that at a gauge of 4½ stitches to the inch, the size for a 40" chest requires 180 stitches. A quick perusal of the chart on page 181 shows that 180 stitches are required for a sweater with a 36" circumference worked at a gauge of 5 stitches to the inch. If you follow the stitch requirements for the 36" size and the length measurements for the 40" size, you'll end up with the proper fit without any additional calculations. This is how the Chenille Yoke Cardigan on page 193 was worked.

Adjusting for Knitting in the Round

Some knitters dislike sewing seams and will go to great lengths to avoid doing so. I've met knitters who have multiple projects in their knitting baskets, just waiting to be sewn together. This book's raglan and seamless yoke sweaters, both worked in the round, are ideal for these knitters, and a number of other books explain how to work additional sweater styles in the round.

The body of any pullover sweater can be worked in the round. Simply use circular needles to cast on stitches for the back and front at the same time, then join the stitches into a round and knit a tube to the armholes. Likewise, the sleeves can be worked in the round to the underarms. At the armholes you have two choices for working the back and front. For some knitters the simplest option is to bind off stitches for the underarms and work the back and front separately (back and forth) to the shoulders. If you choose this method, be sure that you get the same gauge when working back and forth as when working in the round. Some knitters (like me) knit tighter than they purl, others may purl tighter than they knit, so much so that there is a noticeable difference in the fabric below the armholes (where every stitch is knitted) and the fabric above the armholes (where rows of knit stitches alternate with rows of purl stitches). You can minimize this difference by using different needle sizes for the knit and purl rows when you switch to working in rows. For example, because my knit stitches are tighter than my purl stitches, my stockinette-stitch fabric worked in rows can have a striped appearance. However, if I use a needle one-size smaller for my purl rows, the stitches are all the same size.

Another option is to work a steek (extra stitches that are not considered part of the pattern) where you want an opening. After the knitting is complete, secure the stitches on either side of the steek with machine stitching and cut the knitted fabric open. For many, the idea of cutting their knitting falls somewhere between intimidating and terrifying. However, there are many good resources—particularly books on Nordic or Fair Isle knitting in which steeks are the norm—that break the process down into manageable, sensible steps.

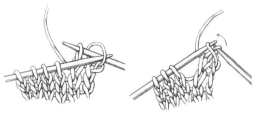

glossary

Figure 1   *Figure 2*

Figure 3

Bind-Offs

Standard Bind-Off

Slip one stitch, *knit one stitch, insert left needle tip into first stitch on right needle (Figure 1), pass this stitch over the second stitch (Figure 2), and off the needle—one stitch remains on right needle and one stitch has been bound off (Figure 3). Repeat from *.

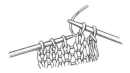

Figure 1   *Figure 2*

Figure 3

Suspended Bind-Off

This method produces a very elastic edge. Slip one stitch, knit one stitch, *insert left needle tip into first stitch on right needle and lift the first stitch over the second (Figure 1), leaving the first stitch on the left needle, knit the next stitch (Figure 2), then slip both stitches off the left needle—two stitches remain on right needle and one stitch has been bound off (Figure 3). Repeat from * until no stitches remain on left needle, then pass first stitch on right needle over the second.

Three-Needle Bind-Off

Place stitches to be joined onto two separate needles. Hold the needles so that right sides of knitting face together. *Insert a third needle into first stitch on each of the other two needles (Figure 1) and knit them together as one stitch (Figure 2), knit the next stitch on each needle together in the same way, then pass the first stitch over the second (Figure 3). Repeat from * until one stitch remains on third needle. Cut yarn and pull tail through last stitch.

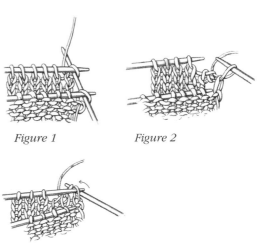

Figure 1   Figure 2

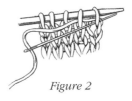

Figure 3

Sewn Bind-Off

Cut yarn three times the width of the knitting to be bound off, and thread onto a tapestry needle. Working from right to left, *insert tapestry needle purlwise (from right to left) through first two stitches (Figure 1) and pull yarn through. Bring tapestry needle knitwise (from left to right) through first stitch (Figure 2), pull yarn through, and slip this stitch off knitting needle. Repeat from *.

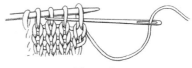

Figure 1

Figure 2

Buttonholes

Simple 2-Stitch Buttonhole (yo, k2tog)

Work to where you want the buttonhole to be, yarnover, k2tog, work to end of row or to next buttonhole position. On next row, work the yo in pattern as an ordinary stitch to leave a small hole and complete the buttonhole.

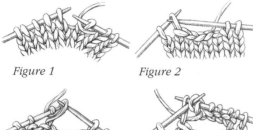

Figure 1   Figure 2

Figure 3   Figure 4

Figure 1   Figure 2

Figure 1   Figure 2

Figure 3   Figure 4

3 (4, 5)-Stitch One-Row Buttonhole

Work to where you want the buttonhole to begin, bring yarn to front, sl 1 purlwise, bring yarn to back (Figure 1). *Sl 1 purlwise, pass first slipped st over second; rep from * 2 (3, 4) more times. Place last st back on left needle (Figure 2), turn. CO 4 (5, 6) sts as foll: *Insert right needle between the first and second sts on left needle, draw up a loop, and place it on left needle (Figure 3); rep from * 3 (4, 5) more times, turn. Bring yarn to back, sl first st of left needle onto right needle and pass last CO st over it (Figure 4), work to end of row.

Crochet Chain Buttonhole

Work single crochet (sc) to where you want the buttonhole to begin, chain 2 or 3, depending on how big you want the buttonhole to be (Figure 1), skip a space equal to the length of the chain just worked (Figure 2), then continue working single crochet to next buttonhole position.

Cast-Ons

Continental (Long-Tail) Cast-On

Leaving a long tail (about ½" to 1" [1.3 to 2.5 cm] for each stitch to be cast on), make a slipknot and place on right needle. Place thumb and index finger between yarn ends so that the working yarn is around your index finger and the tail end is around your thumb. Secure the ends with your other fingers and hold palm upward, making a V of yarn (Figure 1). *Bring needle up through loop on thumb (Figure 2), grab first strand around index finger with needle, and go back down through loop on thumb (Figure 3), drop loop off thumb and, placing thumb back in V configuration, tighten resulting stitch on needle (Figure 4). Repeat from * for desired number of stitches.

Backward Loop Cast-On

*Loop working yarn and place on needle backward so that it doesn't unwind. Repeat from * for desired number of stitches.

Crochet Chain (Provisional) Cast-On

With waste yarn and crochet hook, make a loose crochet chain (see below) about four stitches more than you need to cast on. With needle, working yarn, and beginning two stitches from end of chain, pick up and knit one stitch through the back loop, or bump, of each crochet chain (Figure 1) for desired number of stitches. When you're ready to work in the opposite direction, pull out the crochet chain to expose live stitches (Figure 2).

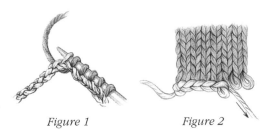

Figure 1   *Figure 2*

Invisible (Provisional) Cast-On

Place a loose slipknot on needle held in your right hand. Hold waste yarn next to slipknot and around your left thumb; hold working yarn over your left index finger. *Bring needle forward under waste yarn, over working yarn, grab a loop of working yarn (Figure 1), then bring needle to the front, over both yarns, and grab a second loop (Figure 2). Repeat from * for desired number of sts. When you're ready to work in the opposite direction, carefully remove waste yarn to expose live stitches.

Figure 1   *Figure 2*

Crochet

Crochet Chain (ch)

Make a slipknot and place on crochet hook. *Yarn over hook and draw it through loop on hook. Repeat from * for desired length. To fasten off, cut yarn and draw tail through last loop formed.

Figure 1   Figure 2

Single Crochet (sc)

Insert crochet hook into a stitch, yarn over hook and draw a loop through stitch, yarn over hook again (Figure 1), and draw it through both loops on hook (Figure 2). Repeat from * for desired length.

Decreases

K2tog

Knit two stitches together as if they were a single stitch—two stitches are reduced to one.

K3tog

Knit three stitches together as if they were a single stitch—three stitches are reduced to one.

Figure 1   Figure 2

Ssk

Slip two stitches individually knitwise (Figure 1). Insert tip of left needle into front of these two slipped stitches and use right needle to knit them together through their back loops (Figure 2). (Some knitters like to slip the second stitch purlwise to make a more prominent decrease line.)

Figure 1   Figure 2

Ssp

Holding yarn in front, slip two stitches knitwise, one at a time, onto right needle (Figure 1). Slip them back onto left needle and purl them together through their back loops (Figure 2).

Centered Double Decrease

Slip two stitches together knitwise (Figure 1), knit the next stitch (Figure 2), then pass the slipped stitches over the knitted stitch (Figure 3).

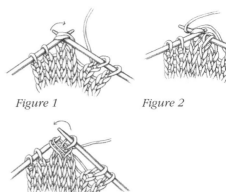

Figure 1   Figure 2

Figure 3

Grafting

Kitchener Stitch

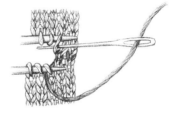

Place stitches to be joined onto two separate needles. Hold the needles parallel with points facing to the right and so that wrong sides of knitting are facing each other.

Step 1: Bring threaded needle through front stitch as if to purl and leave stitch on needle.

Step 2: Bring threaded needle through back stitch as if to knit and leave stitch on needle.

Step 3: Bring threaded needle through the same front stitch as if to knit and slip this stitch off needle, bring threaded needle through next front stitch as if to purl and leave stitch on needle.

Step 4: Bring threaded needle through first back stitch as if to purl (as illustrated), slip that stitch off, bring needle through next back stitch as if to knit, leave this stitch on needle.

Repeat Steps 3 and 4 until no stitches remain on needles.

I-Cord

Standard I-Cord

With double-pointed needle, cast on desired number of stitches (usually 3). *Without turning the needle, slide the stitches to the other point, pull yarn around the back, and knit the stitches as usual. Repeat from * for desired length.

Attached I-Cord

As I-cord is knitted, attach it to the garment as follows: With garment RS facing and using a separate ball of yarn and circular needle, pick up the desired number of stitches along the garment edge. Slide these stitches down the needle so that the first picked-up stitch is near the opposite needle point. With double-pointed needle, cast on desired number of I-cord stitches. *Knit across the I-cord to the last stitch, then knit the last stitch together with the first picked-up stitch on the garment, and pull the yarn behind the cord. Repeat from * until all picked-up stitches have been used.

Increases

Raised Increase (M1)

Unless otherwise indicated, work this increase as M1L.

Left Slant (M1L): With left needle tip, lift strand between needles from front to back (Figure 1). Knit the lifted loop through the back to twist the stitch (Figure 2).

Figure 1   *Figure 2*

Right Slant (M1R): With left needle tip, lift strand between needles from back to front (Figure 1). Knit the lifted loop through the front to twist the stitch (Figure 2).

Figure 1 *Figure 2*

Bar Increase (k1f&b)

Knit into a stitch and leave it on the needle (Figure 1), then knit through the back loop of the same stitch (Figure 2).

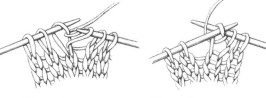

Figure 1 *Figure 2*

Lifted Increase

Left Slant: Knit into the back of the stitch (in the "purl bump") in the row directly below the stitch on the needle (Figure 1), then knit the stitch on the needle as usual (Figure 2).

Figure 1 *Figure 2*

Right Slant: Insert left needle tip into back of the stitch below the stitch just knitted (Figure 1), then knit into this loop (Figure 2).

Figure 1 *Figure 2*

Pick Up & Knit

Along Bind-Off or Cast-On Edges

With right side facing and working from right to left, insert the tip of the needle into the center of the stitch below the bind-off or cast-on edge (Figure 1), wrap yarn around needle, and pull it through (Figure 2). Pick up one stitch for every bound-off stitch.

Figure 1 *Figure 2*

Along Shaped Edges

With right side facing and working from right to left, insert tip of needle between last and second-to-last stitches, wrap yarn around needle, and pull it through. Pick up and knit about three stitches for every four rows, adjusting as necessary so that picked-up edge lays flat.

Figure 1

Figure 2

Figure 3

Seams

Invisible Vertical Seam

(Also called mattress stitch or ladder stitch.) With the right side of the knitting facing you, use a threaded needle to pick up one bar between the first two stitches on one piece (Figure 1), then the corresponding bar plus the bar above it on the other piece (Figure 2). *Pick up the next two bars on the first piece, then the next two bars on the other (Figure 3). Repeat from * to the end of the seam, finishing by picking up the last bar (or pair of bars) at the top of the first piece. To reduce bulk, pick up the bars in the center of the edge stitches instead of between the last two stitches. To prevent a half-row displacement at the seam, be sure to start the seam by picking up just one bar on the first side, then alternate two bars on each side.

Invisible Horizontal Seam

Working with the bound-off edges opposite each other, right sides of the knitting facing you, and working into the stitches just below the bound-off edges, bring threaded tapestry needle out at the center of the first stitch (i.e., go under half of the first stitch) on one side of the seam, then bring needle in and out under the first whole stitch on the other side (Figure 1). *Bring threaded into the center of the same stitch it came out of before, then out in the center of the adjacent stitch (Figure 2). Bring needle in and out under the next whole stitch on the other side (Figure 3). Repeat from *, ending with a half-stitch on the first side. Be sure to work along the same row of stitches on each side for a neat line. If the shoulder is sloped (the final stitches were bound off in steps), there will be jog or stair-step of two rows between each group of bound-off stitches. To give the seam a smooth appearance in these cases, do not follow the exact line of stitches just below the bound-off stitches—use the seaming yarn to visually smooth out the jogs over the distance of two or three stitches.

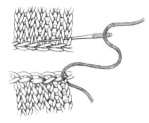

Figure 1

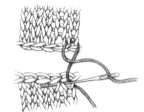

Figure 2

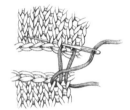

Figure 3

Figure 1

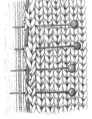

Figure 2

Short Rows

Work to turn point, slip next stitch purlwise to right needle. Bring yarn to front (Figure 1). Slip same stitch back to left needle (Figure 2). Turn work and bring yarn in position for next stitch, wrapping the slipped stitch as you do so. *Note*: Hide wraps on a knit stitch when right side of piece is worked as a knit stitch. Leave wrap if the purl stitch shows on the right side. Hide wraps as follows: *Knit stitch*: On right side, work to just before wrapped stitch, insert right needle from front, under the wrap from bottom up, and then into wrapped stitch as usual. Knit them together, making sure the new stitch comes out under wrap. *Purl stitch*: On wrong side, work to just before wrapped stitch. Insert right needle from back, under wrap from bottom up, and put on left needle. Purl lifted wrap and stitch together.

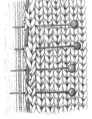
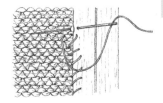

Figure 1   *Figure 2*

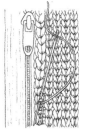

Figure 3

Zipper

With RS facing and zipper closed, pin zipper to fronts so front edges cover the zipper teeth. With contrasting thread and RS facing, baste zipper in place close to teeth (Figure 1). Turn work over and with matching sewing thread and needle, stitch outer edges of zipper to WS of fronts (Figure 2), being careful to follow a single column of sts in the knitting to keep zipper straight. Turn work back to RS facing, and with matching sewing thread, sew knitted fabric close to teeth (Figure 3). Remove basting.

abbreviations

beg	begin; begins; beginning
bet	between
BO	bind off
cm	centimeter(s)
CO	cast on
cont	continue(s); continuing
dec(s)	decrease(s); decreasing
dpn	double-pointed needles(s)
foll	follows; following
g	gram(s)
inc	increase(s); increasing
k	knit
k1f&b	knit into front and back of same stitch (increase)
k2tog	knit two stitches together (decrease)
kwise	knitwise, as if to knit
m(s)	marker(s)
mm	millimeter(s)
M1	make one (increase)
p	purl
p1f&b	purl into front and back of same stitch (increase)
p2tog	purl two stitches together (decrease)
patt(s)	pattern(s)
pm	place marker
psso	pass slipped stitch over stitch just knitted
p2sso	pass two slipped stitches over stitch just knitted
pwise	purlwise, as if to purl
rem	remain(s); remaining
rep	repeat; repeating
rev St st	reverse stockinette stitch
rnd(s)	round(s)
RS	right side
sl	slip (slip stitch purlwise unless otherwise indicated)
sl st	slip(ped) stitch
ssk	slip two stitches individually knitwise, knit the two slipped stitches together through the back loops (decrease)
ssp	slip two stitches individually knitwise, return the two slipped stitches to the left needle in their new orientation, and purl them together through the back loops (decrease)
st(s)	stitch(es)
tbl	through back loop
tog	together
WS	wrong side
wyib	with yarn in back
wyif	with yarn in front
yo	yarnover
*	repeat starting point (i.e., repeat from *)
( )	alternate measurements and/or instructions
[ ]	instructions that are to be worked as a group a specified number of times

yarn**sources**

The following companies supplied yarn for the projects photographed in this book.

Baabajoes Wool

modified-drop shoulder sweaters
PO Box 260604
Lakewood, CO 80226
www.baabajoeswool.com
- NZ WoolPak 14-Ply (100% wool;
  310 yd [283 ml]/250 g)
- NZ WoolPak 10-Ply (100% wool;
  430 yd [393 ml]/250 g)
- NZ WoolPak 8-Ply (100% wool;
  525 yd [480 ml]/250 g)

Classic Elite Yarns

raglan sweaters
300 Jackson St.
Lowell, MA 01852
www.classiceliteyarns.com
- Gatsby (70% wool, 15% viscose, 15%
  nylon; 84 yd [76 ml]/100 g)
- Lush (50% angora, 50% wool;
  124 yd [113 ml]/50 g)
- Montera (50% llama, 50% wool;
  127 yd [116 ml]/100 g)

GGH/Muench Yarns

drop shoulder sweaters
285 Bel Marin Keys Blvd., Unit J
Novato, CA 94949
www.muenchyarns.com
- Horstia Tweed (55% wool,
  27% acrylic, 18% viscose; 121 yd
  [110 ml]/50 g)
- Soft Kid (70% super kid mohair, 25%
  polyamide, 5% wool; 151 yd
  [138 ml]/25 g)
- Via Mala (100% wool; 73 yd
  [67 ml]/50 g)

Louet Sales

saddle shoulder sweaters
PO Box 267
Ogdensburg, NY 13669
www.louet.com
- Gems Opal (100% merino; 225 yd
  [205 ml]/100 g)
- Gems Sapphire (100% merino;
  103 yd [94 ml]/100 g)
- Gems Topaz (100% merino; 168 yd
  [153 ml]/100 g)

Plymouth Yarn Company

set-in sleeve sweaters
PO Box 28
Bristol, PA 19007
www.plymouthyarn.com
- Indiecita Alpaca Worsted Weight
  (100% alpaca; 102 yd [93 ml]/50 g)
- Silk-Merino (70% merino, 30% silk;
  109 yd [100 ml]/50 g)
- Le Fibre Nobili Taj Mahal
  (70% wool, 22% silk, 8% cashmere;
  187 yd [170 ml]/50 g)

Rowan Yarns

seamless yoke sweaters
c/o Westminster Fibers
5 Northern Blvd.
Amherst, NH 03031
www.rowanyarns.co.uk
- Chunky Cotton Chenille (100%
  cotton; 153 yd [140 ml]/100 g)
- Yorkshire Tweed Aran
  (100% wool; 175 yd [160 ml]/100 g)
- Yorkshire Tweed Chunky
  (100% wool; 109 yd [100 ml]/100 g)

index

abbreviations 216

bind-offs 29; standard 204; suspended 204; sewn 205; three-needle 205
buttonholes, crochet chain 206; multiple-stitch 205–206; tips 170; two-stitch 205

Cable Panel Pullover 9, 39, 48; instructions 59–61
cable ribbing 35
Cabled Yoke Pullover 173, 202; instructions 196–197
Cartridge Rib Pullover 107, 108; instructions 132–133
cast-ons, backward loop 207; continental (long-tail) 206; crochet chain (provisional) 207; invisible (provisional) 207
charts, reading 2–3
Chenille Yoke Cardigan 173, 182; instructions 193–195
Child's Fair Isle Pullover 173, 174; instructions 192–193
Chunky Drop-Shoulder Turtleneck 11, 12; instructions 31–32
circular knitting 150, 203
collar, basic 67; front split 67; shawl 68–69; side split 67
color patterns, adding 200–201, tips 180
color tips 180
crewneck, finishes 66–67
crochet, chain 207; single 37, 208
Cropped Cardigan 71, 95; instructions 99–101

decreases 29; centered double 209; k2tog 208; k3tog 208; raglan 171; shaping 104; ssk 208; ssp 208
Diagonal Eyelet Pullover 71, 72; instructions 101–103
Diamond Cable Pullover 107, 118; instructions 136–138
drop shoulder 2
Drop Shoulder Sweaters 10–37

edges, personal touches 35–37; tips 18; hemmed 36, 37
edging, hemmed 36; lace 37; rolled 36

Elizabeth Zimmermann's Percentage System 12

fit 29
Floating Cables Pullover 71, 82; instructions 97–99
funnel neck 66–67

garter stitch 35
Gatsby Cardigan 141, 153; instructions 167–168
gauge 6–8; adjusting 201–203; tips 46
glossary 204–214
grafting, Kitchener stitch 209

I-cord 36, 210
increases, bar 211; lifted 211; raised (M1) 210–211

joins 29
journal 29

Kitchener stitch 209
Knitter's Handy Book of Patterns 1, 5, 6
knitting in the round, adjusting for 203

Lace-Edged Cardigan 39, 57; instructions 61–63
length, sweater 29, 198; sleeve 198, 200

measurements, sweater 4–5
Mistake Rib Cardigan 11, 20; instructions 32–33
modified drop shoulder 2
Modified Drop-Shoulder Sweaters 38–69

patterns, color and texture 180
personal touches, crewneck finishes 66–67; edgings 35–37; raglan decreases 171; V-neck finishes 68–69; waist shaping 104–105
pick-up and knit 211–212

quick tips, for buttonholes 170; circular knitting 150; color and texture patterns 180; consistent gauge 46; general success 29; professional seams 65; tidy edges 18

raglan 2; decreases 171
Raglan Sweaters 140–171
Ribbed Sleeve Pullover 141; instructions 166–167
ribbing 35; shaping 105

saddle shoulder 2
Saddle Shoulder Sweaters 106–139
schematics 3–4
seams, directional ridge 171; gored 171; invisible horizontal 212; invisible vertical 212; prominent ridge 171; subtle 171; tips 65
seamless yoke 2
Seamless Yoke Sweaters 172–197
set-in sleeve 2
Set-in Sleeve Sweaters 70–105
Shawl-Collar Pullover 39, 40; instructions 63–65
short rows 214
size, choosing 4–6
sleeve, indented 38; length 198; raglan 2; set-in 2
stitch patterns, adding 200–201
Striped Crewneck Pullover 141, 142; instructions 169–170
swatches 6–8

texture patterns 180, 200–201
tips, for buttonholes 170; circular knitting 150; color and texture patterns 180; consistent gauge 46; general success 29; professional seams 65; tidy edges 18; turtleneck 66
Tweed V-Neck Pullover 11, 28; instructions 33–34

V-neck finishes 68–69

waist shaping 104–105
Wool Gathering 12

yarn 29; dyelots 29; estimating amounts 8; sources 217; weights 6
yoke, seamless 2

Zimmermann, Elizabeth 12
Zip-Front Jacket 107; instructions 133–136
zipper 214